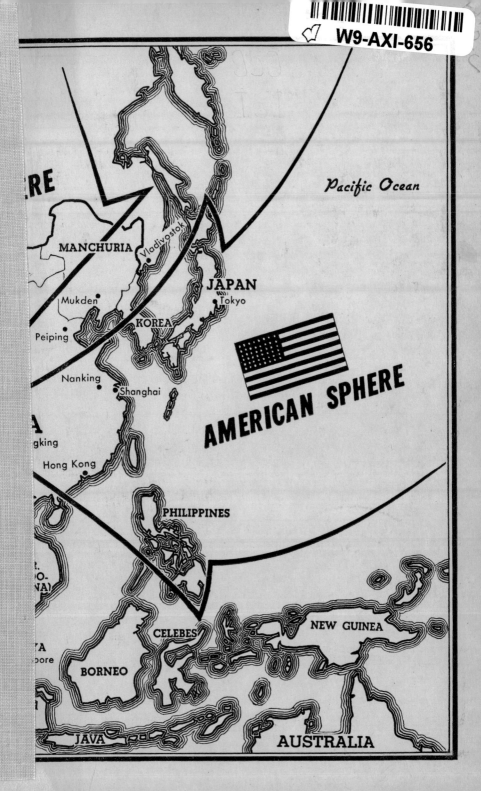

Pacific Ocean

MANCHURIA
Vladivostok

Mukden

JAPAN
Tokyo

Peiping

KOREA

Nanking

Shanghai

AMERICAN SPHERE

gking

Hong Kong

PHILIPPINES

R.
O-
NA)

CELEBES

NEW GUINEA

YA
oore

BORNEO

JAVA

AUSTRALIA

NO PEACE FOR ASIA

By the Same Author

THE TRAGEDY OF THE CHINESE REVOLUTION

HAROLD R. ISAACS

NO PEACE
FOR ASIA

NEW YORK 1947

THE MACMILLAN COMPANY

The people will live on.
The learning and blundering people will live on.
They will be tricked and sold and again sold
And go back to the nourishing earth for rootholds.
The people so peculiar in renewal and comeback,
You can't laugh off their capacity to take it.

—CARL SANDBURG

This book was conceived, complete with title, one night during the British drive in Burma in March, 1945. Shortly thereafter, the Kuomintang government barred me from returning to China, not having approved particularly some of my reports from that country. As a result, changed assignments just as the war ended took me into Korea with the occupying American forces and in following months to Japan, the Philippines, Indochina, Siam, Malaya, and Java. Consequently a study that might have been more limited in scope has become a much broader treatment, taking in much more of the crowded canvas of postwar Asia.

If there are differences in the form and content of the various chapters, they must be understood in terms of the unequal opportunities a working correspondent has to absorb and master the material that lies before him. It is often a temptation for a reporter to make too much out of too little, and this I have done my best to avoid. What I have tried to do is give the broad context of events in the aftermath of the war in Asia and to fill in such details as I feel competent to report. My effort to give a picture, in historic and current terms, of the new power pattern created by the war in the Far East is based, however, not only on personal observation but on fifteen years' continuous study of the subject.

Because there was no place for them in the book and because they might be pertinent here, I should like to tell the story of three conversations. The first was with an Irishman who had lived most of his life in India as a friend, supporter, and follower of the Indian nationalist movement. We worried over the state of the world through a long lunch. He finally shrugged. "I'm not sure of anything," he said, "except that we've got to do the best we can and hope that perhaps in two hundred years the human race will be better off than it is now."

That evening I was with an old friend, a Belgian newspaperman who had wandered over the Far East for many years. We had the same conversation and reached the same inconclusive point. And he said: "I suppose we have to keep on doing whatever we can do. Perhaps in a hundred million years from now the human race will exist on some higher plane." I protested. "My Irish friend," I said, "spoke of two hundred years." He snorted. "Those Irishmen!" he said. "Optimists!"

Some months later, in Java, I had a long afternoon with Hadji Salim, a learned, wise, quizzical old man. We went over much the same ground and he concluded by saying: "The difference between you and me, my friend, is that you will die a hopeless man in a disintegrating world and I shall die a hopeful man in a disintegrating world."

Old Hadji Salim was not quite fair. We have all taken a battering in these years, and events have suggested an attitude more of humility than of hope. But it still seems necessary to keep on raising the unanswered questions and to keep on trying to find the answers. The only alternative would be to accept things as they are. And that is impossible to do.

My acknowledgments are to the editors of *Newsweek,* whom I served as correspondent in the Far East during the war; to *Harper's Magazine,* in which a small part of the material appeared in another form; to my friend S. Mark Smith, for his suggestions; to my collaborator, Viola R. Isaacs, for sharing indispensably in organizing the material and shaping the text.

H. R. I.

New York City,
Oct. 1, 1946

CONTENTS

ix

THE NEW PATTERN OF POWER

NO PEACE FOR ASIA

INTRODUCTION

There is no peace in Asia. From one end of the vast continent to the other, it has seldom been possible since Japan's collapse to escape the sound of continuing gunfire. In every country aggravated political and social pressures collide and tangle in pain and anger and frustration. There has been civil war in China, nationalist war in Indochina and Indonesia, rioting and mutiny in India, political collisions in Korea and the Philippines. And everywhere there are hunger and confusion and economic chaos.

It would be easy and superficial to explain it all as the inevitable aftermath of the Great Pacific War. But it is more than that. The war itself was only an episode, a great and convulsive episode in these continuing conflicts. There is no peace in Asia because the war settled nothing but Japan's attempt to master the continent. A billion people must keep on struggling, as they struggled before, to win even a semblance of political freedom. A billion people must keep on struggling, as they struggled before, against backwardness and chronic starvation.

The Pacific war, like the world war of which it was a part, was a convulsion in an impasse, a planetary impasse in which human society could offer men no manner of renewal except through death and destruction. Millions died amid all the ravage and the survivors are still thrashing around in search of a way out. This is the world picture, and Asia is half the world, a half which has particular and overwhelming importance for all Americans. It still seems difficult for most Americans to realize and accept this fact. But few would have believed only a few years ago that the unsolved problems of the Chinese peasant and the Malay coolie would finally compel Americans from Indiana and Ohio and New York and Utah and from all the states to go as soldiers to the remotest parts of Asia and the Pacific to fight and toil and sicken and die. Yet that is what happened.

1

It did not start with Pearl Harbor. It did not end with the surrender signed on the deck of the U.S.S. *Missouri*. It was not merely a question of Japanese greed and treachery. It started more than a century and a half ago when the Western powers reached out aggressively for the wealth of the East. It goes back into a long and ugly history of empires and slaves, of rival slave masters and of subjected peoples who strained to be free, or at least to master their own fate. The United States has had its part in this history and its share of responsibility for the result. It has been like a gang war that has lasted too long, and we have not yet come to the end of it.

The problem is not an easy one, and because it is so huge, it is complex. Still the essence of it is not so very complicated. In Asia live a billion people. All but a tiny fraction are condemned to live in degrading poverty and primitive backwardness on a continent rich with land and wealth, with all human and material resources. For more than a century the Western powers, and more recently Japan, have vied for the chance to exploit the wealth and labor of Asia. They brought its peoples into subjection. They fought wars, against the Asiatics and with each other, over its territory. They competed savagely for its raw materials and markets. At various times, small groups in different nations have extracted super-profits from their penetration of Asia. But competition was fierce and profits could not be sustained unless competitors were battered down, with the weapons of trade and ultimately, always, with the weapons of war.

In this process of spoliation, the peoples of Asia were never enabled to break with their own dead past. Their renascent nationalism was throttled and deformed. They could never come abreast, economically, of the rest of the world. They were kept in bond to their own archaic traditions and social organization, their primitive modes of life and production. Their native rulers and exploiters were converted into the tools, directly or indirectly, of this or that foreign interest. The land and wealth of Asia could not become an instrument for the well-being of its peoples because it was the committed battleground for contending powers, foreign and domestic, who wanted to exploit it. All the wars fought through a hundred years and more grew into the Great War of 1941–45 and we have emerged from it with nothing better to show than new positions and new antagonists preparing for the next collision. Asia remains a battleground on which power, not peace, is the stake. We are starting all over again, ending one bloody cycle, beginning another.

The war's end opened no other prospect. Northern Asia became the scene of American-Russian rivalry, replacing the American-Japanese rivalry. Southern Asia became the scene of an attempt by Britain and the other older colonial powers to reestablish their old positions. To the backward nations and colonies of Asia, the weaker smaller nations of Africa and Europe, our world still offers only the role of pawns or victims in the interplay of intercontinental power politics. This is no road to peace. It is the road toward a condition of permanent war. This was the condition in Asia in the aftermath of the war against Japan, and a description of it is, in the main, the content of this book.

Yet the prospect of permanent war is not absolutely inevitable. Across Asia I saw more than the drive for power and exploitation. I saw peoples stirred by hope of change. Everywhere, even as in Europe and the United States, ordinary folk wanted to have done with all the travail and destruction. They wanted, if they could only learn how, to build a new structure on new foundations. The cumulative effect of this hope is enormous. Given an outlet, it would inspire the greatest creative effort in the history of man. But it is blocked, hemmed in by hostile circumstance. If it continues to be frustrated, the cost to these peoples and to us will be enormous and perhaps decisive for a whole epoch to come in human history. The future of the American people is decisively involved in the outcome. For as long as the social, political, and economic problem of Asia remains unsolved, Asia will remain the scene of conflict, and while there is no peace in Asia there can be no peace for America or for the world.

It comes down to the question of what kind of world we still have time to build. Can we still organize it more rationally, pool its resources and its needs, federate its races, nations, and cultures? If so, how? If not, what then?

AMERICAN SOLDIERS IN ASIA

1 THE UNWILLING EXILES

There was once an idea that the spread of so many Americans to so many parts of the globe during the war would in the end prove to be a rather well disguised blessing. They would see other lands and learn about other peoples. They would acquire broadened outlooks on world problems. They would return as ambassadors of greater international understanding. Such, at least, was the hope.

Unfortunately, it did not work out that way. Around the world the meeting of the American soldier and other peoples produced not a miracle but a calamity. In Asia, as in Europe, the GI was caught up in a tangle of misunderstanding, angry frustration, mutual prejudice, and contempt. The GI's, with rare exceptions, did not like or understand the Chinese and the Indians. The Chinese and Indians, after short acquaintance, did not like the GI either.

It could hardly have been otherwise. There was not much in the climate of war to nourish the delicate plant of international friendship. War in general fosters callousness and indifference to suffering and death. War grotesquely deforms all human relations, as between men and between men and women. It sharpens all the instincts of self-preservation in their crudest form. For most of the men in it, war is the experience of compromising with unreasonable stupidity. They have to submit to inferior intelligence. They have to put up with the gross indignities of the military caste system. They have to keep sane in the midst of disorder and insanity. They have to adapt themselves somehow to the intolerable senselessness of the whole undertaking. Amid all this, men find it difficult enough to live with themselves. What was there in it, then, that could prepare men to develop sympathetic understanding, if not affection, for the strange and alien peoples among whom they came?

Consider the young American soldier, averaged in the great mass out of the normal percentages: he was decent and generous, small-minded and selfish, keen and perceptive, dull and indifferent. By

7

and large he was a man you respected, for his liabilities as for his assets. But what was there in his whole background, his American environment, his education, his army training, to prepare him for what he found in Asia?

He came from a life of gadgets and movies, schools, mass production, more or less good food, cars, juke boxes, radios, and corner drugstores. He was wrenched from all this and plunged abruptly into the midst of primitive misery. He vaguely expected the Orient to be a lush, glamorous, exciting, and somehow mysterious place. What he found was squalor and poverty and degradation. And so much of it. There was poverty perhaps at home, but never poverty like this. There was nothing in his scale of values by which he could measure and accept the filth and the stench and the bitter subjection in which he found millions of people, crowding about him in their great cities or toiling like dumb animals on the land. It was too much for him to absorb—even supposing he was willing to absorb it. His initial reaction of shock, pity, perhaps even indignation, usually soon dissolved. He got used to it, as you get used to the smell of a stockyard. He had to live with it, adapt himself to it. He found it increasingly difficult to look upon these Asiatics as men and women. Only some subhuman species could live as they did, submit as they did. You could not apply normal standards to your thinking about them. Pity usually gave way to indifference, impatience, contempt, and even hatred.

There is very little in the *mores* of American society or in American education that prepares Americans to be citizens of the world. We do not get it in our school approach to history, economics, languages, religion or philosophy. We do not acquire any real consciousness of other peoples or other social currents. We never completely capture the reality of the whole world that exists across our bounding oceans. It is all remote and inferior and not very important. The fact that we are ourselves of many nations and races becomes a kind of shibboleth, a fine blurry self-satisfying notion that relieves us of all responsibility for what goes on elsewhere in the world. We build out of it a vision of the American genius, of American wealth and superiority, of technical craft and a myth of universal well-being. In America we have the most, the best, the biggest, the tallest, the greatest, the finest, the deepest, the superlative in everything. In all his varied sectional accents, the American is profoundly provincial and profoundly convinced that everything not American is inferior. He is educated into no sense of the proportions of things, or the reasons for differences.

The war came because the country had been attacked by ugly and menacing enemies across the seas, not because the world was sick and in convulsion. When he was dragooned into the army and prepared for his long voyages to distant battlefields, nothing in army "orientation" oriented the young American toward any clearer understanding of what he was getting into. And when he got into Asia, everything he found confirmed his sense of unqualified American superiority. Backward Asia and the backward Asiatics had nothing comparable to American techniques, materials, know-how. Nothing in Asia except the tiny European quarters resembled even faintly the familiar comforts of American life. The rest was staggering slowness and human toil, and people who did not speak English and who did not have sense enough to jump smartly out of the way when a jeep came tearing by. The American could feel like a man from Mars in lands of the water buffalo, wooden plows, and ox carts. He came from another world, and what is more, he came not by his own choice.

For let it always be remembered that these many thousands of young Americans did not travel to these strange and foreign lands as enthusiastic students of human affairs, anxious to learn things, see things, understand things. They were men torn from their homes, from everything that was loved and familiar and secure. They were men forced against their will into the grossness of army life and the war. They loathed the army. They loathed the war. They hated their fate. They were helpless. They were angry. They were frustrated. They were lonely; above all, they were lonely. They idealized everything they had been compelled to leave behind, home, women, a way of life. They had been sentenced to hard labor without appeal, and their balked wrath turned inevitably upon everything and everybody linked to their plight. This included nearly all the new environments into which they came. Whether it was Sicily or Newfoundland or France or Tunisia, or India or China, they hated it and they hated the people in it. All the normal provincial prejudices of the American were magnified a millionfold in this vast enforced migration. The American soldier was neither student nor missionary. He was an unwilling exile.

THE WOGS

In India *wog* was the word. It summed up much when you heard it used. It was a contemptuous epithet apparently not of GI origin nor used only to describe people in India. It was also common during the war in North Africa and the Middle East. The word belongs in that lexicon of social terms which includes "nigger" and "wop" and "kike" and "mick" and "spick" and "kanaka." The wogs were all those brown, unsmiling people who cluttered up a hot and stinking country where there were no soda fountains or drive-in hamburg joints.

"Don't worry about the wogs," the American officer said to the driver of the staff car. "They're expendable." He laughed broadly. You just couldn't avoid hitting them, he explained. There were so many, and they were so slow and so stupid. "They knock off half a dozen or so between the airport and town every week," he said. Each case was usually settled by headquarters for about fifty rupees, fifteen dollars.

"When I first got here," said an American, "I used to be pretty decent to my bearer (servant) but after a while you get so damned sore at these wogs that you find yourself treating them just as the British do." India swarms with bearers. In a hotel dining room there will be three or four to each table, dozens on every hotel floor. Every Briton has his personal servant and every American officer who could do so enthusiastically followed suit. Enlisted men's barracks were likewise amply staffed with servitors who did all the menial tasks that most Americans, particularly in the army, ordinarily do for themselves. Most Americans found that they liked the system, enjoyed its comforts. They found, however, that they could not be breezy and "democratic" with these servants, bred out of centuries to the business of keeping their inferior place. "They take advantage of you, the goddamned wogs," you heard. This was understood to explain why so many Americans gradually adopted the British habit of frigidly distant superiority enforced with abuse when required. I sat once at a table in a Calcutta hotel with a group of American officers when a waiter was trying to explain to one of the party that a certain dish listed on the menu was not available. He was having some trouble making himself understood and grew mildly emphatic. One of the other Americans grew apoplectically red: "Don't let that wog talk to you like that!" he growled. He held his fist under the waiter's nose. "See that?" he asked. "Bring that dish or you'll get this in your face." The waiter left. My neighbor sat back. "Only way to handle 'em," he said.

Brutality was not infrequent and was more or less permissible. The wogs did not know any better. It was the only way to treat them. Such, at any rate, was the common formula. Arguments with Bengalese ricksha coolies over a few annas might end up with the coolie stretched in the street. Sikh cab drivers in Calcutta were involved in so many fights with drunken American soldiers that they began driving only in pairs at night. Tonga wallas in New Delhi, drivers of the small pony carts common in that city, sometimes kept rocks handy to discourage blows. There were always arguments over fares or over prices in shops because Americans felt that they were being gypped. They usually were. They always started out by being lavish spenders. Like lavish spenders anywhere in the world, they were accepted by merchants as legitimate prey. It is a way men of business have. When later Americans tried to be shrewder or more provident, there was almost always trouble. Out of this money relationship affecting individuals and out of the general conviction that the United States was being rooked wholesale on reverse lend-lease came the most frequent complaint: "These wogs are a goddamned bunch of crooks. You can't trust a single one of them."

It is not part of the Great American Myth that Americans ever use force against weaker opponents. But in India it was often simpler to set the myth aside. Adaptation to life in India usually meant, in some form or other, the gradual acceptance of the idea that these miserable people were something less than human, exempt from the "normal" codes of behavior. After all, Americans saw so much brutality around them. They saw Sikh policemen belaboring tonga wallas and ricksha coolies or load carriers somewhere in the streets every day. It affected men who were by no means as a rule casual about such things. A friend of mine who was not a soldier at all, but a government official, told me of coming out of the Imperial Hotel in New Delhi one afternoon. In the entrance, an Indian policeman was unmercifully clubbing a tonga walla. The hapless driver had somehow "insulted" some British officers and their women by coming too close to insist upon a higher fare. My friend stood by and watched the beating. The driver finally got away. Suddenly my friend was aghast at his own thoughts, his own inaction. It had not even occurred to him to interfere. That sort of thing happened, and happened often. Sometimes it developed to extreme forms. One major I knew, a talkative but harmless Texan, once said: "I was allergic to rickshas when I first came out here. Now I want to stand up with a bull whip and make the bastard run faster."

When the Americans first came to India, many Indian nationalists seriously believed that the American mission was to oust the British or, at the least, to assist the cause of Indian independence. They thought the Americans were in the war to spread democracy, to free subject peoples. American high policy, however, remained strictly neutral in Indian affairs and Americans in India did not conduct themselves like apostles of freedom. Some Indians learned this the hard way. When one of the arguments in Calcutta's streets ended with the killing of a Sikh driver by an American soldier, the Sikhs in the city announced that they would give the murdered man a mass funeral and march past the Hindustan Building, the American army headquarters, carrying banners of protest. The American general in command promptly called in the British police chief and the leaders of the Sikh community. He told them he would mount machine guns around the building and would pass the word to his troops that if they broke up the demonstration he would look the other way. The mass funeral was canceled. The American general was quite proud of himself and when the story got around, his soldiers were proud of him too.

Americans in India generally disliked the British as heartily as they loathed the "wogs." The British, who began by worrying somewhat about the "democratic" Americans, were quite satisfied with the way things finally worked out, because in the end the Indians heartily reciprocated the American attitude and it was all one big happy family. When after the war nationalist riots occurred in Calcutta and American soldiers were attacked, a British brigadier announced gleefully to a group of us in Batavia that he had heard the Americans had gone out with machine guns and killed 400 Indians as a reprisal. "That's it!" he exclaimed delightedly. "That's the way to do it! You chaps are finding it out at last!" The report did not happen to be true, although several Indians were killed in clashes with Americans before the latter were ordered off the streets to avoid further collisions. The general GI attitude toward Britons and Indians was probably best summed up in a popular gag: "The thing to do to the British is make them keep this goddamned country!" Or in another version: "If we want to make trouble for the Japs, the way to do is let them have India, and make them keep it!"

There were, certainly, Americans who caught something of the agony and the striving of India, who learned a little of what it meant to a country to be under foreign rule for two centuries and to be caught under the twin burdens of subjection and backwardness. There were Americans who found friends among the Indians, who sought out contacts at Indian universities, and tried to translate their impulsive sympathy into friendliness and information. There were some Americans who did not blame the Indians for their own poverty and tried to understand the immensity of the Indian struggle for survival. But they were rare, as rare as the unshaven sergeant from Brooklyn whom I found in a littered bamboo and palmleaf basha at Ledo, on the edge of the Naga Hills. He pulled out an old English-Hindustani dictionary and started explaining how Hindi phrases are put together. "I just picked it up," he said. "Figured I might as well. Now they all come running to me every time something goes wrong with the wogs, and I go out and straighten things for them. Somehow me and them, we get along all right." A little Indian girl came dashing in, dirty and ragged. She half-climbed to the back of his chair, her arms around his neck, and looked over his shoulder at me with huge, brilliant, gypsylike eyes. The sergeant from Brooklyn spoke to her, sharp and low, in Hindi. She shook her head. He spoke again. She dashed out. "My little girl," he said sheepishly. "Her name's Jamila. About seven years old, I guess she is. Do y' know, I took her down to the pump and scrubbed her clean and then I dressed her up in a whole new outfit I bought, with shoes too. Next day she was back in rags again and just as dirty as before. Her folks probably sold her new outfit back to the bazaar. Jamila's cute, though. I like her." He looked out the door toward the hot, blackened railway shed. "Been here thirty goddamned months," he said in a tired, flat voice. "It's been kind of nice to have Jamila for a mascot."

THE NIGGERS

From the Naga Hills into Burma, over mountains and through jungles, the Americans hacked and cut the Ledo Road. In this remote and unlikely corner of the world beyond Pangsau Pass, thousands of American Negroes trucked supplies, drove bulldozers and graders, felled the great trees, built bridges, and pushed the road steeply deeper toward China. They came to carry the brunt of the toil of a gigantic engineering job. They brought with them to Asia, complete in all details, a field laboratory in American racialism.

Large Negro detachments were stationed around Calcutta. Others staged there before moving westward. Calcutta was also their main leave center. Here Indians could observe the Negro Red Cross Club and the Negro Rest Camp at Howrah, on the city's edge. They had a look at the American color line in operation. They caught echoes of the virulent racism of many white Americans. They learned about the position of the man of color in the American scheme. Competition for the company and the favors of the Anglo-Indian girls was fierce. The whites would explain to these brown-skinned women that the Negroes were the American coolies and therefore unworthy of their attentions. The Negroes were strange and dangerous brutes, they said, and babies begotten by them often had tails. Negroes often said to these women: "You don't understand. You too would be nothing but niggers to these white men back home." But the women were not long in acquiring that thin edge of scorn and rejection. The Negroes were in large part driven back into the worst holes of Calcutta when, on leave from the jungle, they came in search of relaxation.

Up where they were building the road, it was a little different. "We have few social problems here," said a Negro sergeant. He waved at the empty world around him. "It's because we have no society here. No clubs or restaurants or hotels or streets. Most of all, no women." Another Negro boy added quietly: "We get along here because we outnumber the whites here. They're careful. It's not like Tampa."

In a remote little camp deep in the Burma jungle I was taught by a young Negro that there are two kinds of white men, *free* white men and all the others. The free white men were those who were willing to treat the Negroes as though they too were men, without pity, without patronage, but simply with equality. There were not many of the "free" among the white officers along the Ledo Road. They belonged mostly to the "others." The officers stood for segregation, discrimination, for white mastery. "Officers *command* white troops," I was told. "They *handle* Negro troops." And Negroes resented being handled. A simple order issued by a white officer to Negro soldiers was never merely a military act. It was an expression of white mastery. Discipline was not merely the military form of tyranny. It was a racial challenge.

It is a curiously suggestive fact that in this remote wasteland where there was no society to impose its rules, relations between white GI's and black GI's often achieved the quality of genuine and casual freedom. There was more to unite them as GI's than there was to divide them as men. They could make more of their own rules among themselves and try to live together. They could feel freer of the restraints and that faint and hated air of patronage. Despite the enforced segregation, they had to live on common ground, and there were frequent attempts to explore it. Many tried, both black and white, until they ran into the pressure of the officers who "handled" the blacks. An attempt among the enlisted men to start an open discussion forum to fill some of the empty free time in Ledo was quashed by the top command of the base section. "We won't have public gatherings here," the general said, "in which white men and black sit side by side." Some of the Negro units occasionally tried to invite Indian friends they'd made to come and talk to them in groups. One Indian railway employee, a university graduate, invited to come and talk to a Negro quartermaster outfit up the road, was quietly advised to stay home if he valued his job.

Among the Negroes, as among the whites, you found the normal breakdown by the percentages. There were the keen and articulate men, the sharp and the sensitive. There were the tired intellectuals and the silent middle grounders. There were the indifferent men and the toadies. All together they had been thrust into this strange place, an odd layer amid the strata of races and kinds. They had ideas about the Indians too. Many a Negro slid down the easy way and, in aping the white man's attitude, found relief in discovering that there were men held to be inferior, even to the Negro. Many a Negro did not even stop to think about it. He had his hands full accepting his own lot. Still you more rarely heard a Negro use the word "wog." More often the Negroes called the Indians "saabs"—a humorous use of the term "sahib," the respectful Indian term for the whites. And there were Negroes who understood very plainly what they saw: "Whenever we see a white man mistreating an Indian," I was told, "we think of Georgia and Mississippi. None of us likes to see the Indian so dirty and so hopeless, but some of us can see the British in it all the time because we can see the American white man in the South all the time. . . ."

All the twists of racism were there along the Ledo Road. The Negroes writhing and filled with inverted prejudices against the whites; and the white officer who said: "They're nothing but a bunch of damned coolies. They don't give a damn about anything. They're so happy!" And the white captain who chimed in: "Ever see a nigger who wasn't?" And the Jewish GI who thought the wogs were impossible and the niggers little better. And another Jew who nodded grimly and said: "I know about this race thing." And all the Americans, black and white, who could not abide the Chinese. These were all men building a road where none had ever passed before, overcoming the craggy mountains and the great monsoons and the wildness of the jungle. They could drive great steel muscles against a natural wall and break through. But none of their strength, their techniques, or their tools could break through the great walls of prejudice that separated them from each other.

THE SLOPEYS (BURMA)

Along the road that led to the battlegrounds of North Burma, the most virulent of all the many hatreds was the hatred for the Chinese. It was immense and deep and all-embracing. It almost had the force of a natural law because it flowed so wholly from the roots of the situation. In North Burma the Americans abhorred their place and their plight more, perhaps, than anywhere in the whole theater of war. It was foul in itself, by every physical and human standard. What was worse, the Americans toiling and fighting there had no belief in the sense of what they were doing. There was scarcely any faith in the road and pipeline and the link it would make to China. They did not believe it would hasten the end of the war by a day and thereby rescue them that much sooner. They fiercely resented what they felt was the waste and the hopelessness of their job and its irrelevance in the bigger schemes of the real war far away. China was responsible for their being here, building a road and a pipeline where no man had any business building anything at all. They hated China for it; and the Chinese in North Burma represented China.

A host of particulars arose to feed this friction and this pressure. The North Burma campaign was carried out with Chinese troops who had been flown across the Hump, trained and equipped by Americans in India and moved into action against the Japanese in Burma. From the empty-handedness and nakedness of China's weary armies, these men had been plucked and suddenly clothed and given shiny, modern, new arms and fed with full rations. They were trained and taught to acquire confidence in themselves, a confidence justified by their first small victories in action. It was a revolutionary transformation. The small items counted so heavily, like shoes. From a land and an army where only the aristocrats and the generals and the wealthy wear shoes, these soldiers could suddenly discard their torn straw sandals and put on stout boots all their own. They threw away their useless weapons and to them were issued the best rifles American industry could produce. It was the conventional story of rags to riches; and these simple, hungry Chinese soldiers reacted according to the pattern. They were brutalized men, beaten into docility and taught to be cruel to the weak. When wealth miraculously came to them, they discarded their docility with their rags. With their new weapons and their new clothes and their filled bellies, they also acquired new and more daring techniques of bullying arrogance. A lot of it they learned from the Americans. The Americans did not respect the Chinese, as men or as soldiers, and usually showed it. But the Chinese respected themselves more now, and in their new power and new dress they came to demand more respect from others, especially from Americans. They countered the American air of authority with their own air of authority. They countered the American show of power with their own show of power. "When you are weak," explained a Chinese soldier, "the American soldiers will take the upper hand over you. But if you take a strong attitude, they will concede."

The trouble with this brash and cynical truth was that the Chinese interpreted it as license to flash their weapons on little or no provocation. The result was a rash of incidents which infuriated the Americans involved. To make matters worse, General Joe Stilwell had issued the strictest orders to Americans to lean over backward in any dealings with the Chinese. So in addition to everything else in their overflowing bitter cup, the Americans had to taste thwarted vengeance and to pass over without resort a host of real or fancied wrongs.

Many of the incidents arose out of the simplest kind of misunderstanding: the language difficulty. Here was a typical occurrence: Two trucks pulled up to a barrier along the lower section of the Ledo Road. The first was filled with an American road crew, the second with Chinese soldiers. The American guard at the barrier waved the first truck on, and it went through. The Chinese truck he gestured aside and pointed to a detour, a narrow track that cut off to the right through the jungle. The Chinese in the truck flared up in instant indignation. If the Americans could proceed on the main road, why couldn't they? The guard tried to explain. The Chinese grew louder in their protests and more menacing. A minute later the guard was looking into the muzzles of half a dozen tommy guns. He fingered his inadequate .45 and then took his hand away and shrugged. It was hardly worth dying for, and he stepped back. The Chinese truck drove on through, the troops aboard smiling in triumph. The frightened, angry guard glowered back at them. Two miles farther up the road the truck came to a dead end. It was a road section under repair. The American truck had been taking a crew up with some additional supplies. The Chinese had to go back and take the detour after all and pick up the highway a few miles beyond.

Supply-drop parachutes were highly prized by the Chinese. They were used for tents and for clothing, for barter and sale to the local tribesmen, and were profitably shipped back over the trails to cloth-hungry China. At forward drop fields far beyond the road's end it was usually some time before there were airstrips capable of accommodating anything larger than L-planes, small liaison craft. The siege of Bhamo had been under way for some time when a transport strip was finally laid out. Orders came down from American headquarters at Myitkyina to salvage all the drop chutes and send them back for further use. An American lieutenant was duly sent down to the drop field to retrieve that day's chutes. He and his detail arrived at the field at the same time as a Chinese squad which had come, as usual, to pick up the chutes—which were disposed of, incidentally, for the private profit of the local Chinese commander. The American officer tried to explain, in his limited Chinese, what the new orders were. The Chinese in charge shook his head. His orders, he said, were to get the chutes. The American impatiently demanded the chutes and started his detail across the field. Whereupon the Chinese drew up their tommy guns, trigger-ready. The Chinese officer indicated plainly that his next order would be to fire. The American flushed and stood his ground uncertainly. After a long instant, he chose discretion. Under the mocking eyes of the Chinese, he ordered his detail off the field. Pulling a gun is a court-martial offense in the American army. Nobody likes to have it done to him, especially an officer. The young lieutenant and the other American members of that detail were sulphurous in their comments. Most of their language about the incident was unprintable. "The sons of bitches," said a sergeant through his teeth. "I hope the day comes when we go to war against the Chinese. I don't give a damn if I'm sixty years old. I'll be the first to volunteer. Right now I'd rather plug one of those dirty Chinks than any Jap in Burma."

There was always the matter of stealing. The Chinese stole.

There was no doubt about it. They stole whatever they could lay hands on and carry away. The evidence was overwhelming, and the top Chinese commanders did not deny it. "They'll steal you blind" was the phrase you heard up and down the road. The Chinese, for their part, called it *fa yang tsai*—"to acquire some extra foreign wealth." The Chinese had a way of picking up anything loose, and the Americans had a way of leaving a lot of loose things around. American profligacy with equipment was something that appalled and baffled most Chinese soldiers. Americans would make the most ridiculous barter arrangements. At least they seemed ridiculous to the Chinese. They would swap valuable pieces of clothing and equipment for Japanese souvenirs. They would give up almost anything they had for anything that looked and acted like liquor. "The Americans don't seem to care about the quality of wine at all," said a puzzled Chinese soldier. "Whatever it is, they'll take it." Americans would swap Indian rupees for Japanese invasion rupees. This, to the provident Chinese, was the final measure of absurdity. "You can buy things with the regular Indian rupee," said the Chinese soldier, "while the Japanese rupee is worthless. Yet the Americans seem to think that the Japanese rupee is worth more than the regular rupee!" The Americans were wasteful. Astonished and somewhat horrified Chinese would see Americans cut off the sleeves of their shirts or the legs of their pants. They would see them sometimes cut down para- chute boots. Once on the march the hand generator used by the signal team was damaged beyond repair. The American officer in charge, in front of the shocked Chinese, ordered his men to throw their now useless radio transmitter into a river.

This prodigal and careless American attitude did not excuse but it did explain in part why so many Chinese soldiers often felt justi- fied in taking what they found so easy to take. All these gadgets and items of equipment represented fantastic wealth to the Chinese. The Americans, without a black market handy, seemed indifferent to their value. This did not go for rations, however, and the Chinese did a lot of ration stealing, especially up at forward drop fields where Americans would often arrive to find that their rations had entirely disappeared. That was never funny. Neither was the fact that out of the sum of these experiences, most Americans in North Burma were convinced that all Chinese were incorrigible thieves—and the Americans hated them for it.

In some cases there were Americans who had fought and slogged their way together with the Chinese through one snafued battle after another, from Shimbwyang all the way to Bhamo and beyond. They had won some degree of field comradeship, which is one of the few decent things that can ever happen to men in war. An American captain up front who had been talking bitterly for twenty minutes about his hatred for the Chinese and all their crimes and failings suddenly stopped and said: "Now I'm not talking about my own boys. They're all right. They're swell. We understand each other and like each other and we get along fine. But they're exceptions. As for all the rest of those bastards . . ."

It was pretty rare that anybody understood anybody else along the North Burma front. The social and racial tangle was thicker and more impenetrable than the jungle undergrowth. Friction smoked between American whites and blacks, between Americans and British, and between everybody and the Chinese. You could never cut through it or find your way out. One night at a hospital in Myitkyina a group of correspondents led a discussion about China for an audience of several hundred wounded and sick GI's. The talk and the argument went on for hours and finally ended. When it was all over, an American infantryman walked up in his hospital robe. He looked us over wonderingly and with a little pity. And he said: "I been out twenty-four months and you know, you're the first guys I ever met that had a good word for the Chinese."

THE SLOPEYS (CHINA)

Slopey was the word for the Chinese. The word "Chink" was officially frowned on, so the GI coined his own substitute. "Slopey" was a contraction of "slope-eyed." It was used in the same tone and with the same connotation as "wog."

In Burma the American contact had been with the troops of five Chinese divisions in a land foreign to both American and Chinese. Across the Hump, in China itself, the picture widened. There were greater differences, more gradations. Most Americans felt a sense of relief when they came over the great mountains from India to China. The poverty was just as great, the filth and squalor no less pervasive. But the climate and the people were different. Except in a few places, China does not have the dank and sodden atmosphere that India has. The Chinese are much less beaten down. In Bengal, where so many Americans served in India, they rarely heard laughter or saw adults playing with children. In China the dreariest village is brightened by the noisy, racing, gleamy-eyed children and the smiling toleration of their elders. In both countries the children, like the elders, toil, but in China a certain vitality has been retained that in India so frequently seems to have disappeared. It is often said that the Chinese are a smiling people, with a sense of humor. What this really refers to is the genius the Chinese have for adapting themselves to adverse circumstances. The Chinese *hsiang fa-tze*—they find a way in almost any conditions. They know how to yield much to misery without yielding the inner core of their self-assurance. Call it dignity, if you like, although that is an overworked word. But it is something you glimpse, and it commands respect.

It was not uncommon to hear American soldiers say: "This is pretty lousy, but compared to India it's paradise." Sometimes this meant nothing more than a comment on the weather. It wasn't so hot and sticky. Or it sprang from the fact that in China the American soldier ate fresh eggs, a wondrous emancipation from the powdered eggs he got in India. But sometimes, however remotely, it reflected something more, something caught by a marine lieutenant I met in Kweiyang. He turned up with his team in the midst of the frenzied evacuation in the path of the advancing Japanese. We drank tea in a shoddy little restaurant filled with slick young officials and Chinese army officers and their fur-coated camp followers, listening to outdated jazz on a wheezy phonograph. They were a fine specimen collection of the leeches and sons of leeches that abound in China and who always seem at their most prosperous when the rest of the people are suffering the most deeply. But the marine was speaking of the others, all the numerous others who filled the land and the roads that night with fear and anxiety and cold and hunger and death.

"They're great people," he said. "I've been out east for a year and I know, because it takes a little time to find it out. You know, I don't think that after this I will ever depend on anybody or anything else in my life. I've learned from these Chinese what it means to endure, to be reduced to the absolute minimum, and yet get along. I get along on less, yet I share more. I feel emancipated somehow because of it. I'm for these people. I've learned things from them I'll never forget. They're pretty beat up all the time, war or no war. But they have something. How shall I describe it? When an Indian cringes before superior force, he cringes not only outside but inside himself as well. The Chinese may cringe sometimes, but you always know he is bending only to an external necessity. Inside he's always standing up straight."

I never met another American soldier who caught that thing about the Chinese in quite that way. I think it was so rare because Americans so rarely had any daily living contact with the vast *laopaihsing,* the common people of the towns and the countryside of China. There were some Americans and some Chinese who became friends. There were many acts of kindness and generosity. Many a fighter group or lonely supply team or liaison outfit adopted its orphan, and men gruffly vied with one another to give the lucky youngster food and clothing and even a chance for the future. But the rare currents of sympathetic understanding and friendly fellow feeling between Americans and Chinese in the war years were utterly submerged under a torrent of aggravations, of misunderstandings and irritations, of angry and disgusted contempt, of hostility and hate.

The normal American contact with the Chinese was with shopkeepers, restaurateurs, merchants, brothelkeepers, and the blackmarket thieves; with the various brackets of the Kuomintang bureaucracy, the most corrupt in all the world; with the Chinese army, whose higher ranking officers are the most venal, the most criminally incompetent of all the ruling elements in China. There were the small-scale aggravations of the market place and the large-scale aggravations of wholesale stealing and grafting in American war supplies. Many an American in China, as everywhere else in the world, joined the blackmarket jamboree. But a great many more Americans felt personally affronted by the trafficking in materials flown across the Hump with such great effort and at such cost in lives. There were endless accounts of medical supplies diverted into private channels at fantastic profit, of gasoline hoarded and sold, of weapons and ammunition taken out of circulation and hoarded for use in future civil war. And almost all these stories were quite true. They were taking place before your eyes all the time. I was on the Salween front at a time when many Chinese soldiers' lives depended on the flow of ammunition and supplies from the rear. One convoy of twenty-nine trucks left a supply depot a few hours' drive from the forward area. Only six arrived at their destination. There was not a single item of American supplies for China that could not be bought on the black market in Kunming, including 2½-ton trucks. Graft was epidemic. Fortunes were made by a favored few who speculated in gold, in currency, in contraband of every kind, out of American stocks that came across the Hump or in exchanges with the Japanese and their puppets across the gray zone of inactivity known as the "front." Explained away always as the "tradition" of Chinese "squeeze," the system operated from the lowliest foreman of a working gang up to the highest reaches of the Chungking government. It was paralyzing. It was stifling. It cost lives. And it caused Americans on every day of their service in China to damn and triple damn the hopeless slopey sons of bitches.

One of the worst examples of official Chinese graft and inefficiency hit every American soldier in China in his most vulnerable spot: his stomach. No American who served there will ever forget the WASC hostels. When Americans began arriving in China, the Chungking government undertook to house and feed them and asked for $6 per day per man credit for it in the reverse lend-lease accounting. The United States Army rejected the rate as unconscionably high, whereupon the Chinese insisted that the Americans would be their "guests" until the matter of price was settled. The negotiations went on fruitlessly and, as far as I know, the question was still unsettled when the war ended. It became part of the whole inextricable tangle of exchange rates and lend-lease bookkeeping. But meanwhile the War Area Service Corps was set up and operated as only corrupt Kuomintang officials and businessmen can operate an undertaking from which fabulous profits could be made.

There were inadequacies which nobody could help. A relatively small establishment of American soldiers could normally eat more meat and vegetables in a week than all the people in a crowded

Chinese city might eat in a year. They could burn more charcoal in one night than most of the ordinary folk in a city like Kunming would burn through half a winter. In the end deficiencies in food and living necessities were largely met by the army out of its own supplies. But the main problem was not shortage. It was filth. It was unsanitary and inefficient operation. It was the endless graft involved in every purchase made, from the largest items to the smallest needed to operate the billets and the mess.*

The result was not merely hunger and discomfort but sickness. Americans in WASC hostels all the way from Chengtu to Kweilin suffered chronically from diarrhea, dysentery, from every variety of gastro-intestinal disorder, as a direct result of conditions in the WASC hostels. American medical officers inspected, reported, protested, recommended . . . all in vain. They repeatedly demanded that various WASC hostels be declared out of bounds and that the army set up its own messes. The chief surgeon of Y Force in West China drew up a detailed report on unsanitary conditions and the resulting sickness. His exasperated conclusion: "It is recommended that as long as the use of the present mess setup is persisted in, the Medical Section of YFOS (Y Force Operations Staff) be not held responsible for resulting disease, morbidity, or mortality of US personnel." The general in command sent the report along to headquarters with this endorsement: "For over two years WASC has repeatedly demonstrated that under the best conditions it cannot operate. . . . It is the opinion of this headquarters that US Army installations have suffered unnecessary illness and unnecessarily poor living conditions long enough. If we are to attempt to 'save face' for this organization, as the Chinese authorities have insisted in the past, the effort is a hopeless

* Trading companies or "cooperatives" were set up and WASC made all its purchases through them. The formula was simple. The company would buy cups, for example, at CN$20 apiece and sell them to WASC for $40 apiece. Precise margins of graft, established by investigation in Kunming, included items like bread tins bought at CN$300, supplied to WASC at $480; sheets bought at CN$1,000, supplied at $1,600; charcoal purchased at $16 per catty, supplied at $19 per catty. On the charcoal supply to one Kunming hostel alone, the daily graft came to CN$60,000. The WASC purchases were credited to the Chinese reverse lend-lease account. The official government exchange rate was first CN$20 to US$1 and later CN$40 to US$1 at a time when the black-market money rate ranged from CN$500 to CN$1,000 for one American dollar. Construction costs for buildings, airfields, etc., were billed in astronomical figures which Chungking hoped to write off its account with the United States at the official rate. The whole American operation in China was relatively small, in wartime terms, but there was nothing small about the graft involved.

one, inasmuch as the WASC has long since lost all face, not only for itself but for the Chinese government among all personnel who are familiar with its operation." In one month at one establishment of 400 Americans there were 329 cases of diarrhea. In every month at every American establishment there was 100 per cent morbidity. Nothing was ever officially done about the repeated protests. Conditions were finally improved when Americans arbitrarily in many places assumed control and supervision of the messes. Sanitary conditions, if not the food quality, were improved and the sickness rate went down. But WASC graft, echeloned back through half a dozen connected Kuomintang politicians and agencies, went on unchecked. It was an open scandal. The chief of WASC, General J. L. Huang, was a personal friend, it was said, of the Missimo herself. He and his organization were untouchable.

But that did not prevent thousands of American soldiers from acquiring, via WASC, an unforgettable impression of the Chinese and their way of doing things. You are not generally inclined to feel kindly toward people responsible for giving you chronic diarrhea. I will not soon forget the first GI I spoke to in Kunming the day I arrived there. He was on guard duty at the gate of Hostel No. 1. I asked him what he thought about the Chinese. He looked at me sourly. "I don't know," he growled. "I put in my working time here and the rest of my time I spend in the latrine." I slept and ate in WASC hostels in many parts of West China after that, and I got to understand what he meant. I looked into the records, the medical reports, the confidential army complaints about filth and corruption. It was not difficult to establish that the whole shoddy business was part of the general rot of the régime of Chiang Kai-shek. But the GI, for his part, wrote it all down to the unforgivable crookedness and sloppiness of Chinese in general. It is no exaggeration to say that the greater part of the violent hatred for the Chinese felt by so many Americans was directly traceable to Madame Chiang Kai-shek's friend, General J. L. Huang, and his WASC.

Another thing was the brutality practiced on the people. It was a common sight on the streets. Everyone in Kunming saw soldiers "requisitioning" ponies from cartmen. It was done with heavy bamboo sticks. If the cartman or cartboy protested, he was beaten across the hands, over the head, and across his stomach. He was kicked in the groin and his face when he doubled over. Finally he would usually be led away under arrest; and nobody ever came out of a Kuomintang prison without scars to carry for the rest of his life. The sight of dying or dead people, untended and unnoticed in the streets or by roadsides, was likewise not uncommon. This was shocking enough, by American standards, but most Americans did not know that this was by no means a wartime peculiarity or confined to the backward western provinces. In the prewar days in lush Shanghai there was a benevolent society whose sole mission it was to retrieve corpses from the streets. In an average year they picked up 50,000, mostly the bodies of infants. In West China there was no benevolent society of any kind, and there was much more occasion for people to hunger and die out of normal want and out of the abnormal excesses of the war. Death, of the stiff or the living variety, is a familiar fixture of the Chinese scene.

The same standards existed in the Chinese army. There was never much concern for care of the wounded. Men died in droves from neglect of minor wounds. The devoted efforts of a few Chinese doctors and occasional foreign well-wishers had availed very little through the years of the war. During the Salween campaign American medical teams radically changed this picture. They brought competent medical service to within gunshot of the front lines. But once they left the forward areas, the wounded returned to the unsupervised care of the Chinese army authorities. The wounded were carried back to the river, and there they were loaded on trucks driven as a rule by men of the old Burma Road gang, the worst bunch of cutthroats and bandits ever assembled in West China. They bounced their vehicles along the rough road, heedless of the wounded men packed like pigs in the back of the truck. It was a common sight to see them stopped for long periods by the roadside while the drivers salvaged parts from wrecked cars and trucks. They would stop in villages to trade, to eat, to drink, to sleep with whores. They almost never bothered about the care or feeding of their charges. If trucks stalled anywhere on the road, which they frequently did, the wounded men simply lay there through the hours, trying to survive. And many did not survive. I have watched those trucks drive into the Chinese army hospital near Paoshan where an earnest little team of Friends, doctors and nurses, was trying to help. In any truckload of sixteen or twenty men, half a dozen or more as a rule would lie stiff and dead by the time they were driven into the muddy courtyard. The rest would soon be stretched out in the straw in the foul-smelling hospital shed to be victimized there by orderlies who took whatever little the soldiers had in return for performing some of the necessary services. Most of the mangled men lay still in their own filth. When they died, it was some time before they were taken away.

It did not help much to understand this kind of thing, to understand that in China the struggle for survival was too fierce to permit the luxury of Western standards about life and death; or to understand without nausea the spectacle of persecution, of brutalized soldiers and policemen riding roughshod over paupers. It did not help much to understand that this stemmed from the higher to the lower orders of a ruling tyranny, of a surviving medievalism, and that the people and the soldiery were themselves the chief victims of this tyranny. Impressionable American soldiers read into what they saw the quality of the whole land. They made a national thing of it, a racial thing. They made a new and raging prejudice out of it, and it came to them out of their own indelible experience.

The American in China saw the Chinese soldier in many different shapes. He saw him as a ragged, starving, hopeless, and largely incomprehensible feature of the Chinese countryside. He saw him as a miserable, groveling, and insensible nuisance or as a stupid dog who could not learn new tricks. He saw him as a brute, maltreating and robbing his own people. He saw him as a beast of burden carrying his nondescript loads along the mountain trails. He saw him, more rarely, as an uncomplaining sacrificial offering, dying needlessly when he was told to do so. The American saw the Chinese soldier as everything but a man.

An army can only mirror the social régime of which it is part, and the Chinese army was no exception. It was made up of hordes of men drawn from the great pauperized masses of the land, conscripted helots, caught like trapped animals, dragged away in bonds and beaten into subservience. The army had no conception of a service of supply, no communications worth noting. Its commanders were almost universally corrupt and incompetent. Chinese generals and their supporting hierarchies down the line fattened on graft out of army funds under a system legalized by long practice. The Chinese soldier paid in hunger and disease and nakedness for the cupidity of his officers. He often paid with his life for their stupidity. The Chinese soldiers were poorly led, poorly trained, poorly armed. With ancient or faulty rifles and occasional odd pieces of obsolete artillery, they faced a powerful enemy. How often Chinese soldiers fingered American carbines with envy! I crouched once next to a calm little Hunanese boy who took my carbine, aimed it over the rubble and fired it. He handed it back to me. "Does it really shoot every time you pull the trigger?" he wanted to know. He picked up his old piece. "With this one you never know," he said. In the fighting in the east, the Chinese soldier never had a chance when it came to the test of battle. His commanders were always cowardly or confused, or both. After doing everything possible to contrive their own defeat, they would sometimes make sudden and futile and heroic "last stands." More often they would simply dissolve in the face of their responsibilities. It was never remarkable that in these conditions Chinese troops broke up in confusion. It was remarkable only that they fought at all. And along the vague front across Central China, from the Yellow River bend to the outskirts of Canton, it is true that they seldom fought from the time of Pearl Harbor to the last year of the war.

When General Stilwell set out to train and equip a limited number of Chinese divisions, he encountered all the stolid obstacles of an entrenched medievalism. He met the effective resistance of grafters and jobholders and the stubborn and phony problem of "face" among the Chinese leaders, from Chiang Kai-shek down. Americans from the top headquarters through the lowest echelon of the remotest liaison team met the same obstacles, and grappled with them just as fruitlessly. The Americans, to be sure, were too often imbued with a rather exaggerated sense of their own ability and their own superiority. Their scorn of the Chinese was often a convenient substitute for recognition of their own shortcomings and failures. But by and large they made an honest and sometimes even heroic effort. Whatever results they gained came despite the Chinese high command, never because of it. In the little-noted and little-remembered Salween campaign, Chinese soldiers went into battle with a few more advantages than they ordinarily had. They had some American weapons, including light artillery. They had some training. They had front line medical service. And for what it was worth, they had American tactical advice. But they had the same hopeless officers and were victimized by the same brutal disregard of their most elementary interests. The troops that crossed the Salween and scaled the great Kaoli range under fire climbed into the bitter cold, snow, and ice of the passes while blankets that had never reached them circulated in the black markets. Raincoats destined for them had disappeared far up the supply line. They went without food, without cover. The healthy, well clothed, well shod Americans who made that crossing and that climb will remember it as the most rugged physical and moral test they ever faced. They, at least, will never forget the show the puny, ragged Chinese made of simple endurance and devoted stoicism.

One day west of the river at one of the many little battlefields of this remote war once again Chinese soldiers had advanced, standing up, against the pillboxed Japanese. They had been cut down, rank after rank, by Japanese crossfire. From a covering position of a neighboring hilltop a young American machine gunner had fired to cover them until his gun was too hot to handle. He slumped, sick with exhaustion, onto the heaps of shells and links around his feet. "They just kept on going up," he said. "Just kept on going up. Did you see them? Just kept on going up . . ." To an American captain on this front I said that the Chinese had courage that deserved better leadership. "Courage?" he snorted in angry disgust. "All right, courage. But do you say a mule has courage because he keeps on going until he drops?" Did he mean, I asked, that the Chinese soldiers had no more sensibility than animals and did what they did only because they were lashed to it? "I didn't mean it that way exactly," he said. "But I did mean that they act out of dumb submission, not out of conscious will." He was unwilling to give them their due as men.

In American eyes the Chinese did nothing right. They used

ammunition wantonly. They did not take care of their weapons. Once I found an American officer almost in tears from angry exasperation. A Chinese gun crew on a .37-mm. gun which had been laboriously packed over the hills had fired a hundred rounds without swabbing the barrel, and had wrecked the gun. They seldom aimed at enemy targets but liked to fire indiscriminately and at random in the general direction of their foe. The American liaison teams, which had purely advisory status, fumed and raged and argued and never got anywhere with the Chinese colonels and generals. The Chinese soldiers died in useless droves because of this failure. Americans often acquired, out of sheer self-defense, a kind of callous indifference to the whole thing. I remember a snatch of an argument in a tent at field headquarters. One American was describing with some passion the course of operations across the river. "They threw away three thousand men," he said. "Three thousand men!" One of the others looked at him contemptuously. "So what?" he said. "Since when are you bleeding for three thousand slopeys? *They* don't bleed about it, do they?"

The American ground force combat teams formed a relatively small part of the American forces in China. They were in a far better position to see the distinction between the victimizers and their victims. Yet they were most often scornful and impatient and, in the end, indifferent. Only occasionally did they feel, almost without witting it, the fleeting touch of the respect which these ragged little *laobing*— common soldiers—really had every right to command. The Salween force finally fought its blundering slow way down to the Burma border, giving up the prodigal total of 50,000 dead and wounded as they went. The day they finally entered the town of Wanting, looking more like a mob of tired refugees than like an army of victors, an embittered, weary, gray-haired American colonel who had been through the whole campaign broke out some hoarded liquor and after a while he found words:

"They look like a bunch of bums, don't they?" he said. "Sure they look like bums. But we kind of like our bums, do you hear that? We're proud of our bums. Get that? These goddamned *laobings*, they fight. They keep attacking, keep attacking. Can you imagine it? Can you explain it? I can't. I'm a colonel in the Regular Army of the

United States. I ought to be ashamed of being associated with an army that looks like this one. I don't know why an army that looks like this one, eats like this one, is equipped like this one should go on attacking, go on attacking. But they do, and, Christ, you go down the road and it's a smile and 'ting hao!' all the time. God, every time I see those fellows going in with their lousy rifles and bayonets and a few grenades apiece . . . Did I tell you the story of the *hsiaobing*, the little fellow only fifteen years old? He was too small to carry a rifle. He had just three grenades. He went up the hill and lobbed one at a Jap and got him. Then he got so close the Japs grabbed him. We saw it happen, and we figured he was a goner. But that goddamned kid, a little while later he comes sauntering down the hill, grinning like a jackass. I don't know even now what happened. Or that other time we ran into a soldier wandering right across a line of fire. We yelled to him and he came back. Lost his outfit, he said, and he was looking for the enemy. Imagine that! That ragged stupid bastard was out there with his rifle looking for the enemy! That's the kind of bums they are. Do you think we need any help from those slick bastards on the other side of the border, with their shoes and good rifles and helmets and rations? Hell! We don't have anything. No shoes, no helmets, no rations, not a decent rifle in the whole army. The only thing we've got here is a mob of crazy bums who will fight no matter what kind of commanders they've got."

The old colonel's head drooped to the table. "A bunch of bums," he muttered, "a lousy bunch of slopey bums."

But even such half-glimmerings of sympathy and pride were rare. The whole was a snarl of friction, prejudice, and hatred, and it has deepened since the end of the war, particularly in China where Americans stayed on in large numbers. This fact cannot be blinked away, nor can it be dismissed as simple misunderstanding. On both sides the feeling is based more on fact than on fancy, on at least half as many truths as half-lies. The American who now abhors the Chinese as he has known them, has a case. So has the Chinese who has lost his respect and admiration for the Americans as he has known them. This may come from the twisted and distorted experience of wartime. The whole picture may sorely lack proportion or any simple reasonableness. But it is nevertheless a fact. The results of it will be felt for a long time to come.

Consider what has happened: the previous direct contacts of Americans with Chinese in China were confined to a small number of missionaries, officials, businessmen, scholars, and students. These were abruptly widened to include about a quarter of a million young Americans drawn from a cross-section of the whole American population. This large and significant body of men emerges from the experience nursing violent prejudices. They return to their homes attributing to the Chinese people as a whole all the brutality and venality and ugly viciousness of China's ruling cliques, its big and small officials, its generals and many of its soldiers, its exploiters. They bring to the traditionally amorphous American feeling of sympathy for China a sharp and bitter and explicit contradiction. Taken together with the families and friends whose ideas about China will undoubtedly be shaped by what they have to tell, they represent a new and important body of American opinion touching millions of the people. Their experience will inevitably find expression in books and stories and novels which in time to come may reach many more. The returning soldiers will be able to speak with all the factitious authority of men *who were there*. Right or wrong, they will not easily be contradicted.

Take the other side of the picture. Millions of Chinese who never saw an American before, or saw only the isolated missionary or business traveler, have now seen and encountered Americans in large groups. They were enormously impressed by American power and the marvels of American technical efficiency. But they also found that Americans too can be coarse and brutal, contemptuous of the weak, prone to depend on brute strength to get what they want. The Chinese, in short, had a lot of their myths about America dispelled by their contact with Americans. As this change percolates through the rest of the population, the standing of America in the Chinese mind is going to be increasingly revised. Whatever new form it takes, it will certainly not be a change for the better.

This was not the least of the tragic consequences of the war. It paralleled, at the level of direct personal and human contact, the broader divisions and friction and baleful entanglements of the nations emerging from the war. The times called desperately for some small measure of greater common understanding, of greater common purpose. This was, apparently, too much to expect. There was no sign of it in Asia in the events swiftly unfolding after Japan's collapse.

AFTER JAPAN'S COLLAPSE

2 RUSSIA: THE BIG NEW FACT

Japanese soldiers had not yet laid down their arms when Russia swept in to take Japan's place as a major contender for control in Asia. The Russians re-entered Manchuria in a swift, triumphant occupation. Here Japan had started its long march of conquest. Here the Russians picked up where the Japanese had finally been compelled to leave off. Russia re-entered the Asiatic arena. This was the big new fact after Japan's collapse. This was the beginning of the new cycle.

Six months earlier, in February, 1945, at Yalta, President Roosevelt and Joseph Stalin and Winston Churchill had signed a secret agreement. Roosevelt wanted a Russian commitment to enter the war against Japan. Stalin laid down his terms. They bargained territory and power across the table. Everything the Czar had long ago taken from China and everything the Japanese had subsequently taken from the Czar was returned to Stalin by American agreement and at Chinese expense. "The former rights of Russia violated by the treacherous attack of Japan in 1904 shall be restored," the agreement said. These "rights" included restoration of southern Sakhalin, recognition of Russia's "pre-eminent interest" in the port of Dairen, restoration of Port Arthur as a Russian naval base, and an arrangement for joint Sino-Russian operation of the Manchurian railroads formerly controlled by Japan. In addition the Kurile Islands were handed over to Russia and Outer Mongolia's status as an independent republic was formally recognized. China's "concurrence" would be needed, the agreement acknowledged, but "the heads of the three Great Powers have agreed that these claims of the Soviet Union shall be unquestionably fulfilled after Japan has been defeated." In other words, with cynical bluntness, the agreement left China no choice in the matter. Under American dictation, the Chinese ratified the Yalta deal by signing a treaty with Stalin in Moscow embodying all the pertinent Yalta terms. This treaty was signed in the week of Japan's surrender, in August, 1945. Thus Japan's long struggle to carve out and maintain its "special position" in Manchuria came to an end and Russia's "pre-eminent position" in Manchuria took its place.

Down the Manchurian railway corridor, in Mukden, in Dairen, in Port Arthur, affairs quickly assumed the shapes of the brave new world. Where the Japanese ruled and expanded before under constant American challenge, the Russians now prepared to rule and expand and would soon come under constant American challenge. China, still the hapless victim, had to get along under the new dispensation as best she could. This was the new pattern, and it prevailed everywhere. The end of the war transformed northern Asia from an area of friction between the United States and Japan into an area of friction between the United States and Russia. There was no interval. The transfer was immediate. It determined the shape of things not only in Manchuria, but in Japan, Korea, and in China itself.

Japan, the defeated power, became for the time being a political cipher on the map of Asia. Its armies and its manpower, so lately the chief enemy, were dispersed, docile masses of confused men. They were readily disarmed, concentrated, and repatriated, except where the victor powers had other uses for them. The Chinese and Americans tried to use them in the race with the Chinese Communists for postwar position in North China. The British, French, and Dutch used them as mercenaries against the insurgent nationalists in Indochina and Java. The Russians deported them in long trainloads to toil as forced labor in Far Eastern Siberia. Japanese businessmen beat a disheveled retreat toward their homeland, carrying with them what little they could salvage from the ruins of the co-prosperity sphere. In Japan itself the rulers of the land, the princes of finance and the princes of military might, the pullers of the imperial strings, drew long breaths before accepting the submersion of defeat. The more conspicuous among them committed suicide or were handed up for trial as war criminals. The remainder concentrated on preserving the essence of rule while they surrendered its trappings. This did not prove difficult, because the Japanese were a numbed and hynotized people. They stolidly began paying the harsh price of defeat, just as they had paid the cost of the many empty victories that had gone before.

The social régime in Japan—the imperial system, the enormous concentration of wealth, the medieval tenure on the land—astonish-

ingly took the shock of catastrophic defeat with scarcely a tremor. It
was not challenged by the people nor really touched by the American
conquerors. Under MacArthur the "democratic transformation" of
Japan was turned into a preposterous and macabre comedy, a business
of decrees and directives, of fabricated constitutional revision drafted
by the old rulers and imposed upon a docile and suffering mass un-
shaken from the grooves of the old way of life. Perhaps this was
traumatic shock that would wear off as the harsh consequences of the
defeat made themselves felt. Or else it was a remarkable demonstration of how far a mass could be conditioned to subjection. New influences would sooner or later stir the great victimized peasantry and
the masses of the homeless and the hungry in Japan's pulverized
cities. But now submission was the thing, adaptation the only possible
course, and the Japanese régime dug out a new group of pliant
politicians to carry Japan somehow across the rough spots to come.
For in submission there was survival, and survival would clearly be
served by collision between the victors. There was flickering encouragement in the early Russian-American friction over the control of
the occupation policy, in the early outbreak of Russian-American difficulties over Manchuria and in Korea. There was promise for Japanese politicians in the remark frequently heard around the MacArthur
headquarters in Tokyo that Japan had to be regarded as the "staging
area for the next operation." It was necessary only to survive, for there
would surely be ample room for maneuver by Japanese politicians
when the future would have taken the sharp edge off the disaster that
had befallen them. No longer a king or even a knight on the Asiatic
chessboard, Japan could still have a role to play as a pawn.

In Korea the new pattern was visible in test-tube proportions.
Here the new element of Russian-American relations in the Far East
could be observed taking shape. Korea had all the necessary components. It was territory adjacent to Russia, and therefore a peculiar
object of Russian interest. It was occupied by Russian and American
troops facing each other across a line arbitrarily halving the country. It was a country with a strong nationalist tradition, a powerful urge to regain its own independence. Here it was all put together
in neat capsule form: Russian and American power and a small subject people wanting to be free. Here was a testing ground for words

and deeds, for motives and actions. If the freedom of peoples from foreign pressures and foreign domination is the crux of the problem of Asia, then in Korea it would be possible to see plainly whether the great war had brought that goal any nearer or had driven it to a still remoter future.

If Korea was a test-tube showing of the new era, Manchuria was an applied demonstration on a far larger scale. Nobody got to know much about Manchuria in the months after Japan collapsed. The open door clanged shut by the Japanese in 1931 was kept shut by the Russians. It was six months before even American correspondents were allowed to cross the Great Wall to have a look at the place where the great war had actually begun fourteen years earlier. They found that the Russians had carried out as a matter of deliberate policy an additional piece of wanton destruction that not even the war had required. Claiming it as war booty, the Russians had stripped a good part of Manchurian industry. Numerous factories were reduced to hollow shells and warehouses were emptied. Plant machinery, raw materials, and even food, were shipped in large quantities across the Siberian frontier. The Russians did a systematic job of deindustrializing the most highly developed area in eastern Asia. This was plain, high-powered looting accompanied by tommy gun terror. If, as widely thought, it was also part of the Russian system for assuring "security" by leveling out a vast glacis beyond all its frontiers, then it simply demonstrated once more the brutal and heavy-handed character of the new Russian nationalism. By this act, the Russians further crippled the meager industrial potential of a weakened and exhausted China and made still bleaker the prospect of Chinese rehabilitation.

Whatever else this was, it was hardly "liberation" of Manchuria. The empty factories and boarded-up shop fronts and lifeless streets of Manchurian cities six months after Japan's surrender did not suggest that conditions after Japan's defeat were any improvement over those that existed under Japanese control. The Russians, after accomplishing their own immediate objectives, finally did evacuate from the broader area of occupation while settling down in Dairen and Port Arthur to consolidate their newly won "pre-eminent position" and to wait future developments. And as they evacuated, Chinese Communist forces moved to take over. Chinese central government

forces, transported by the Americans, were able to reestablish themselves in Mukden; but from Mukden northward the Communist
strength, enhanced by Japanese weapons and artillery and other equipment secured during the Russian occupation, proved too much for
Chiang Kai-shek's troops. Changchun, the Manchurian capital, fell to
the Communists after a sharp battle, and Harbin, in the far north,
fell into their hands by default. They later yielded Changchun but
held tenaciously to their gains farther north. Thereby the prospect
opened of a new Manchurian separatism under Russian-dominated
Communist auspices which, whatever the legal fictions devised, would
amount to another division of China and the creation of a Soviet-
sponsored buffer state. Similarly in the west, in Inner Mongolia, the
old long-standingly unsuccessful Japanese-inspired separatist movement was replaced by a new Russian-inspired separatist movement
which could, if the Russians wished it, extend into the large Mon-
golian sections of western Manchuria. Obviously the practical terms
of Russia's "pre-eminent position" in northeastern Asia were only beginning to be worked out.

What it amounted to was the beginning and the development of
Russian penetration, of Russian acts and policies carried out for sufficient Russian reasons. These would, in due course, bring Russia into
conflict with the United States. The United States for *its* sufficient
reasons wants Manchuria to remain open to *its* penetration, *its* acts,
its policies. And the deploring, the debating, the editorial writing and
the diplomatic note writing has begun. There is nothing new in
it. Whole libraries are filled with identical literature in which Japan
was featured as the main antagonist. The new and fateful file of
Washington notes to Moscow about Manchuria begins at a date when
there has scarcely been time to relegate to some dustier, remoter ar-
chive the old series that started with John Hay's Open Door notes in
1899 and ended with the declaration of war in 1941. The old bootless
and tragic business has begun all over again. There is no peace. There
is only a deepening of China's overlong travail.

For Manchuria cannot ever be regarded apart from China. Any
Manchurian question is a Chinese question. Control of Manchuria
can determine in large measure the shape of things in China proper.
Manchurian coal, iron, lumber, and other resources are indivisible

from China's hope and need to rebuild itself. Manchuria has the greatest part of all Chinese industrial development, actual and potential. Before it was stripped by the Russians, Manchurian heavy industry represented seventy per cent of all such industry in China. It has steel mills and machine shops and the most extensive net of railways in the whole country. It is the only area in China where coal and iron exist in sufficient quantity and quality to form the basis of an indigenous heavy industry. Built up in large part as an integrated part of Japanese warmaking economy, Manchuria became capable of producing heavy and light metals, weapons and ammunition, locomotives and rolling stock, ships, textiles, chemicals, cement, paper, processed foods, automobiles, and airplanes. It has extensive hydroelectric power resources and facilities, and some of the best ports on the China coast. Converted from serving Japan's needs and reintegrated with a generalized economic program serving China's requirements, Manchuria would be the heart and center of a new era in Asia. By the same token, Manchurian industrial resources are no less essential to the long-thwarted American dream of selling American goods to four hundred million Chinese customers. That is why, ever since the day of John Hay, the American effort has been to keep Manchuria open, at least to the potential possibility, if not the actual fact, of American exploitation. That is why the clash between Japan and the United States so inevitably had to come.

In the crazy mosaic of geopolitical and economic rivalries in Asia, Manchuria is the central piece. In many ways, it is the key to the puzzle, the clue to the outcome. Notched into Asia's most strategic corner, it has been the elusive prize, the heart's desire of eternally unresolved triangles. For many centuries the Chinese, the Manchus, and the Mongols were the contenders. Later the Chinese, the Russians, and the Japanese fought a series of wars, between 1894 and 1905, to control it. After that the triangle was Chinese-Japanese-American. In the new cycle now just opening it is Chinese-Russian-American. China remains now, as before, the passive element, the petitioner and the victim. Russian-American relations are the new dominant factor in all the affairs of northern Asia. They will color and determine, from now on, almost everything that happens in all quarters of the continent; and of these the most crucial is occupied by China.

3 CHINA: THE LONG TRAVAIL

NEW WARS FOR OLD

In China the collapse of Japan brought on civil war. The unresolved conflict between the Kuomintang régime of Chiang Kai-shek and the Chinese Communists was resumed in the mad dash to exploit the sudden victory. The immediate goals were the territories so long occupied by the Japanese and now yielded without a struggle: the rich ports of the east coast, the heart of the Yangtze Valley, the northern provinces, and Manchuria. The Communists reached out for the arms of the defeated Japanese. Chiang Kai-shek moved to keep those arms from falling into Communist hands. It was a deep lunge for position. Chu Teh, the Communist commander, demanded the right to accept the Japanese surrender in regions that the Communists could reach. Chiang Kai-shek sharply denied this right. He ordered the Japanese and the 800,000 Japanese-controlled Chinese puppets in the north and the east to hold their ground until the Kuomintang troops could reach them to take over. At a dozen tangled points fighting began between the government and puppet and Japanese and Communist troops.

From the rich Shanghai-Nanking area, where the Communists had been expected to make a strong bid for power, they unexpectedly withdrew, filtering northward. From Shensi and Shansi and northern Hopeh they moved north and east, into Suiyuan and Jehol to swell their partisan bands in Shantung and Manchuria. The Communists' strategy was simple and obvious. They wanted to back themselves up against the Russians, concentrating on the northern provinces adjacent to Manchuria and on Manchuria itself. They figured on implicit or explicit Russian support if the civil war should become generalized and prolonged. The Kuomintang, on its part, counted on and received strong and immediate American support. American air transports flew whole Chinese armies to key areas, to the Shanghai-Nanking triangle, to the Peiping-Tientsin area in the north. American troop-ships were loaded in southern Chinese ports and in the Indochinese port of Haiphong to move Chinese government troops to Manchuria. When the Russians blocked their entry at Dairen, they landed at North China ports instead. American marines landed on the Shantung coast. American planes flew patrol over the Tsinpu Railway. The old Yang-tze River naval patrol was reestablished. Where contact was made with Communist or other non-Kuomintang partisan bands, there was usually shooting.

This was conflict that China could hardly sustain. China was a weary country, buffeted and ravaged, a land of famine and uprooted people, doomed to turmoil it could not abide. Fourteen years of Japa-nese invasion, of battering attacks and air raids and constant plunder-ing; eighteen years of Kuomintang tyranny grinding out the life sub-stance of the land; thirty years of intermittent civil war; a century of hammering by all the imperialist powers: such had been the long travail of China. It was as though the whole country were being sub-jected to the prolonged torture of the thousand cuts. Out of its deepest silent suffering came the will for some kind of pause. While contend-ing armies and factions could trample at will across the prostrate land, they could not wholly ignore nor be free themselves of this powerful impulse. It had some part, at least, in the long, hesitant, inconclusive negotiations, in the readiness to entertain a truce if within that truce they could hold positions, or gain as much as pos-sible, or lose as little as possible, depending on the changing circum-stances.

Back of the contending Chinese factions, moreover, the greater forces in play more or less equally desired a quieter interim. Russia had signed its treaty with Kuomintang China. Russia had secured its enormous gains in Manchuria, and in return had pledged non-inter-ference in China Proper and unqualified recognition of the sover-eignty of the Chinese Central Government. These were formal phrases and diplomatic promises, to be sure, subject to any convenient and expedient change, and did not in any case bind the Chinese Com-munists. But still, they reflected an important fact: Russia wanted to establish its new footholds in Asia without having to fight for them, without colliding too soon and too harshly with the United States.

The United States, equally and for its own reasons, was anxious to limit the burgeoning Chinese civil war. The prospect it opened up was nothing less than a masked war between Russia and America in the form of an American-supported Kuomintang fighting Russian-supported Communists. This was neither necessary nor desirable, at least not so soon. The United States wanted its positions in China secured also without having to fight any more for them. And this, undoubtedly, had been the sense of the Yalta agreement. Whether tacitly or explicitly we do not know, but American acknowledgment of the broad Russian sphere beyond the Great Wall was presumably matched by Russian acknowledgment of the American sphere in China Proper. All the pushing and pulling and maneuvering and countermaneuvering that followed the war's end was simply part of working out the *modus operandi* for this broad agreement. But this required that the Americans should achieve some kind of balance within their own sphere, and this they had failed to do. Instead, by virtue of the American policy of all-out support of Chiang Kai-shek, they found themselves embroiled in the civil war. For the Great Pacific War had settled nothing in China. All the unresolved conflicts remained unresolved.

CHIANG KAI-SHEK: THE MYTH AND THE MAN

The struggle between the Kuomintang and the Communists in China has by now accumulated a history nearly twenty-five years long. In its changing faces, it is the frame and the substance of all the unfinished business in China's fight for real national freedom and for its emergence from its clinging past. In all its twists and turns and agonies, this quarter century of travail has been largely dominated by the single personality of Chiang Kai-shek. His has been the central role. He has deeply stamped his imprint on these years, and the demands of nations and classes in conflict have placed their mark upon him. The annals of China in the time of Chiang Kai-shek are annals of enormous suffering, of disintegration, of frustrated growth. He was a part of these, and with them he will always be identified. In an epoch marked the world over by destruction and cruelty, Chiang Kai-shek occupies a peculiar eminence among the men who have contrived the chaos we live in. In this gallery of the dubiously great, he is undoubtedly one of the greatest.

Chiang Kai-shek is peculiarly the product of his China. He has represented in his own person all the elements that have come to bear on the tortured body of the country. He has epitomized the ruling class that shaped itself out of the formlessly crumbling society of the old China and attached itself to the new like some huge, insatiable parasite. As member and leader of this class, Chiang Kai-shek is militarist, politician, landlord, banker, racketeer, extortionist, and executioner. In the mirror held up to Chiang Kai-shek by his admirers, he can see himself as soldier, statesman, leader, and even— for foreign consumption only—as a democrat. But in the mirror of living history, he is the product and the artisan of incalculable violence. His story dominates two decades of slow death and sudden death on a vast scale in China. It is a story of malevolent terror and grinding privation, of an archaic social system not allowed to die and a suffering people barely allowed to live, of foreign invasion and of warring cliques contending with one another across the prostrate land. These are the threads that form the pattern of Chiang Kai-shek's career.

The myth built up around the personality of Chiang is one of the remarkable creations of our time. He has enjoyed in his latter years the services of an ardent claque made up of a variety of people who for policy, group, or individual interest, prefer not to see him as he is. In this country he has enjoyed the generous and influential praise of government leaders like President Roosevelt, Cordell Hull, and Donald Nelson; powerful publicists like Henry Luce; popular interpreters of Chinese life like Lin Yu-tang; sentimental humanitarians on occasion, like Pearl Buck; the hosts of the organized Christian mission bodies too delighted by his conversion to the faith to look too closely into his works; and from time to time even the American Communists and their fellow travelers, when it suited this or that zag of their quick-changing policy, have billed Chiang as the "father of his country."

Out of the whole has emerged a fine and misty portrait, scarcely marred by the occasional accidental exposure of the starker reality in transient news stories and articles. Here in this picture is a heroic leader of his country, dedicated unto the death to the task of national unity, self-defense, fruitful growth and modern progress. Here—in the more exaggerated versions—is the towering and peerless and wise and long-suffering and indispensable man of good will, the personification of Chinese virtue. Sometimes there is slight acknowledgment for such slight difficulties as the pervasive corruption and venality of his régime, the rapacity of his followers and henchmen, the absence of the most elementary democracy, the hounding of liberals and students, the imprisonment and execution of political opponents. But almost invariably, Chiang Kai-shek is absolved of any responsibility for these "shortcomings." It is not he, but a cabal of evil men around him who screen his lofty eminence from the lowlier facts of life and go their nefarious ways balking his higher purposes. He remains the unique and irreplaceable leader, the chief and even the only unifying force in the land, the professing and practicing democrat who wants only to lead his people along the path of freedom and righteousness.

It is quite possible that Chiang Kai-shek has come to regard this portrait of himself with great seriousness and considerable admiration. He has had years enough in power to be uncontent merely with satisfied cupidity and personal aggrandizement. His lust for place in power has been transmuted in recent years into a lust for virtuous greatness, for an assurance of his heroic place in history. Chiang has identified himself, increasingly, with China. He sees it in his image and looks upon himself as China personified. He must be the man of whom the story tellers for generations to come will spin their tales and make their songs. He must be the great ruler who held the country firm against foreign invasion and who must lead it, like a child, toward its destined greatness.

History, being more often a capricious muse than an exact scientist, may employ sufficient poetic license to offer such a picture to posterity. This would come under the heading of "gaining perspective" on men and events. But there will always be the galling necessity for footnotes. It will not be possible, one hopes, that all history shall be written with an airbrush. Some of the real lineaments of this man would have to show through.

Chiang Kai-shek never felt too seriously the need for buttressing himself with principles or appeals to the traditions of the past. He began his career and built his power as a brash and brutal and able brigand, a new and more effective kind of militarist who would not content himself with a provincial satrapy but took the whole country for his domain. He is a man, however, whose success was never complete. He never achieved security in his conquests or tranquillity in his achievements, for his conquests and his achievements were always brittle, always more apparent than real, even though he exacted them at appalling cost to his country and his people. He had to remain lean and vigilant under constant threat, from rival militarists and politicians, from rebellious peasants and struggling workers, from recurring foreign attacks. His tenure has been one of permanent crisis in which he has distinguished himself chiefly by his unflagging devotion to his own interests. To win power, to maintain it against all challenges, to outconspire all conspirators, to keep in his hands the perquisites of place, these have been his satisfactions and he has possessed the particular skills, the cruelty, and the singlemindedness he needed to realize them.

Ideas and ideologies have been a matter of changing convenience in his career. From Sun Yat-sen he inherited a set of doctrines liberally sprinkled with ambiguities and justifications for tyranny. Old Sun was something of a paternalist, and Chiang could borrow from him the notion that China was like an unruly, difficult ward, badly in need of stern, parental care. Sun Yat-sen fathered the idea of a period of "political tutelage" through which the country would be governed by a Kuomintang one-party dictatorship until it was "ready" for constitutional democracy. This in itself was a sufficient fig leaf for an all-out military dictatorship. Chiang Kai-shek has kept this idea of "tutelage" going for twenty years now. In this time there have been proposed national assemblies which were in no real sense national and usually did not assemble. There have been drafts of constitutions in which democracy, a tender delicate plant, has been surrounded by all sorts of authoritarian barbed-wire fences. But even these drafts never became the law of the land. There was legality for the dictatorship only, and consequently all opposition to the dictatorship has been "illegal." The country was ruled only by the sanctions of armed force. Hence all serious efforts to change it have had to be made with arms in hand.

In some fairness to Chiang, let it be said that his repute as a demo-

crat is something of an importation. It was built up for him by
foreign admirers, chiefly American, who had to justify the American
policy of supporting Chiang's régime against all opponents. Thus,
such keen judges as Patrick Hurley, Donald Nelson and Henry Luce
have perceived in Chiang Kai-shek a profound yearning, a conse-
crated dedication to the ideal of transforming China into a genuine
democracy in the image of the United States. But somehow he has
always been thwarted in the attempt to consummate his dream.
Either time was lacking, in these twenty years, or Japanese invasions
intruded, or small knots of Chinese peasants with premature and un-
dignified insistence tried to win democratic rights for themselves and
had to be suppressed; or the people as a whole, more likely, were
stubbornly unready for the great dispensation. Whatever the cause,
the dream of democracy remained, safely, a dream.

It is quite possible that in talking to such people as Hurley, Luce,
Nelson, or other visiting American dignitaries, Chiang has on occasion been prevailed upon to confess his devotion to the democratic
idea. It was convenient, useful, politic; it cost him nothing and
there was something to be gained from it. Chiang Kai-shek was never
a man to overlook such opportunities. His career is rich with examples
of this kind of sagacity. He was just as dedicated once to the ideals
of communism. It is not often remembered now that at the outset of
his public life, Chiang first appeared in the foreign public prints as
the "Red General" who swore frequent fealty to the cause of the
world revolution. He waded out of that phase of his career up to his
hips in the blood of his betrayed comrades but managed to find
quick respectability, if not total absolution, by immediately thereafter
embracing Christianity.

It may, of course, only have been the overwise cynics who
regarded Chiang's conversion to Methodism as a fine stroke of public
relations, similar in kind if not in content to his previous espousal
of communism. It may, of course, have been a purely incidental fact
that at the time he saw the light he was a man who badly wanted and
needed American patronage. It could, of course, have been purely
incidental proof of the goodness of God that he got it. It is equally
possible that he never dreamed that he would win the everlasting
praise of the American evangels of Christ in China whose influence

on American opinion, through the churches at home, is not negligible.

In the same way as he has used communism, Anglo-Saxon democracy, and Christianity to serve his purposes at different times, Chiang Kai-shek in the early thirties borrowed extensively from doctrines and practices of European Fascism. He allowed some of his most devoted disciples—some members of that evil cabal that somehow always has surrounded him—to become fascinated with the Leader principle. His most powerful and most dreaded secret police organization of those years even borrowed the colored-shirt motif from Europe. It was known as the Lan I-shan—the Blue Gowns—and alongside the gun, knife, headsman's block, it used the techniques of Fascist propaganda in publications and carried those methods particularly into the universities to terrorize dissident students. The capital at Nanking drew corps of German and Italian advisers, military and political. Chiang's best prewar armies were the product of training by the Reichswehr general, Hans von Seekt, and a German mission which he retained in his service until the European war began. In methods of repression, Chiang had little to learn from these Fascist mentors, but they contributed whatever they could. Although Chiang's government dutifully declared war on Germany after Pearl Harbor, Nazis continued to receive friendly treatment in China, and Chinese military students in Germany did not have to interrupt their education. Connections between high-ranking personages in Kuomintang military and civil circles and Nazis remained close during and after the war. This was only natural, for while the Chiang Kai-shek dictatorship exists in a setting and in social conditions which make it difficult to use the label Fascist except in the loosest sense of the term, Fascism was the foreign doctrine and social political system with which Chiang found his closest affinity.

But communism, Anglo-Saxon democracy, Christianity, and even the more formal doctrines of Fascism are all foreign creations quite alien to the set of ideas which Chiang Kai-shek appears finally to have adopted as his own. In search of a justification for his past and a rationale both for his future place in history and for the state of affairs he will bequeath to his country, Chiang has sought more native roots.

The margin of Chiang Kai-shek's known thought beyond the

limits of his intense egocentrism is extremely narrow. His motivations are in terms of himself. Ideas he must borrow. He has reached out now to find a foundation for his thinking amid the ruins of China's past. Like a lord surrounded by portrait painters, he has finally looked with favor on a representation of himself dressed in the shimmering glories of China's golden ages during which power, as now, was built on the docility of the subjected mass. He has drawn upon the ancient philosophies and the ancient ethics, and with these he would design his permanent monument. He would glorify the past and embellish it with firm authoritarian principles. For Chiang, the ideal government is the all-powerful state. The ideal condition of the people is one of thankful docility while benefits are, in due course, conferred upon them. He rejects both Western democracy and Western communism in favor of the Confucian ideal, the "ancient Chinese heritage" in which everything under the sun has its appointed place. Such is the philosophy given to us by Chiang Kai-shek as his own in a little book called *China's Destiny* published in China in 1943.

The central theme of the book is the rejection, from the most reactionary point of view, of all foreign influence upon Chinese thinking and ways of life. By judicious selection and re-writing of history, both ancient and recent, it draws from China's past a justification for present tyrannies.

From the writings of Sun Yat-sen, in which almost anything can be found, Chiang extracts a passage in which old Sun said that China suffered from "too much liberty" and therefore deteriorated into "a sheet of sand." From this Chiang draws the obvious moral. "Whether in wartime or in the postwar period," he writes, "individual liberty that is like a sheet of sand cannot continue to exist."

All the political and ideological ferment among Chinese intellectuals during the past thirty years he dismisses as the product of slavish acceptance of foreign doctrines:

Since (1919) ideas of liberalism and communism have spread in China. . . . The struggle between liberalism and communism is nothing more than the opposition of Anglo-American thought to the thought of Soviet Russia. Such theories are unfit for the national life and people's livelihood of China and are opposed to the spirit of China's native culture . . .

This "native culture" Chiang translates into a wondrous idyl. In ancient China, according to Chiang, "the distribution of agriculture in the whole country was even and balanced." The social system, built around family, clan, and village responsibility, served the public benefit "without interference of the law." The wisdom of the sages was such that "we are still able to maintain in our social customs the elements of faith, honesty, hard work, plain life, esteem or propriety and righteousness and comprehension of purity and modesty."

These values, which alone account for China's survival, were rooted, he goes on, in ancient Chinese philosophy and ethics, which he describes as follows:

Ancient Chinese philosophy and ethics revealed deeply and in detail how the relationships of mankind and society were maintained. Though social organization is constantly evolving, the following are the immutable, universal rules of social life, *i.e.,* the way of fathers and sons, husbands and wives, brothers and friends, and the order of the upper and the lower, superiors and inferiors, men and women, elders and juveniles, as well as the principles of mutual assistance among neighbors and in adversity. . . . The original philosophy of life of China, created by Confucius, developed by Mencius, and explained by the Confucian school of the Han Dynasty, formed a lofty system of its own and is superior to any philosophy in the world.

The blow to this way of life, the retreat from these values, the onset of corruption and suffering and disintegration, came, according to Chiang, wholly and exclusively as a result of the imperialist invasions of China during the last hundred years. Crime, graft, venality, lawlessness, all originated in the foreign concessions which the imperialists extracted from China by force. The travail of China, its lack of peaceful growth, the breakdown of its society and its economy were due exclusively to the unequal treaties imposed by the foreign powers. This yoke, he concludes, has only now been thrown off. The virus of foreignism has been rejected from the sick body of the country and only now, Chiang says, can China really begin to reconstruct itself on the basis of its great past.

By this argument, ingeniously compounding truths and half-truths, Chiang Kai-shek completely absolves the Chinese ruling class, past and present, from any share in the responsibility for the present chaos. By that token, he absolves himself. The throwing off of the foreign yoke—by which he means the final rendering of extraterritorial rights by the powers in 1943—is his achievement and he would crown it by guiding the country into the future via its great, its Confucian, past.

But this Confucian past, it is interesting to note, along with the unequal treaties and the privileged foreign position in China, was the main target of renascent Chinese nationalism in this century. The stifling and hidebound precepts of Confucianism, used in that distant past to rationalize the old imperial hierarchies, were recognized as a prime stultifying factor in the stunted growth of modern China. In his day even Sun Yat-sen and indeed the whole school of ardent Chinese nationalists going back even to the days of Liang Chi-chao at the end of the nineteenth century, recognized that the Chinese people had the twin task of throwing off the heavy hand of foreign imperialism and the dead hand of China's past. As a philosophy, Confucianism was a social straitjacket, stifling any movement toward progressive change. Its precepts were empty, futile, and reactionary in a time of upheaval and growth. As a political system and a way of thought, it glorified a status quo in which, in that distant day too, the great masses of the Chinese people were held in ignorance and helotry and the privileges of wealth and civilization were reserved for the chosen few. Chiang Kai-shek, the modern statesman and reputed democrat, summons it now to serve the same purpose.

Chinese nationalism began by setting its face resolutely against the old Confucian system. But it failed to fix China in a new place in the modern context of social, economic, and political circumstance. This has not been entirely the fault of the Chinese nationalists nor even of Chiang Kai-shek, because China's struggle does not go on in a vacuum. The world of these decades has not offered China or any other backward country a fit and fruitful place in the scheme of things. So out of Chinese nationalism, thwarted and stunted, came the military dictatorship of Chiang Kai-shek and the Kuomintang. And Chiang, casting about in his aging years for a firm structure of which he can be the builder, offers China the greatness of . . . Confucius.

CHIANG KAI-SHEK: THE PROCESS OF SELECTION

Considering his world prominence, Chiang Kai-shek is remarkably little known outside of China except as a distant myth. His biography is almost wholly a closed, even an unwritten, book. Yet, since crucial decisions must still revolve around this man, it may be of some use to recall the principal details of his career.

Chiang's rise was a process of selection, natural and induced, fathered by his own cunning, his skill at intrigue, his shrewd sense of people and politics, his total lack of scruple. He won position and power by a series of well timed coups and he held it by brute force, causing the land to run red with the blood of those who opposed him. He had the sagacity and daring to do successfully what no other Chinese general of his time could do: he made use of a gigantic mass movement to further his ends, and when he had used it, he smashed it. Once in power he balanced himself between contending groups and individuals in his own camp. Out of their clustering discord, their clashing greeds and ambitions, he fashioned the single, consistent theme of his own leadership. In the midst of snarled-up plots and oppositions, he drew always in the right measure from his own strength and from the weakness of others. He knew better than any when to retreat, when to advance, when to speak in his own voice and when to let others speak for him, when to buy and when to threaten, when to dismiss and when to patronize. He was and is, by all odds, one of the most extraordinarily able politicians who ever lived.

The son of a fairly well-to-do merchant-landlord of Chekiang province, Chiang was a military student in Tokyo in 1911 when the Manchu Empire fell apart. He returned at once to Shanghai to begin his military career, but in the temporary absence of profitable employment as a soldier he turned to other pursuits. There is always a discreet curtain, in the official biographies, over these first years. Under the patronage of a few powerful Shanghai bankers and merchants, he dabbled obscurely as a broker on the Shanghai Stock Exchange. Through the old secret societies—the Green and Red Circles—he was initiated into the teeming underworld of which later he would make so much use. The first lines of the portrait the world later came to know were drawn in these years by gangsters and bankers, smugglers and brothelkeepers, the money-changers and the scum of the treaty ports. He apparently dipped a little too deeply into the fleshpots, because he had to be rescued from imprisonment or worse by his benefactors, the compradores Yu Ya-ching and Chang Chin-chiang. They made good his losses and shipped him south to link his fortunes to those of Sun Yat-sen.

This occurred amid the freshly burgeoning nationalist moods just after the first World War. The great anti-Versailles student demonstrations that began on May 4, 1919, had given body and impetus to these moods. Sun Yat-sen was at this time also establishing contact with the young Soviet régime in Russia. Invited to send a staff officer to Moscow, he selected Chiang Kai-shek. The spare, silent, youthful Chinese soldier in 1923 spent six months in the Bolshevik capital. Whatever else he learned and observed there, Chiang caught something of the magic of an idea: the power of the aroused masses as a political and military weapon. Upon his return to China, Chiang— then, as always, a bold gambler—plunged on his findings. He promptly became the dark-haired darling of Borodin and the other Russian advisers who had come to help Sun Yat-sen revive the moribund Kuomintang. When the Whampoa Military Academy was set up in May, 1924, with Russian funds and under Russian auspices, Chiang Kai-shek was the logical choice to head it. At Whampoa he began to build the foundations of his power. To that school flocked some of the best youth of the land. From it came some of the sturdiest fighters of the national revolution. But out of the Whampoa officers' corps Chiang also fashioned a personal machine, a private fraternity of men joined by their ambitions and by the interest of their merchant-landlord families. For years afterward, these men of Whampoa formed a solid core at the center of Chiang's carefully built machine.

The Kuomintang, meanwhile, was completely reorganized and equipped with a new and moderately radical program: for abolition of the unequal treaties with the foreign powers; for a 25 per cent reduction in land rents; for abolition of the militarist satrapies and creation of a nationalist central government. With this program the Kuomintang was embarked, under Borodin's direction, upon a vast campaign for organization and arousing of the masses. This task fell largely to the Chinese Communists.

At the dictation of the Communist International, the newly formed Chinese Communist Party had joined Sun Yat-sen's moribund Kuomintang and devoted itself wholly and unreservedly to the business of building up the Kuomintang as the leading national force in the country. This was the time, Borodin said then, for Communists to "do the coolie work for the Kuomintang." This policy was based upon the idea that the nationalist leadership belonged without question to the "revolutionary bourgeoisie," that the Chinese workers and peasants were not "ripe" to become the leading force in the national struggle. Russia, already even then beginning to move under Stalin's leadership away from the ideas of the world revolution, wanted a strong, friendly ally in Asia. It wanted to deal a blow to the Western powers who were its enemies, and it believed this could best be done through the bourgeois Kuomintang. Hence the Chinese Communists were directed to subordinate their own aims and their own organizational possibilities to the Kuomintang leadership. So as the mass movement rose, of its own momentum, out of the fertile soil of age-old exploitation and the sudden onset of hope for great change, the Communists offered it no revolutionary leadership in terms of the masses' own interests but gave precedence instead to the more limited objectives of the Kuomintang.

The mass movement rose swiftly, like a gathering tidal wave. When on May 30, 1925, British police fired on students demonstrating in Canton, killing a number of them, the answer was a general strike which paralyzed Hong Kong, the great British port on the South China coast. In the countryside, the peasants began to stir, to organize in their own behalf against the heavy inequities they had borne for so long. The Communists were the sinews, the organizers, and the leading fighters of this great revolutionary wave. Chiang Kai-shek rode the crest. He was obedient to Borodin. He became a highly vocal and "reliable" ally of the Russians. At public meetings he raised the clenched fist and cried: "Long live the world revolution!" At the head of Nationalist troops he won quick and easy victories over dissident local militarists who were rendered impotent by the mass movement in the villages before he ever attacked. Chiang was marked as one of the "new" Chinese military men, and he won quick promotion. A fortuitous assassination in Canton won him the command of the Cantonese army, and from there on out Chiang Kai-shek worked tirelessly to gather political as well as military control of the movement into his own hands.

The seat of control had to be made clear and explicit. Although the Communists practiced their self-effacing policy with complete fidelity, the logic of the rising mass movement required a firm decision. It could not be allowed to get out of hand. The Chinese bankers and merchants and compradores (agents for foreign firms) in the treaty ports were anxious to increase their share in the system of economic exploitation dominated by foreign capital. Struggling Chinese industrialists, smothered by foreign competition and foreign control of Chinese tariffs, wanted protection for their infant industries, wanted freedom to develop. To accomplish this, the system of unequal treaties, of extraterritoriality, of foreign-controlled treaty ports and concessions, of restrictions on the tariff, all had to be broken down, or at least strongly modified. The difficulty and the danger was that the masses of workers and peasants being used as a weapon toward these ends would begin to ask for too much. To the peasant in the countryside the term "unequal treaty" meant his contract with the landlord which took 50 to 70 per cent and more of his crop for rent. To the worker, the fight for freedom was the fight to emerge from helotry in the factories, whether they were foreign-owned or Chinese-owned. It was necessary to insure, in short, that the nationalist movement remained within the desirable limits. To this end the wealthy Chinese, inside and outside the Kuomintang, organized with a remarkable degree of consciousness of their problems and their needs, and it was soon recognized in these circles that Chiang Kai-shek was their man.

In Canton in the first months of 1926, Chiang Kai-shek gave a masterly demonstration of his special talents. He was like a three-headed Cerberus standing guard before his own and his class interests. He faced right, giving patronage and protection to a cabal of conservative politicians who represented the treaty port wealthy. Through them he sponsored a widespread campaign of anti-Communist propaganda. He faced left: "We cannot deny that the Chinese revolution is part of the world revolution," he told a graduating class of his Whampoa cadets. "Realization of the Three People's Principles means the realization of communism!" How Borodin must have applauded! And Chiang also faced squarely forward, above all and before all the jealous and vigilant guardian of his own sprouting ambitions. He built up his organization in the army and in the Canton government. He brought his old mentors down from Shanghai to stand by him with counsel and assistance. He fused their political interests and his consuming aspirations, his envy of his rivals, his unmistakable and unerring lust for power. He drew all these threads into a knot and before dawn one day, March 20, 1926, he cut them sharply to make them over into a new pattern in his own image. On the convenient pretext of an imaginary Communist plot, Chiang had his soldiers seize power for him in Canton. The left-wing Kuomintang leaders and their Communist associates capitulated with protestations of innocence and apologies. Wang Ching-wei, the leader of the left, gave up his top offices in the government and the Kuomintang to Chiang and departed for foreign exile. Chiang reorganized thoroughly, putting his henchmen into all key positions and establishing a new set of stringent limitations on the activities of the Communists. The Communists, on the advice of their Russian mentors, accepted all of it without question. It was a shuffle, a shift and a determination of power at the summit. The masses of people never knew the difference.

As a result, Chiang was able to take command of the Northern Expedition and head for the Yangtze Valley and glory with the full momentum of the mass movement to sweep him forward. Through the fall and winter of 1926 and into the spring of 1927, there was a majestic and awesome rising of the Central China peasantry. The advancing Nationalist forces were carried from victory to victory, scarcely ever having to fight. The opposing armies of the old militarists either melted away or were absorbed. When Chiang Kai-shek approached Shanghai in March, the workers of that city rose in insurrection under Communist leadership. They seized power from the local ruling militarists and handed that power over to Chiang when he entered.

In Shanghai, Chiang had arrived at the citadel of the bankers and merchants and the foreigners, who were ready enough now to make a deal if the radical wing of the movement could be eliminated.

Chiang had the south in his control and the whole Yangtze Valley within grasp. He moved with decision and boldness. With the Communists blindly protesting their friendly good will up to the last moment, he struck again, and this time he struck to crush the mass movement. In the early morning hours of April 12, 1927, he turned the Shanghai gangsters loose on the workers' movement. In pre-dawn attacks, hundreds were seized and shot. Protesting demonstrators the next day were met with machine guns, and their blood mingled with the rain coursing down Shanghai's streets. At nearby Lunghua, Chiang's executioners worked ceaselessly night and day. Down the line, in cities newly occupied by the victorious Nationalist advance, the pattern was repeated. There were wholesale killings that spread across the country as his minions took their cue. For a brief interlude, stretching into the summer, the Left Kuomintang, so-called, and the Communists, took respite at Hankow; but the Hankow leader, Wang Chiang-wei, serving the same interests as Chiang, capitulated in his turn to the generals and the landlords. The terror spread across the provinces. In a convulsive reaction which swung them from the extreme of blind capitulation to the other extreme of futile adventurism—both under the direction of the master brain of Stalin in Moscow—the Communists attempted a series of uprisings, culminating in the Canton Commune of December, 1927. They were drowned in blood.

"Here are the facts of the suppression," began a contemporary report in the pro-Kuomintang, American owned and edited *China Weekly Review*. "For four months a systematized massacre has been going on in the territory controlled by Chiang Kai-shek. It has resulted in the smashing of the people's organizations in Kiangsu, Chekiang, Fukien, and Kwangtung. . . . In Hunan . . . subordinate generals have carried out a clean-up of 'Communists' that Chiang Kai-shek can scarcely parallel. The usual methods of shooting and beheading have been abetted by methods of torture and mutilation which reek of the horrors of the Dark Ages and the Inquisition. The results have been impressive. The peasant and labor unions of Hunan, probably the most effectively organized in the whole country, are completely smashed."

As Chiang Kai-shek set up his own government at Nanking, the principal activity then and for long years afterward remained the suppression of the opposition. No one can estimate fully how many died under the scourge of this terror, or how many choked stinking jails from one end of the land to the other. There are only partial figures for the record, culled from official announcements and from the official press. From April to December, 1927, according to one summary, there were 37,985 known dead and 32,316 known political prisoners. Between January and August, 1928, 27,699 were formally condemned to death by Kuomintang court-martial and more than 17,000 were imprisoned. At the end of 1930 one estimate put the total dead at 140,000. In 1931 a study of data from cities in only six provinces showed that in that year 38,778 had been executed as enemies of Chiang Kai-shek's régime.

Chiang Kai-shek substituted a new militarism for the old. His government was a ruthless military dictatorship, decked out in nationalist trappings and quoting Sun Yat-sen as source and godfather of the one-party system under which the Kuomintang ruled. In behalf of the landlords, this new government preserved the hopelessly backward and oppressive and semi-feudal system of land tenure which drove great masses of the peasantry into wandering pauperism, into the swollen armies of the militarists, into banditry. In behalf of the bankers, it floated huge loans from which enormous profits were made by favored individuals. In behalf of the military, it drained the national resources, swallowed up huge portions of the revenue, and carried out wholesale requisitions, which stripped the country and poured into the bottomless drain of the officer group the proceeds of the national loot. In behalf of the bureaucracy and the politicians, the provincial satraps and the tax collectors, it sucked up the vitality of the people through the land tax, the salt gabelle, and the unofficial opium monopoly. China passed wholly into the hands of a rapacious band of rulers made up of militarists turned landlords, landlords turned bureaucrats, bureaucrats turned bankers, bankers turned politicians, and politicians turned militarists turned landlords. Over the whole sat the Leader, Chiang Kai-shek.

As the most effective instrument of his class, Chiang became also its most powerful member, its chief arbiter, its all-powerful master. After the first days of power, when tribute was exacted openly in the form of ransom and "protection" money, the acquisition of wealth was regularized. Chiang Kai-shek, personally and through the family group of the Soongs and Kungs allied to him by marriage, became immensely wealthy. The term "Soong dynasty" applied to the Kuomintang government was hardly an exaggeration. While individuals of the clan came and went in favor before the throne, the whole régime functioned in some respects like a family corporation which controlled the whole banking system, tapped the national and provincial revenues, derived income directly or otherwise from smuggling and racketeering, and drew tribute in one way or another from all other sources of profitable activity which it did not directly control. H. H. Kung, T. V. Soong, and all the lesser Kungs and Soongs and their host of satellites, and even Sun Fo, the "liberal" of the clan, have all enriched themselves in these years. Power has been profitable.

It was a bastard monster, this ruling class, born out of the union of thwarted Chinese nationalism and the persistent semi-medieval order of Chinese society. It was the godchild of foreign imperialism which for a century had balked the growth of any healthy new economy and new social system capable of replacing the outworn régime of the ancient past. By backing one clique against another, one satrap against another, the rival Powers had kept the country divided. Within the Kuomintang after it took power, there were pro-Japanese groups, pro-British groups, pro-American groups. There was everything, actually, but a pro-Chinese group, for under the rule of the Kuomintang, China was driven deeper and deeper into the morass.

Kuomintang "unification" was a fiction. Chiang disposed of some of his rivals in a series of civil wars. Others he bought over, outwitted or absorbed. His "national unity" was nothing but a complicated and insecure system of alliances superimposed upon the old system of provincial satrapies. The local leaders, in large sections of the country, held full provincial power, sometimes by fief from Chiang, sometimes without it.

Kuomintang "reconstruction" was a myth used to cover the wholesale plundering of the country's waning wealth. China's languishing economy was dealt new and nearly mortal blows. Peasants, hopelessly ground down by taxation and usury and outright requisitions, were driven off the land in great numbers. The cities could not absorb them. Unable to extract even bare subsistence from their toil, they died in chronic famines, became soldiers or bandits, or passed into open rebellion in the hinterland. Ricelands became wastelands over great areas. Natural and man-made disasters successively destroyed more and more of China's capacity to sustain itself.

Between 1927 and 1932, Chiang Kai-shek's government ran the internal debt up to $1,100,000,000 (Chinese currency then valued between $2.50 and $4.50 per US$1) and used all but one per cent of this sum for the military and bureaucratic machine. The index of foreign trade (1912: 100) fell from 277 in 1931 to 118.6 in 1934. The index of unfavorable trade balance was 91.92 in 1927 and rocketed to 542.62 in 1932. By 1932, industry and agriculture had declined to the point where food and clothing accounted for more than 50 per cent of the total imports. The Chinese cotton and silk industries disappeared or passed into foreign hands. Prices of agricultural products declined 25 to 50 per cent, and land rents soared 50 to 100 per cent. The onset of the world economic crisis in 1931 had completed the process which was already bringing China to the point of total collapse.

The country was prostrate when Japan, shrewdly picking its moment, began its conquering march into Manchuria toward the end of 1931. For nearly six years after that, in the face of recurring Japanese blows, Chiang Kai-shek tried his best to find a basis for collaboration with the Japanese that would satisfy Japan's demands and leave Chiang enough of his power intact. In the Shanghai truce of 1932, the Tangku truce of 1933, the postal and customs agreements with Manchukuo in 1934, and the Ho-Umetsu agreement of 1935, Chiang Kai-shek signed away territory and sovereign rights, hopeful each time that Japan would accept a final settlement. The considerable popular resentment against this "non-resistance" policy was held down with blood and iron. Students who held anti-Japanese demonstrations were shot and cut down. The prisons filled with young people whose only crime was their desire to resist Japan's incursions. Unable or unwilling in these crucial years to make a stand against the Japanese, Chiang employed the best of his troops, the bulk of his weapons and resources, in successive campaigns against insurgent peasant armies in Central China led by the Communists.*

The peculiar conditions of Chinese life and the conservative-national evolution of Russia imposed upon the Chinese Communists no less distorted a history. They had organized the great and thunderous rising of the people in 1925–27. They had, at Moscow's order, subordinated themselves wholly and supinely to the Kuomintang leadership of Chiang Kai-shek. They were defenseless and demoralized when he turned and struck them down, smashed their unions and peasant associations and drove them into the remote hinterland. There they found refuge and they also found splintered sections of the insurgent peasantry and rebellious units of the Kuomintang armies. Commanders of two of the latter were Mao Tse-tung and Chu Teh. These leaders gathered their splinters together and out of these in the years 1928 to 1930 they fashioned a guerrilla fighting force. In the provinces of Central China—Kiangsi, Hunan, Hupeh, Honan, and Anhwei, the Communists reemerged as the leaders of a radical agrarian movement. Under their leadership, the peasants seized the land where they could, resisted the depredations of Kuomintang landlords, militarists, and tax collectors. They blended into the rich and ancient tradition of peasant war in China.

They furbished it, to be sure, with Muscovite absurdities. They filled the air with fantastic exaggerations. They painted themselves as "proletarian leaders." In the narrow little zones they could control, they struggled against suffocating limitations and the overwhelmingly greater force of the enemy. They claimed for themselves the national revolutionary leadership they had forfeited during the great movement of the preceding years. They tied themselves from afar to the growing super-nationalism of Stalin's Russia. Like all their fellow parties in other lands, they careened from one political fetishism to another in accordance with the current and constantly changing requirements of Soviet foreign and domestic policies. Having been weakest in program

---

* Citations of source material for this sketch of Chiang Kai-shek's career will be found in the author's *Tragedy of the Chinese Revolution* (London, 1938).

and policy when they were strongest in power and popular following during the great revolution, they turned ultrarevolutionary at a time when they were isolated in the provinces and cut off from the masses of workers in the cities. They proved incapable, as a result, of regrouping the revolutionary forces of the country. In their remote hinterlands instead they employed all their energies in the arduous and often spectacularly heroic business of fighting a peasant war.

Of this business they became superb masters. Their agrarian radicalism—seizure of the land and expulsion of all landlords—won them the support of the poorest peasants wherever their armies could penetrate. With great devotion and under practiced, skilful fighting leaders like Chu Teh, Ho Lung, Fang Chih-min, Peng Teh-huai, they successfully fended off wave after wave of Kuomintang invasion of their territories. Always outnumbered, always vastly inferior in arms and equipment, these Chinese Red Armies invariably outwitted Chiang Kai-shek's legions and made utter fools of Chiang himself and of all his generals. But time and circumstances worked against them. Hemmed in, isolated, kept to the back country of the hills and paddies, they could never take the offensive, could never capture even a fair-sized town. Within their areas, in these conditions, they could not solve any of the basic problems of the liberated peasant. Nor could they hold out against the forces of the Kuomintang indefinitely. By 1934, when Chiang's armies moved in for the sixth time, they were freshly reorganized and trained by the German military mission headed by General Hans von Seekt. They were directed tactically in the field by German specialists. Their striking power was enhanced by American and European planes and weapons. The Communists finally had to retreat from their Central China areas. They foiled Chiang's announced purpose to exterminate them by slipping through the cordon he threw around them. They made their famous long march across Kiangsi, Hunan, and Szechwan, and re-established themselves finally in the barren remoteness of Shensi province in the far northwest.

Under the pressure of the approaching showdown with the Japanese, both Chiang Kai-shek and the Communists began to adapt themselves to changing circumstances. Chiang Kai-shek had dearly hoped to wipe out his Communist enemies before having to face the Japanese in search either of a final compromise or failing that, of a fight. He had publicly announced that the Communists were the primary enemies and had to be dealt with first before any other national issue could be touched. But his string of compromises with the Japanese was running out. The Japanese had not proved content with their gains in Manchuria and the northern provinces. It became quite plain that they wanted to bring all of China under their direct control and that this would mean erasing entirely the power of Chiang Kai-shek.

The Communists, on their part, had offered Chiang a united front against the Japanese. A new turn in the international communist movement, the shift from ultra-radicalism to the People's Front idea which began on a world scale in 1935 after the Seventh—and last—Congress of the Comintern, enabled them to water down their own domestic program and to make themselves acceptable once more as allies of Chiang Kai-shek. In the interests of this alliance, they abandoned their land program, modified it until it was mild enough to be quite acceptable to most landlords. Chiang Kai-shek finally accepted the proffered truce, although not until after he had been "kidnapped" in Sian and rescued from some fate worse than death by the timely intervention of his old Communist enemies.

The new "united front" thus formed early in 1937 was a tenuous thing, a façade of uneasy collaboration scarcely concealing all the legitimate mutual distrust, all the suspicions and hatreds carried over from the years of the revolution and the civil war. It never solidified. When the all-out Japanese attack began in July, 1937, Chiang's resistance was feeble and far less effective than it might have been, even with his meager resources. For one thing, the Kuomintang split on the issue of collaboration with the Japanese. A large section of the party, headed by Wang Ching-wei and including some of the most prominent leaders of the government, threw in with the invaders and formed a puppet government at Nanking. Chiang Kai-shek was unwilling to adopt the social reforms that might have mobilized far greater popular support. He was even more unwilling to let the Communists reap the benefit of doing so. He still feared the Communists more than he feared the Japanese. He preferred to have the Japanese occupy territory rather than see the Communists grow any stronger. His own military weakness, compounded by the inner rot of his régime and incompetent leadership, was quickly translated into shattering defeats.

As Chiang fell back westward under Japanese blows during 1938, he was concerned chiefly with preventing the Communists from exploiting his reverses. As best he could, he kept them blockaded in the northwest while the Japanese completed their conquest of the coastal provinces, the railroads and river systems. Chiang Kai-shek retired behind the craggy Yangtze Gorges to Chungking. The Japanese held their lines in the river valley. By 1940, except for sporadic Japanese attacks and equally sporadic Kuomintang resistance and for a continuing Japanese attack from the air, the war was stalemated across broad gray zones that extended from the Yellow River bend across the land to the port of Canton.

The Communists meanwhile fought their own kind of small-scale partisan war against the Japanese, largely behind the Japanese lines. From their bases, where they entrenched themselves with limited popular reforms, administrations free from corruption, and rigid authoritarian party rule, the Communists made deep forays into the many hinterlands. While Japanese troops held the main lines of communication, the Communists filtered past them, brushed and skirmished with outposts, raided supply trains, cut railroads, mobilized new bands in the unoccupied back country. Ill armed and scattered, they could make but a small impression on the over-all military situation. Not only did they receive no support from Chiang, but they were constantly colliding with his blockading forces in border region battles that were always inconclusive. Behind the ill kept truce, the war within a war went on almost without interruption. Chiang Kai-shek was neither willing nor able to carry on an effective war of resistance. His only refuge was in geography. The Communists, for their part, were willing enough but not able. The Japanese were quite content with the result.

This was the state of affairs when the China war finally became part of the bigger war between Japan and the United States which began on December 7, 1941. For Chiang Kai-shek, the hour of Pearl Harbor was the promise of coming rescue if he could hold on where he was. He knew now more definitively than ever before that his future rested with the American future in Asia and he was intelligent enough to realize that American power would finally triumph. In this he simply showed foresight superior to that of some of his closest political and military associates who after Japan's initial great sweep of victories wanted China to sue for peace. For this resistance to the "peace party" in his own camp, Chiang Kai-shek has received great plaudits and praise. Yet it was simply another demonstration of the reasons for his becoming and remaining the leader of this band of self-seeking politicians and generals. The margin of Chiang's superiority to them was represented by his superior ability to recognize the winning side even when it was losing. He held on to the shreds of his power and bided his time. The Communists had to do likewise. The relative positions of the Kuomintang and the Communists would be decided now, plainly enough, by the way the Americans decided to fight their war in Asia.

THE AMERICAN WAR IN CHINA

For nearly three years after Pearl Harbor, the United States fought only a token war in continental Asia. The early Japanese victories had severed the Burma Road, the last land link between China and the outside world. The job of trying to reopen the road and of seeing whether Chinese troops could be regrouped to play any effective part in the over-all anti-Japanese strategy was handed to the American general who had been driven from Burma by the advancing Japanese in the spring of 1942. Joseph Stilwell, onetime American military attaché in China, became commander of the China-Burma-India theater of war.

Stilwell was a simple military man who had lived long enough in China to discover the difference between a Kuomintang general and a Chinese soldier, between a Chungking bureaucrat and a toiling farmer. He had watched the early battles of the Sino-Japanese war as an observer. He knew what he was getting into. Stilwell was an impatient, puritanical soul, hating liars and grafters and men in pinstripe suits. He had learned the Chinese language but had never adopted or accepted the Chinese notions of indirection and face-

saving. He believed in simple solutions and in an oddly uncompli-
cated way he was for good against evil and, in his own particular
terms, he was for progress of some kind against reaction of any kind.
As theater commander in China-Burma-India, Stilwell had many
limitations. He was a fearless and inspiring fighter on the battlefield.
He achieved a kind of crusty greatness in his memorable retreat from
Burma at the beginning of the war and in his return to Burma before
the war's end. But there were many arguments about his ability as
a strategist and his broad sense of timing. We all listened in those
bleak months of 1944 to long and dreary arguments on this score,
and it usually seemed to me that all the real and fancied experts
managed to cancel each other out.

The chief issue revolved around the use of the limited materials
that could be flown across the great Himalayan Hump, whether to
employ them for greater air operations in China or for land operations to break the Burma Road blockade. This argument raged un-
endingly from month to month between the partisans of Stilwell on
the one side and the air commander, Claire Chennault, on the other.
In the end, the sudden Japanese collapse rendered the whole argument bootless and made it seem that much toil and many lives had
been expended for very little. But few of the experts had been expert
enough to predict and gamble on the precise manner of the war's
ending. Had events gone otherwise, Stilwell's decisions might have
gone down in the military tomes as the essence of daring foresight.

Whatever Stilwell's abilities as a strategist, he was undoubtedly
an execrably poor administrator. Even a correspondent who laid no
claim to being a military expert could see that. He had a peculiar
genius for tolerating incompetents on his staff. This was probably
due to his abiding hatred of staff work in general. He liked to say that
he did his staff work under his old campaign hat and carried all
necessary staff files in his head. This often made Stilwell an engaging
character to everybody but the members of his own staff. It did not
exactly win him laurels as an organizer.

But with all his limitations, Stilwell as a man towered far above
the numerous small fry wearing generals' stars in the American army.
He could never conceal his contempt for the autocratic, conniving
Chiang Kai-shek, or the debonair, ineffectual Mountbatten, with

both of whom he shared the command of the war in Asia. While Mountbatten flustered about all the impossibilities of waging war in Burma, Stilwell went ahead and waged war in Burma and finally compelled the British to follow suit. In China, Stilwell hammered at Chiang and Chiang's minions for more effective cooperation, for less graft, less inefficiency, less calculated sabotage. This looked a lot like American power-pressure on the Chinese government and, of course, in the fundamental sense that is just what it was. Having finally been brought into jeopardy itself, the United States wanted to squeeze every bit of military assistance it could out of exhausted and war-weary China. But as applied by Stilwell, this policy exposed the ironic paradox of the American relationship with the Kuomintang régime. Stilwell, certainly, was not primarily animated by any broad social or political aims: he wanted to fight the Japanese. But to fight the Japanese in China, he found that he had to start by trying to reform the whole Chinese régime. He had to buck the vast, sodden system of backward tyranny. It was a peculiar little one-man challenge doomed in advance to failure.

The challenge was a sum of many things: problems of manpower, of supply, of effective communications, of a reasonably decent and competent command in the field. The Chinese army, again, could only mirror the social régime of which it was a part. When Stilwell tried to tackle its deficiencies, he tangled automatically with the whole rotten, worm-eaten structure of Chiang Kai-shek's dictatorship. He got into trouble by trying to get the Chinese army rationalized and reorganized. Combining below-strength divisions was a business that drove too many generals out of their jobs and cut off the revenue that came from collecting ration allowances for full-strength rosters. Stilwell's pressure for efficiency and honesty was simply absorbed by the shapeless, resistant, pulpy morass of Chinese military politics. He got into more trouble by trying to keep a tight rein on distribution of the meager supplies flown across the Hump from bases in India. He stubbornly resisted the constant Chungking demand for more weapons and ammunition, insisting instead on earmarking all arriving equipment for specific purposes. There was a tendency for American war material to disappear from the regular channels into private hoards. Stilwell wanted to be sure that the supplies brought into

China at such great cost would be used not in the future against Chinese dissidents, but in the present against the Japanese.

This, in fact, was the heart of the matter: Stilwell was trying to organize a fight against the Japanese with Chinese manpower. The Chungking government, weary and weakened and fearful of its precarious internal position, did not want to fight at all. Chiang Kai-shek considered that he had gone through enough: it was up to the Americans now to take the Japanese off his back. What he really needed was to build up his strength with an eye to the internal balance of power, with an eye to the future necessity for dealing with the Communists. So it was the crowning and conclusive and finally decisive challenge when Stilwell decided he wanted to use Communist troops against the Japanese and to arm them for that purpose.

At that time—spring-summer of 1944—the broad strategy of the anti-Japanese war had not yet taken shape. It had not yet been decided whether American forces would make a direct assault on the Japanese home islands or whether they would have to land first on the China coast and fight their way through the strong Japanese continental armies before approaching the Japanese homeland. The amount and kind of possible Chinese assistance in the latter case was naturally a crucial factor. So far the experience with the Chinese had been vexatious and disappointing to the Americans. It had taken Stilwell nearly two years to get five Chinese divisions under his control and to get them sufficiently re-equipped and trained to face the relatively small Japanese forces in North Burma. Other divisions were in training on a more limited basis in China. The creation of the Salween Expeditionary Force had been one long heartbreak, and its campaign, ultimately successful, to push the Japanese out of the southwestern corner of China to help clear the Burma Road was a triumph of persistence over enormous and unnecessary obstacles.

After long pressure, Stilwell finally got permission to send a mission of observers up to the blockaded Communist areas in the northwest. They sent back glowing reports on how much could be done there with how little: a supply of rifles and machine guns and ammunition and a coordinated command. The Communists claimed to have more than 500,000 fighting troops, and the American reports

largely supported these claims. The American officers saw rich possibilities of using these widely dispersed forces to break up Japanese
communications in North and Central China, to infiltrate to the coast,
to build up forces there capable of assisting prospective American
landings. Stilwell finally went to Chiang with the proposal that the
Communists be armed, supplied, and drawn into a common strategy
against the foe. To this end he proposed administrative and political
reforms in the government that would admit the Communists into a
working partnership with the Kuomintang.

The generalissimo blew up. He was not interested in the tactical
possibilities against the Japanese. He was interested in the political
necessities for safeguarding himself. Armed, spread across the entire
country, free to operate under American auspices on a large scale in
territories loosely held at best by the Japanese or by Chinese puppets,
the Communists would beyond any further doubt tip the scales of
domestic power. The end of the war would have found the Kuomintang in the minority position. Chiang's position in 1944 as an isolated
satrap bottled up in the western provinces would have become his
permanent fate. He would have none of it. Let the Americans find
their own way of fighting the Japanese. He had not waited this long
just in order to preside over the liquidation of the Kuomintang
régime.

It was at this juncture, in September, 1944, that Patrick J. Hurley
came on the scene as President Roosevelt's special envoy, accompanied
by Donald Nelson. Hurley was quickly taken into camp by the persuasive T. V. Soong, who had become Foreign Minister. He soon
saw the whole picture Chiang's way. After a complicated intrigue
in which everything looked briefly like its opposite—including
Chiang's momentary agreement to hand total command over to Stilwell—the situation resolved itself with Chiang requesting Stilwell's
recall. Hurley endorsed the request, and the White House acceded.
Chiang Kai-shek had gambled again and had won. Clarence Gauss,
the American ambassador, resigned and followed Stilwell home.
Hurley became ambassador. Major General Albert Wedemeyer, a
careful and mediocre military diplomat, succeeded Stilwell. Hurley,
always resplendent in his uniform, his ribbons, and moustache, assembled the embassy staff and read them a lecture: he was here, he

said, to bolster the government of Chiang Kai-shek by any and all means. He would entertain no critical comments, no critical reports. Cowed, the staff filed out in silence and remained silent. Before long, they all disappeared, one after another. Virtually all American diplomatic and military personnel in China with long China background and experience were weeded out. It was a curious and arresting development: at a most critical period of the war and of the American position in China, all the men trained for the purpose proved inadequate or unsatisfactory instruments of American policy. "It's amateur night in China now," said one disgusted officer as he packed to go.

As an amateur diplomat, Hurley wrote a bizarre little chapter of his own in the history of American policy in the Far East. It was soon realized that Hurley was a strange old man, often a little too old to follow clearly in conversation. All who questioned or criticized his acts were automatically Communists or traitors or, obviously, both. Starting with a few humble correspondents as charter members, the Hated-by-Hurley Club in Chungking was soon a large and relatively distinguished company, including diplomatic secretaries, OWI propagandists, and American staff officers ranging in rank from two bars to two stars. One of his victims, preparing to leave China, said: "Well, I've been hurleyed out of China," and the phrase promptly entered the current political lexicon in the Chinese war capital. It was indiscreet to cross Hurley, for his was the wisdom, no matter how obscure or devious or simply incomprehensible it was to his listener. In Hurley's day in China, the conversational version of American policy was one long anecdote about pioneer days in Oklahoma, punctuated by Choctaw war whoops and vituperative adjectives.

But even senility can be consistent. For what came to be known as the Hurley policy in China was a fixed policy of unqualified American support of the Chiang Kai-shek régime, including toleration of its tyrannies and acceptance of its primacy on its own terms. But this was not a Hurley policy. It was the policy of the United States Government. After all, the Hurley ambassadorship lasted for more than a year. The policy-makers in Washington were certainly not uninformed, despite Hurley's ban on critical reports. Support of Chiang Kai-shek had long been the pillar of the American China policy, and Hurley represented no departure from it. He simply demonstrated in a particular situation and in somewhat spectacular fashion how thoroughly reactionary and even dangerous to American power-political interests that policy actually was.

However, the issue had ceased to be pressing. For military purposes, China was by-passed. Stilwell's recall coincided with the end of any plans for serious, large-scale military operations against the Japanese in China. It had been decided instead to throw the weight of the American assault against Japan itself. In the spring of 1945, when these plans were already in execution, General George Marshall told this writer in Washington that as matters then stood, the American relation to the internal situation in China would not matter. Japanese pressure on China would be relieved in direct ratio to the increased American pressure on Japan. Whatever the consequences of American policy in China would be, he said, it could no longer affect the outcome of the war. It would become, instead, a major postwar headache.

And so it proved. The pressure on the Japanese homeland, the incessant bombing, and in the end the atomic bomb and the Russian entry, brought Japan's surrender many months earlier than the most optimistic had expected. But the Japanese surrender did not usher in peace in China. American policy had instead helped usher in civil war. This was the sizable postwar headache that Marshall himself finally was sent to China to cure if he could.

In the fall of 1944 Ambassador Hurley initiated negotiations to bring about Kuomintang-Communist settlement. "I've got it settled," he said and we looked at him incredulously and saw that he really thought he had it settled. It was to be accomplished by some obscure Choctaw system of hypnosis of which Hurley alone was master. For weeks Hurley continued his lonely insistence upon his success. But his Couélike repetition of his formula failed somehow to produce the desired result. For there were more things in the Chinese heaven and on the Chinese earth than ever Hurley dreamed of.

Hurley first presented himself as a mediator. He never tired of quoting what Molotov had told him in Moscow. Molotov had "disowned" the Chinese Communists and solemnly affirmed that Russia

had no interest in them whatever. "So you see?" Hurley would beam,
"it is really all quite simple." But as the talks proceeded—Hurley
had brought Chou En-lai as chief Communist negotiator down from
Yenan, the Communist capital—it became more obvious that Hurley
was not so much mediator as chief Kuomintang advocate. His idea
of a compromise was a Communist capitulation. He presented Communist demands to Chiang, found Chiang's objections eminently
reasonable and tried to bluster the Communists into retreat. The
Communists, favored by all the actual and prospective circumstances,
were not impressed.

The Communists were many things: they were hardened fighters,
they were political hacks, they were ruthless totalitarians, they were
patriotic social reformers. But they were not naïve. The years had
at least given them that. They were not anchored in any principle or
tied to any program. Long practice in supple switching of ideas had
liberated them from the simpler revolutionary approach. They
bandied words like "democracy" and "the people" and "popular
rule" around with studied ease. Whatever they were, they confidently
knew that they were no less and possibly a little more democratic
than the Kuomintang, that they depended more on some of the
people than the Kuomintang and could count on more popular support than the Kuomintang could. They did not suffer from the
cancerous inner rot of corruption in the same sense that the Kuomintang did. But these factors were all secondary. They came to the
bargaining table primarily as representatives of an independent army
with territory of its own, with strategic position, with an important
following. Like wary traders, diplomats, and strategists, they matched
these against Chiang's armies, Chiang's territories, Chiang's strategic
position, Chiang's following. They measured positions strictly by
relative force—and it did not take them long to measure Patrick
Hurley. What they sought to discover was what American policy
held out for them as a perspective for the immediate future.

This was the drift of a conversation one night in the Chungking
Communist Party headquarters, which was established in the Kuomintang capital like the embassy of a hostile country with which diplomatic relations have not yet been broken off. Chou En-lai, in his
bouncing, vigorous, nervous way, went down the list of the Com-

munist demands: a coalition government, a coalition military staff, elimination of one-party rule. He was interrupted by a question: "Is the Communist Party now programmatically against one-party rule?" Chou stopped. "Programmatically?" he repeated. "No, we don't think that way. We think of the immediate and present necessity. You can't be abstract and settle all future questions with a program. Who knows the future? We speak only of now." He grinned. "And right now we're against one-party rule."

"Then how about the Bolshevik doctrine of the one-party dictatorship?" Chou En-lai waved that aside with an impatient gesture. "Doctrine? That is again abstract. That is . . ." He fumbled for the word, and asked a young bird-faced assistant who sat there for the English equivalent. "Dogmatism," the young man said. The pragmatic and undogmatic questions, it seemed, at the moment had to do with American policy only, and the rest of the conversation went as follows:

Chou: "Will the Hurley policy continue, the policy of playing only Chiang's game?"

Correspondent: "There is no Hurley policy. It's Washington's policy."

Chou: "You mean it would be Washington's policy to sacrifice its military interest in China to some political interest?"

Correspondent: "That would be one way of putting it."

Chou (stops pacing and stares): "Then in that case we would have to expect the United States to help the Kuomintang in a civil war."

Correspondent: "Undoubtedly."

Chou (throwing up his arms): "But that's ridiculous. Then we couldn't do anything or get anywhere!"

Correspondent: "Where do you want to get?"

Chou: "We want to defeat the Japanese and drive them out of the country."

Correspondent: "And then what?"

Chou: "Then all together we'll build a strong democratic China. That's what the United States says it wants. How are we going to get it, if the United States supports only the Kuomintang and takes sides against us?"

Correspondent shrugs.

Chou: "But surely you're not being realistic. Does America want civil war in China? Is that being realistic?"

Correspondent: "The Americans may be thinking of the Russian position in all this."

Chou: "Russia? What has Russia got to do with it?"

That was always the rub. What did Russia have to do with it? It was more than a rub. It was a stumbling-block. Trying to get over it or around it, many earnest American liberals fell flat on their faces. It was a preview of things to come, for the very question implied that Chinese internal politics was not and would not be a purely Chinese affair, nor a Chinese-American affair, but fundamentally a Russian-American affair. Many an American officer or junior diplomat went up to the Communist areas and came back convinced that, for good or ill, the Chinese Communists were by far the most dynamic force in the country; that they had on their side a more progressive program, efficient administration, freedom from graft and corruption, and the relatively willing support of a large section of the population under their control. Nowhere could this much be said of the Kuomintang régime.

These observers would often be a little dubious or uncertain about the democratic pretensions of the Communists. They would be disturbed by the specious features of Communist democracy as practiced in Shensi. They observed that the Communists were always capable of adjusting themselves to criticisms from more conservative elements but turned with ruthless wrath on critics from the left. On the whole it seemed no more healthy in the Communist areas to be an active opponent of the Communist Party than it was elsewhere to be an active opponent of the Kuomintang. Nevertheless, the over-all impression favored the Communists by a broad margin over the decrepit Kuomintang as the hopeful leadership of the country. It was wrong to call these people Communists, the argument usually ran. They were not Bolsheviks. They were simple agrarian reformers, respectable folk in any country except a backward and feudal land like China. Here were the people upon whom the United States should rely because they were the real hope of the future. Either by themselves or as a powerful leaven in a coalition, these were the people capable of building the "strong and democratic" China which was stated to be the main theme of America's China policy.

The only trouble with all this was the Russian tie-up. It was understood, implicitly and explicitly, that the future of Asia would henceforth be determined by the development of Russian-American relations, by the relative play and counterplay of their influence and position in the country. And the Chinese Communists were . . . well, Communists. They had a long history of dutifully compliant membership in the Communist International. After the dissolution of that body, they had no trouble in following with the same religious blindness every twist in the international political "line" dictated by the transient interests of Soviet diplomacy. Thus in Yenan, China, as well as in London and New York and Paris, the war between the Western powers and Germany was an imperialist war until June 22, 1941, when, with the German attack on Russia, it became a great crusade for the liberation of all men from the Fascist yoke. Yenan followed the party line. Stalin was as sacrosanct in the Shensi caves as he was in the Kremlin. It did not matter whether emissaries passed or did not pass between Shensi and Moscow, whether secret radios operated, or the traditional Moscow gold changed hands, or whether arms were somehow transported across the mountain and desert wastes from Russian Turkestan or Outer Mongolia to the Communist strongholds. The political affinity was the fact, and with the war's end it was understood that political affinity would be enriched by practical opportunity. Russia would stand at the Great Wall. If the Communists were strengthened in China, it amounted to strengthening the Russian position in China. And strengthening the Russian position in China was not, by the canons of power politics, the best way to serve American interests.

The younger liberals, the junior American foreign service officers and military men, wrestled with this unhappy paradox. "Do you think," one of them once asked, "we could wean the Communists away from Russia?" If the United States, he went on, gave arms and political support to the Chinese Communists, if it allowed the warped and rotting régime of Chiang Kai-shek to die on its Szechwan vine, would the Yenan reds be grateful enough to become tools of American influence rather than tools of Russian influence? Or in another variant, the question would be put like this: "If the Communists cannot be wholly weaned from the Russians, can the United States neutralize the Russian influence? Can it by its great political and economic weight draw the Communists into a new Chinese combination that would better serve the American interest?" Yes, the answer went, with a proposed policy summed up as follows: The United States should seek to bring about a genuine absorption of the Communists into the ruling régime of the land. To do so, it had to wring concessions out of Chiang Kai-shek instead of wringing them exclusively, as Hurley planned, out of the Communists. Chiang Kai-shek had to be compelled to liberalize his régime whether he liked it or not. He had to be made to agree, as up to now he had stubbornly refused to agree, to end the one-party Kuomintang dictatorship. He had to loosen the heavy curbs on free speech, free press, free assembly and organization. He must accept a realistic coalition in power with the Communists. Such a course, it was argued, would avert the civil war which was inevitable as soon as Japan was defeated. It would also soften the sharp edge of American-Russian friction in China which would just as surely result from a Chinese civil war.

This, in substance, was the policy urged by the more "liberal" group of China men in the State Department at Washington. It was embodied in a memorandum sent to Washington from Chungking early in 1945 at a time when Hurley had returned to Washington to report. This memorandum was favorably received by the State Department's Far Eastern Division and went up the line of hierarchs until it actually, by report, reached the presidential desk. But China was not very high on the Washington agenda in those days. Rooseveltian power politics was operating strictly on the basis of short-range expediency. The end of the German war was in sight. The end of the Japanese war was not. It looked to all the military experts like a long pull. At Yalta, Roosevelt had already bought Stalin's promise to enter the war against Japan; and he paid heavily, at China's expense directly. There would be inevitable consequences for America, it was understood, in this free cession of Russia's "pre-eminent position" in Manchuria, but sufficient unto the future the problems thereof: the great American military-political-economic position in the world after the war would be sufficient to counter any Russian advance into Asia. The need now was to hasten the crushing of Japan. Internal developments in China would be taken care of in due course. Such, at least, seemed to be the official American reasoning.

But the war ended abruptly. Japan folded six months after Yalta. It surrendered less than a week after Russia marched into Manchuria. Instead of a long exhausting pull that would have further depleted its strength, Russia paid nothing for its great gains in Asia underwritten at Yalta. While in Manchuria the Russians swiftly and easily took over, in China the consequences of the American policy rose and smote its makers.

The mad dash for position and power and arms began. The Kuomintang-Communist civil war began. The Russians could act equivocally: with the newly signed Sino-Soviet pact in their pockets, with occupation and control of Manchuria theirs, they could afford to watch the pot boil over in China Proper. The Chinese Communists, filtering into Manchuria by thousands, would be a handy lever in working out the pattern of the new position there. South of the Great Wall, meanwhile, the Americans under General Wedemeyer acted in terms of the prevailing American policy of all-out aid to Chiang Kai-shek. The civil war was in full cry, and the Americans were deeply involved.

Patrick Hurley, who had been to such an extent the artisan of this tangle, was in Washington when the big war ended and the little war began. With characteristic irascibility, he blew up. He flailed about him at Communist traitors nestling in the bosom of the State Department. He resigned as ambassador to China, and after failing to making himself coherent at a Congressional hearing, he faded from the scene. But what had really blown up was not Hurley but the whole American policy as pursued up to that time on the ground in China. General Marshall, selected for his great personal prestige, was quickly sent out to China to see what could be done. Marshall was given the mandate to preserve the power of Chiang Kai-shek by making him yield enough to avert civil war. Since in China both sides were blaming each other for the outbreaks, neither would assume the responsibility for refusing to compromise. Accordingly Marshall had what looked like a staggeringly swift success. He brought about a truce agreement, and this was followed by parleys which resulted in formal liquidation of Kuomintang one-party rule, reduction and combining of the opposing military forces, a "grant" of democratic rights, and a pledge of a new régime based upon a brand new democratic constitution. It was a dazzling bit of sleight-of-hand that could have happened only in China. All the externals of an accord were down on paper. Marshall left for Washington. But he had no sooner left than the conflict resumed. The Communists charged Chiang Kai-shek with bad faith in the agreements made. Chiang Kai-shek charged the Communists with trying to seize Manchuria for their own. Both sides were right. Marshall returned to China to try again to force the conflict into some quieter groove where the friction could continue with a little less heat. It was a question of making northeast Asia look a bit less like the first battlefield of a third world war already begun. If that could be done, it would look somewhat more like the first potential battlefield of a third world war that would start a little later on.

Such were the prospects opened in China by Japan's collapse. Nothing in it promised peace. The internal dissolution, aggravated fearfully by a man-made famine, continued. The struggle between the contending factions in the land continued because of all the unsolved problems of Chinese economy and society. It was also now decisively a matter of the "American interest" and the "Russian interest." China was back where it had been, the buffeted victim of Greater Power rivalries which now, as for a century, prevented her from achieving a viable internal balance. Infinitely the worse off for the travail of the war years, China entered the postwar years with new shadows over her future far longer, far darker than any ever cast by Japan.

4 KOREA: BETWEEN THE MILLSTONES

To Koreans the end of the war was like a miracle. They felt as the faithful would feel if the resurrection suddenly took place in the middle of a hot summer afternoon. The voice of the Emperor announcing the surrender heralded the end of a long night. It was the close of the ordeal of the damned, and the coming of the Americans would be the coming of the glory. There was rejoicing in the streets of Seoul and across the Korean countryside, and sudden fear among the Japanese. But the wonder was that not a single Japanese was seriously attacked, not one killed. It could have been the numbness come of long passivity, or joy that was too full, expectations too high to admit ordinary vengeance. Or perhaps it was the fact that armed Japanese soldiers still held the country. It was necessary to wait for the liberators. When they came, up the road from Jinsen port, the Americans were like shining knights descended straight from heaven to strike away a people's shackles, to throw open the gates to their own, their promised land.

It was like that, the religous fervor, the unreasoned excitement of salvation. American soldiers marched into Seoul that September day between thick ranks of applauding people, massed shining faces. They could feel for a moment like knights in armor. They could participate, even if a little sheepishly, in a moment of unthinking release. For it was a time of naïve joy, and it belonged to everybody. This was more than the clamor of momentary liberation that sounded through so many cities briefly occupied for three of four years by a hated enemy. This was more than the end of a short, abnormal episode. This, for Koreans, was the lifting of a weight already borne for more than a generation.

The rich little peninsula, jutting downward into the Sea of Japan, had been under Japanese rule for thirty-six years. Its twenty-five million people had been reduced to slavery. The land, the wealth, all the resources of the country passed into Japanese hands.

Japanization carried on through the years culminated in 1937 in the banning of the Korean language from the elementary schools. "Think and live in Japanese!" was the official slogan. It was enforced by police spies who haunted the streets and pulled in children who thoughtlessly lapsed into the Korean vernacular still spoken in their homes. The campaign never wholly succeeded, but still the language of the home and the streets was a limited language. A whole generation of children now entering their teens were acquiring all their broader knowledge through the Japanese tongue and seeing the rest of the world only through Japanese eyes. It was a deep wedge. In another generation, Korean would largely have been the familiar speech of the old folks alone.* But thanks to the teachers who had written their texts in prison and the intelligent interest of the American officer assigned to education in the military government, there was, in this one field at least, swift and real liberation. It was an exhilarating sight for all Koreans on that day in late September when their children trooped noisily back to the reopened primary schools from which all Japanese teachers, Japanese language, Japanese curriculum had been wholly purged.

In another respect, too, reality fed the illusion of sudden freedom. The great weight of the Japanese police régime was lifted. All the old controls disappeared. The restraint on every movement, every spoken, heard, or printed word, was removed. It was a dazzling thing, far too bright at the very beginning for people to see much else around them. On an evening during the second week of the occupation I had dinner at a Chinese-Korean restaurant with a group of women educators, aspiring feminist leaders, wives of some of the leading citizens of Seoul. The talk turned on some of the problems already harshly intruding upon the honeymoon of the liberation. One of the guests, dean of a girls' middle school, brushed misgivings aside. She turned to me and said: "Have you any idea what it means to us to sit here in a restaurant with friends, to talk freely among ourselves, to say anything we please?" She described the old system

---

* "I worried deeply about it," one educator told me, "until in 1938 I was lucky enough to go to Europe and I made a special trip to Ireland to find out what had happened to the Gaelic tongue. I found it had almost entirely disappeared. Yet the Irish kept on fighting for so many hundred years to be free. I felt more confident after that about Korea!"

under which the Japanese police had to be notified of any gathering of three or more persons, in any public place or in any home. A police agent would attend and sit by throughout the evening, a forbidding monitor to see that no vagrant free thoughts found their way into words. "Can you imagine what it means to us to be free of that?" she asked. "I don't see how you can possibly know. But we know. This looks like an ordinary dinner gathering to you. To us it's a miracle. Can you blame us if we're a little dizzy?" She threw up her hands and gave a little shriek of plain excitement. She laughed. "I've never been drunk," she said. "But I think I must know now what it feels like." At another party that week a Korean newspaperman, who knew exactly what it felt like, came up to me and said, "Welcome, liberator!" I replied: "I'm no liberator." He smiled in polite disbelief. "All Americans are our liberators," he declaimed, "and now the pen shall at last be mightier than the sword." He bowed and navigated away. "Yes, we're dizzy," said a professor soberly, "and we have to get our heads down from the clouds."

Many Koreans descending from the clouds landed with a rough jolt. Whatever it was that had come to Korea, it was not liberation. At the Cairo Conference in 1943, the powers had promised Korea its independence "in due course." But that time, evidently, had not yet come. The war's end brought to Korea neither real freedom nor any substantial promise of it. Instead it brought partition. The country was crudely cut in two at the arbitrarily chosen line of the 38th parallel north latitude. Korea north of that line was occupied by Russians. Korea south of that line was occupied by Americans. The northern zone was controlled by the Russian headquarters set up in Heijo, subject to the Russian command in Mukden and thence to Moscow. The southern zone was controlled by the American headquarters set up in Seoul, subject to MacArthur in Tokyo and thence to Washington. The distance between Seoul and Heijo, a bare hundred miles on the ground, was no shorter than the distance between Washington and Moscow. It was greater, in fact, because there was some communication between Washington and Moscow, while Heijo and Seoul might have been on two different planets. Between them no trains ran, no radio sparked, no voices passed. This was not merely partition. It was dismemberment.

When the tumult began to die down after the American landing, the first questions heard on all sides were: "What happens at the 38th parallel? What does it mean? Who decided on this partition, when and where? How long is it to last?" Korean leaders and newspapermen and American correspondents as well put these questions to the American commander, Lieutenant General John Hodge. He knew none of the answers. Neither, as it turned out, did MacArthur. Nor, as far as anyone could learn, could the State Department in Washington offer any clear explanation. Nobody would identify any agreement, written or verbal, in which the partition was arranged, nor would anyone admit that any such agreement existed. From the evidence made available to anxious Koreans and others in those first days, it appeared that the Russians swept into the country from the north and the Americans entered from the south and both stopped at the 38th parallel by some telepathic accord arrived at during some mystic game of numbers attended by nobody.

There seemed reason to believe that Korea was part of the price paid by Roosevelt at Yalta for Stalin's promise to enter the war against Japan. Korea fell within the broad sphere of Soviet influence staked out by Stalin and conceded by the American President. The main terms of the secret deal at Yalta were well known in Chungking, Seoul, and Tokyo long before they were published at Washington, amid general embarrassment, six months after the end of the war. No reference to Korea appeared in the written document of Yalta nor in the documents attached to the Sino-Soviet pact which implemented the Yalta accord. Still it is known that Korea figured in the talks as a conceded portion of the Soviet sphere of influence. One story goes that President Truman was confronted with this concession at Potsdam. He is supposed to have repudiated it there, insisting upon the Cairo Declaration as the guiding basis for the powers' policy on Korea. Nevertheless, when the American, British, and Russian foreign ministers met in Moscow in December, four months after Potsdam, the Korean problem was written off—to the outraged astonishment of the Koreans—with a vague proposal for a five-year trusteeship which left the partition intact.

The fact seems to be that the division of Korea arose out of military arrangements paralleling the diplomatic poker playing. In plans made for concurrent Russian and American military operations against Japan, the 38th parallel was marked off as the northern boundary for American operations and the southern boundary for the Russians. As events turned out, Russia was at war against Japan for only about a week. Plans for joint operations had to be transformed into plans for joint occupations. United States Department of State spokesmen have said that the 38th degree was a military line which was to be maintained for a short period of divided responsibility for disarming and repatriating Japanese forces. But more than a year has passed, and the line is still there. Talks between American and Russian military commissions in Korea were finally organized some months after the Moscow Foreign Ministers' Conference. The stated object was to restore some intercourse between the two halves of the country as a prelude to setting up some kind of unified régime. But even the simple problem of arranging for railroads to carry goods back and forth seemed too difficult to solve. The commission meetings stretched out at intervals for many weeks, with small results. The commission's nominal task, the setting up of an interim provisional government, was not aimed primarily at hastening Korean independence but at establishing if possible a Russian-American modus vivendi in Korea.*

But whether it was a military line or a political line to begin with, whether it was designed to be temporary or permanent, and no matter where or by whom it was conceived, the partition has been utterly ruinous for Korea. On that artificial boundary line, Korean hopes for freedom and independence were hung like a ragged scarecrow on barbed wire. By it this little country was economically and politically hamstrung.

* The quality of "self-determination" for Koreans was cynically underlined at the Soviet-American Commission meeting which began in Seoul on March 23, 1946. The commissioners were all Russian or American military men. They agreed magnanimously "that representatives of Korean democratic political parties may attend the commission meetings by special invitation upon mutual agreement of the two chief commissioners." The sessions were conducted in English and Russian, and all documents were to be in those two languages. Any incidental proclamations to the Korean people, it was noted in an official communiqué, would of course be translated into Korean.

Taken as a whole, Korea is a relatively rich land, capable not only of feeding itself but of growing an export surplus. It proved to be industrially developed to a degree that surprised American economic intelligence officers. During the years of Japan's drive for continental conquests, Korea had become a crucial cog in the war machine. Rich in food, coal and timber, serviced by well developed hydroelectric power plants, and with a host of heavy and light industrial establishments, Korea had contributed heavily to the strengthening of Japanese economy. It could now readily turn these resources and assets to the use and the benefit of Korean economy. But it could not do so as long as the country was halved. For northern Korea has two-thirds of the country's coal (including all the industrially important bituminous), all its extensive sources of hydroelectric power, all its chemical, iron, and steel plants, and the great bulk of the mining and timber industries. Southern Korea, on the other hand, is the country's rice bowl. Its rich crops feed the north. In addition the south, aside from machine tool and shipbuilding facilities, has most of the lighter industries: textiles, electric parts and equipment, airplane and automobile assembly plants. The effective use of these economic resources in Korea is dependent entirely upon the integration of the country, the free movement of railroads, goods, and people.

Under Japanese rule, Korea functioned as such an integrated economic unit. Under the victor powers, after Japan's defeat, the country was cut in two and promptly paralyzed. The 38th parallel became a sealed frontier. Railroad traffic across the line stopped. Coal and food shipments ended. Even chemicals produced in the north and urgently needed to purify the water supply system in the south could not be brought across the line despite repeated urgent requests. After the Russian occupation, northern Korea's only export southward was refugees. The new line was like a boundary between two hostile countries that have severed all relations. To this serious extent Korea was worse off after Japan collapsed than it was under Japanese control. "Liberation" was a peculiar gift when it meant that in the south people could eat but freeze. The United States Army brought some coal in from Japan as emergency rations. In the north people could keep warm but had to go hungry. What the Russian Army did about getting food in to tide over the winter we never learned.

Politically, the division was no less injurious. It sanctioned and deepened a traditional sectionalism of long standing in the country. But far beyond that, it created two opposite polar attractions for the new political currents that began to flow when Japan's rule ended. In the south the American military command became the gravitating center for the most conservative and reactionary political elements. In the north the Russians ladled out power to Communists or pseudo-Communists. In the south the Americans contrived chaos with an air of benevolent good intentions. In the north the Russians dispensed with the benevolent air. Details were always sparse about the north. It was never easy to sift the stories of refugees. But it seemed plain enough that the new power in the north, whether wielded by the Russian military or by Korean Communists, followed the familiar totalitarian pattern. It seemed equally plain that the Communist Party program, whatever it held forth socially or economically, revolved around the central idea, openly proclaimed in the north, that "the Soviet Union is our fatherland." We heard little that was reliable about what happened in northern Korea, and saw even less. No opportunity was given for any adequate firsthand look. Months after the occupation, the Russian refusal to admit correspondents to the area was still categoric. It was only in the confusion of the first days that a few correspondents were able to cross the line and get brief glimpses of the new dispensation in the north. We had no chance to get any rounded or truly factual picture; but whatever it was we saw there, it was not liberation for Koreans.

The unauthorized one-car special train chugged northward through the Korean countryside, through rich fields of ripening rice and beans and tasseled corn, between gentle hills rising toward the great distant mountains. White-clad farmers in the green fields and the women washing at the streamsides stared and the children came running, for a train was a rare sight those days on the long-quiet rails. We stopped in the neat town of Songdo, nestling in the elbow of a hill five miles below the 38th parallel. The whole town turned out to greet the party of six correspondents whom they mistook for liberators. They told us the Russians had been there for ten days. When they retired to their own side of the line, they took with them everything movable, clothes and cotton goods and money from the local bank vault, wine and chinaware and an immensely valuable stock of ginseng, the medicinal root heavily grown in the area and normally exported all over Asia. To these people the brief Russian incursion across the new boundary had been like a bandit raid. They were confused, angered, and outraged by it. They wanted to know what the Americans, who had not yet arrived to take over, would do about it. We said we didn't know. They paraded us back to the railroad station, where a smiling white-toothed boy thrust a flag into my hand, a Korean banner hastily made by painting over part of the red-balled Japanese emblem. They cheered as we pulled out. We wished we deserved their homage.

A few minutes later we crossed the line, an imaginary thread across the rice paddies and over the round summits of the tree-covered hills. West and east it cut through tiny clustered Korean villages with their toadstool roofs of thatch. It dropped across power lines, telegraph lines, the railroad, across streams and old natural boundaries. Heedlessly it bisected three provinces. Here was the new, invisible frontier where Russian and American sentries would soon take up their positions. Here, in some ways, was the most fateful boundary line in Asia. When we passed, there was still nothing to mark the spot and it was at Kinko, fifteen miles farther on, that we ran into our first Russian soldiers. They were round-faced peasant boys in dusty gear, swarming around flatcars, unloading battered vehicles, artillery, and military stores. They were ragged, untidy men from Siberia, most of them, plain boys and men who crowded around to swap smiles and greetings. We had no one with us who could speak Russian and none among them could speak English, so on both sides we spoke with that loud, precise enunciation which mysteriously is supposed to substitute understanding for blankness but of course never does. Back from the siding near the railway yard barrier little knots of Koreans watched silently from a respectful distance. They were the first somberly unsmiling Koreans I had ever seen.

We walked up through the village. Red Army soldiers filled the street. The village folk watched from the doorways or from behind the unglassed windows. They followed the Russians with their eyes and they looked at us without greeting. I can testify to nothing but an atmosphere in that village street, to the demeanor of people and the unseen currents of mood and feeling. I had felt that atmosphere before in remote Chinese villages where Chinese troops had come to conscript soldiers and labor and to take away for the army all available stocks of food. It spoke of fear and fright, of confusion and uncertainty. There was no relief, or welcome, or pleasure in the faces of the people of Kinko village.

At the headquarters at the top of the street—it was the former police station—we met the officers of the detachment. Here were men different from the peasants in the railway yard. Here were sharp, natty officers in immaculate green uniforms, their chests glittering with decorations from the war in the west. They were lean, or barrel-round, all hard-muscled, bold, and faintly scornful—of their surroundings, of their own enlisted men, of the Koreans, and of us. The greeting was stiff, the conversation limited for lack of any adequate common tongue. We went back to the railway station, where we found we had to wait for someone coming down to see us. On both sides of the track, well back from our waiting train, huddled several hundred Koreans, men, women, and children. Hungrily they eyed the locomotive and the coach. Through our Korean interpreter I managed to glean the fact that some of these people had come all the way from Manchuria. Others were local people. All wanted to go south. "Can't we get some flatcars here and take them along?" I asked. Our Korean engineer shrugged. "The Russians won't give us any cars," he said. Asked to make the effort anyway, he shook his head. Then our visitor arrived. He turned out to be a smart young officer who wanted to know what we wanted. He brought a Japanese-speaking interpreter with him. Through half an hour of talk, strained from Russian into Japanese into English and vice versa, we explained we had merely come to see what was going on in the Russian zone. He replied that notice of such visits had to be given, that permission was needed and had to come from the main headquarters farther up, but as long as we were going right back . . . he shrugged politely. It would have been rather difficult, it was plain, to go any way but back. It was nearly nightfall when goodbyes were finally said.

We boarded the train, and as we did so the huddled waiting people made a dash for it. They tried for the cowcatcher, for the engine cab, the coal car, the windows of the single coach. A Russian officer shouted, and Russian soldiers moved in to drive the would-be travelers back. They picked the clambering figures off the car and off the engine and shoved the rest back, away from the station platform. The officers stood in their tight group, smiling and saluting, seemingly quite oblivious of the hustling and the roughhouse going on around them. They clicked heels smartly and bowed as the train pulled slowly out. The disconsolate figures of the people who had wanted to come along melted away in the dusk.

Several other correspondents made contact with small groups along the boundary. They ran into somewhat warmer hospitality, but their impressions were largely hidden behind a fine vodka haze by the time they got back to Seoul. Three others actually got as far as Heijo, the Russian headquarters town, but were held under hotel arrest there and were refused permission to look around the town or talk to people and were finally shipped back to Seoul. American military personnel who ventured north received mixed receptions. One B-29 which flew in to drop food to a prisoner-of-war camp was actually shot down by Russian Yaks. An official party from the American headquarters was royally entertained and sent back, without answers to any of its questions. They brought back stories of swaggering Russians and frightened, bowing Korean hotel attendants—the only Koreans they saw. They had received cordial invitations to visit distant Moscow, but they were given no chance to visit Heijo, the town they were in. They all shared a common impression that they had been visiting enemy territory under a white flag of truce.

These assorted glimpses and fleeting impressions did not yield much. Yet through them all, if one could hear it, ran a low and torn theme, a tumbling muted discord. It carried, faintly, from down the years a reminiscent phrase from the *Internationale,* grotesquely distorted, and something of the mood of a far time when the hammer and sickle was a liberating symbol and when men who wore it could be looked upon as the vanguardsmen of a new world and, indeed, a

new race. Such men, coming into a land newly freed from a generation of slavery, would have been different from the men we met in
Kinko and there would have been traces of something different in the
faces of the Koreans we saw there. Somehow, I think, there would
not have been huddled refugees in the railroad yard or soldiers with
rifles to bar their escape. Or if there had been refugees, they would
have looked more like people who had something to lose.

In the Russian north many Koreans were confounded and
frightened. In the American south Koreans were confounded and
confused. In the beginning particularly, the confusion was monumental. The day the Americans landed old Governor General
Noboyuki Abe faced General Hodge at the government palace,
retched into a handkerchief and then signed over Japan's richest
colony to the victors. On the walls of Seoul they were posting General
MacArthur's Proclamation Number One, which contained the phrase:
"Until further orders, all governmental officials and employes . . .
shall continue to perform their usual functions and duties." This was
plain enough, but it took a little time for many Koreans to realize
that this meant that Governor General Abe signed the surrender and
then went back to work as Governor General. It meant that Japanese
police, still walking the streets armed with guns and sabers, continued to do so under American direction. Not freedom was the
word, but law-and-order was the fetish. That first night in flag-decked
Seoul there would have been dancing in the streets in honor of the
liberators, only the liberators clapped on an 8 P.M. curfew and the
liberated had to contemplate their joys indoors.

The Americans had approached Korea in the most abysmal
ignorance of the country. They came unarmed with policy or even
with personnel faintly familiar with the land or its people. Hodge
had only his orders from MacArthur, tablets from the mount on
which were written the words "law and order." Hodge was to preserve
the existing governmental machinery, just as MacArthur was doing in
Japan, and he was by all means to preserve public peace. Hodge, a
simple infantryman, tried to carry out his orders literally. The results
were appalling. As the troops of Hodge's 24th Corps approached the
Korean shore, the senior Japanese commander in Seoul radioed:

"Communists and independence agitators are plotting to take advantage of this situation to disturb peace and order." He appealed for authority to keep troops on hand to back up the Japanese police. To this appeal the reply was promptly made:

> It is directed that you maintain order and preserve the machinery of government in Korea south of the 38th degree north latitude until my forces assume those responsibilities. . . . You are authorized and directed to retain in the Jinsen-Seoul area the minimum Japanese armed forces necessary to preserve order and safeguard property therein.

To this the Japanese commander replied:

> Am extremely grateful to have received your understanding reply with regard to the keeping of law and order in Korea.

A few days before the landing, Americans dropped leaflets over southern Korea calling for implicit obedience to "orders passed to you through the current Korean government" and added the astounding warning: *"Do not participate in demonstrations against the Japanese or in welcome to American armed forces. Go about your normal pursuits. . . ."*

So when Koreans organized a march to the Jinsen waterfront to welcome the landing Americans, Japanese police fired into the crowd, killed two and wounded ten. They were acting with the authority of the United States command.

During those first days other bizarre things happened in this freshly liberated land. Japanese remained in control of the newspapers and the radio. They were still broadcasting Domei news from Tokyo a week after the occupation began. Japanese policemen stood armed guard over Japanese property. They even blossomed forth with armbands marked "USMG"—United States Military Government—and with this authority stalked in groups through the streets of the city before incredulous Koreans. Armed Japanese soldiers rode around town in trucks bearing the signs: "Japanese Army Detachment: Understood by the US Army." In the countryside, Japanese soldiers were tearing down Allied flags put up by Koreans. They were seizing Korean flags which bloomed everywhere, appearing in the land for the first time since the annexation. There were minor clashes in which the Japanese always won because they were armed and the Koreans were not.

In Seoul, Hodge wrestled as best he could with the confusion. He countermanded the order which put USMG armbands on Japanese policemen, and he appealed to MacArthur for release from orders that obviously did not fit the situation. It came as something of a revelation to the Americans that the Koreans stubbornly believed they were being liberated. To General Hodge at a press conference a Korean newspaperman blazed: "You are now utilizing the existing machinery of government which has been exploiting, destroying, and squeezing the Korean people for the last thirty-six years. Do you realize how the Koreans hate this government? Do you think this is the machinery for maintaining law and order?" Hodge replied unhappily: "I am making reports and recommendations, and I will have to wait for my instructions." Hodge had by this time asked for authority to dismiss the Governor General and his principal aides, and he had also seen that if he was to maintain order he would have to get rid of the Japanese police. By the week's end, Hodge was free to ship old Governor Abe home and to clean out the top rungs, at least, of the Japanese régime. Recruitment was opened for Korean policemen, and the Japanese police were marched out of the south gate in long, black, straggling lines, heading for repatriation ports.

An American military government took over, under another infantryman, Major General Arch Arnold. Arnold started out with 109 military government officers, not one of whom had been trained in any way for service in Korea. Not one of them could speak Korean. They had been trained to run a military government in Japan, but there the emperor had been left to rule instead. So they were passed on to Korea, where the liberated Koreans were not yet "fit" to rule themselves. Japanese were fit to rule Koreans. So, apparently, were a band of American officers. Only Koreans were unqualified. They lacked the necessary number of "experts." A good number of these American "experts" had learned a smattering of Japanese and could talk to the Koreans only in the tongue which Koreans hated and never wanted to hear again. English-speaking interpreters were rare and soon had key jobs for which their only qualification was their knowledge of English. The Americans in charge tended inevitably to lean on their interpreters, who quickly acquired peculiar power. It was not long before the military government was scornfully referred to as the "interpreters' government" by a great many Koreans. The government was inadequately and incompetently manned by men who could not be blamed, after all, for not being Koreans or not knowing anything about Korea. Arnold had one Korean "expert" on his staff, the son of a onetime missionary who had left the country twenty years before. His word was taken for gospel by the grateful infantrymen who ran the show. The government was bumbling and inefficient, and it had no policy about anything. Its sole function was to fill the artificially created political void in southern Korea.

But good, bad, or indifferent, it was military government, under a military governor general, supported by an army of occupation. To a great many Koreans this looked like anything but "liberation." It was not what they had expected. It was not what they wanted. In fact, it looked a great deal like the Japanese régime that had just been ousted. Only it was a little more benevolent, slightly more democratic, somewhat less efficient and it covered only half the country. This was not freedom nor did it look like any prelude to freedom. What Koreans wanted was a government of their own, and they did not agree that they were not ripe enough to form one. "We did all right for 4,000 years," said one of them. To be sure the American goal was stated to be assistance to the Koreans in preparation for their independence in due course. "But," commented a Korean editor, "that's just what the Japanese said in 1910!" It was around the issue of the early creation of a new central Korean government that all the new politics of the country revolved.

In southern Korea political life stirred in many layers after the Japanese lid was lifted. In a natural ferment rising swiftly to the surface, numerous groups and parties came into existence. Some were designed to contend for Russian or American favor on the basis of serious programs, others reflected the views or ambitions of particular individuals. Out of the tumult of new voices, finding relatively free expression for the first time in so many years, there quickly emerged a rough division into a conservative right and a radical left.

The Democratic Party was the largest of the right-wing groups.

It was the polar center for Korea's relatively few men of wealth and position. They included the business men who had won advantages under the Japanese and anticipated greater opportunities under the Americans. They eyed Japanese property with glinting anticipation, and they expected a good part of it to pass into their hands under some natural law which entitled them to the major gain. Here too were the Korean landlords, the comparatively small group which had been permitted to share in the exploitation of the peasantry. They, for their part, counted on acquiring a heavy share of the lands held in bulk by Japanese companies like the Oriental Development Corporation. Also gravitating toward the Democratic Party were the professional politicians, intellectuals, jobholders, people who had compromised in greater or lesser degree with the Japanese régime and found places in it for themselves. It was the only way they could have become community leaders, no matter how much they chafed under their alien rulers. As their political opponents scornfully said in a published leaflet: "How could a patriot make a fortune under the shrewd rule of the Japanese? If a man was a 'respectable gentleman' under the Japanese, he could not have been a true patriot, for the rest of us were all poor slaves." This was factual enough. The Democratic Party was primarily a party of "respectable gentlemen" who earnestly wanted a free and independent Korea in which the principal political and economic privileges would be reserved for them.

There were too in this right wing a fair number of honest liberals, by political impulse and program progressive and even socialist, who were repelled from the left wing by their fear of Russian totalitarianism. They were united with the bourgeois conservatives in a common mistrust of Russia, a fear that Russian designs were a threat to Korean independence. To all these groups, in general, Russia was the northern colossus that had tried to absorb Korea fifty years before and was now, they feared, trying again. Russia was also the menace of communism which threatened their places in society. By these same tokens, their impulse was to lean on the United States if they could. The United States did not turn out to be the active liberating force they had hoped for but at least, they felt, it could not be credited with designs on Korean independence and Korean territory. The United States represented the kind of safely capitalist democracy on which they wanted to remodel the renascent Korea. The United States, above all, was the great counterweight to Russia, the great pillar on which they could lean in their resistance to control from the north.

The left wing of Korean nationalism was more of an amalgam. It was dominated by the Korean Communists but included many radical nationalists of different non-Communist hues. Here too the dubious mingled with the earnest, the clean-handed with the heavily spotted. Among the leftists I met Koreans who fought almost alone in the mortally dangerous underground against the Japanese. Here were Koreans who had spent the best of their years in Japanese prisons. But here also were Koreans who had managed to get along quite well as placeholders under the Japanese and now shrewdly calculated they could do quite as well with the Russians if they got on the band wagon early enough. There were also radical nationalists who quite genuinely identified the interests of Korean independence with a radical and socialist program for the workers and peasants. They did not see that interest served by throwing in with the "respectable gentlemen" of the bourgeois right. They did not see that interest served by the Americans, who favored the conservative right. So they stayed in the left wing, looking anxiously to the north and wondering what happened to freedom under the Russians. They were divided and vacillating, and consequently it was the Communists who guided the leadership and fixed the policies of the movement as a whole. The Communists were at best radicals who seriously believed in the progressive character of the Soviet power and considered therefore that Korea's future as an independent nation was bound up with the future of Russia in Asia. At the worst, the Communists were simple stooges for a foreign government, a pressure group for Russian national interests who did not hesitate to make cynical use of a radical agrarian and industrial program in Korea to further Russian ends. Thus, in the south, the Communist leader spoke in favor of a one-nation trusteeship over Korea, if that one nation was Russia. In the north, Korean Communists more unreservedly sloganed: "Russia is our fatherland."

Between these two wings of Korean politics, there was no doubt of the position of the American military command. General Hodge and some of his aides were, in their own way, men of limited good will, but they were military men trying to serve the vague power interest of the United States in Asia as best they could. They were unequipped to swim in political currents, and they were guided by nothing but their instinctive prejudices. That meant that they were instantly sympathetic to all the "respectable gentlemen" who were anxious to play along with the United States, and suspicious of all the dissident radicals, whom they suspected of being tools of Russia. Their impulses were scarcely shaken when the leftists put out a pamphlet consisting largely of compromising quotations made during the war years by some of the most prominent of the pro-American "gentlemen." They quoted recruiting speeches, addresses to Korean youth asking that they lay their lives down for the Emperor, newspaper articles denouncing Americans as vultures and baby-murderers. Repentant respectability was still preferable to unrepentant radicalism.

The issue of a new central Korean government was the main issue that lay between these rival groups. The conservatives passionately sought American recognition of the provisional government in exile, long headed abroad by Kim Koo and a group of fellow exiles who waited out most of the war in Chungking under Chinese government sponsorship and protection. The Americans did not go as far as recognizing this government, but they did bring its members and supporters back to Korea. Kim Koo and his associates were flown back from China. Syngman Rhee, another long-time exile and greatly venerated nationalist leader, was flown back to Seoul from Washington. Their function was to solidify the moderate nationalist wing, to weaken the lefts, and to lay the basis for a safely conservative government.

The left wing, on the other hand, was unwilling to give a blank check to the government in exile or to its leaders. The left wing went ahead on its own and formed a provisional government in which the exiled leaders were invited to participate. They established a provisional commission for a Korean People's Republic and actually nominated Syngman Rhee to be president. But the two groups did not succeed in getting together. At one stage the People's Republic group tried to force the issue by calling for an election, an act which brought forth repressive action by the American Military Government. There were highly undemocratic bans on public meetings and demonstrations, and crude, bumbling attempts to muzzle or at least control the left press.

Actually the political divisions in Korea cut far deeper than they had any reason to and this was because every domestic Korean issue became directly or indirectly a Russian-American issue and was thus enlarged and aggravated. In Korea, if anywhere, it seemed possible to start from scratch. The segment of the Korean population enriched by Japanese rule was insignificant. The great bulk of the wealth and property of the land—approximately 80 per cent—had been in Japanese hands and was now in the process of being confiscated. This expropriation would not take place at the expense of any domestic Korean class and therefore it could and should have proved easier to place the country's wealth at the disposal of the whole people. These intentions were written into almost every party program. Even the rightists of the Democratic Party gave a socialist slant to their economic platform. But their translation into fact was made far too remote from immediate political realities. These realities, above all, were the partition and the occupation of the country by two armies facing each other in an attitude of suspended hostility. It was on the rock of partition that Korean hopes for a fruitful independence were being smashed to pieces. Many Americans in the military government picked up the facile argument that Koreans would be "ripe" for freedom only when they had shown that they could unify themselves. To this Koreans could and did answer: "You Americans say we are still unfit to rule ourselves. Yet you indicate by your policy in Japan that you consider the Emperor and his politicians still fit to rule that country, even though they led it into war, chaos, and destruction. We have our differences and our serious problems. That is evident. But how else does one grow? How do you learn to rule except by ruling? You say we are divided among ourselves. Divided? Who divided us? Who split our country and our people in half?"

Korea's misfortune is its geography. Its unhappy lot is to be a small country occupying a crucial corner of the cockpit of Asia.

Long held tributary to the Chinese Empire, it became in the last century the victim of the rival ambitions of Czarist Russia and Imperial Japan. Japan won and annexed Korea for its own. Now Japanese rule has ended. Russia has returned to the Asiatic arena to pick up where it left off in 1905. Korea is a small country bordering on Russia. That brings it automatically into the "security" zone in which Russia clearly intends by any means to establish its decisive influence or control. This need not mean literal absorption of Korea into the Soviet Union. Korea might be independent—as independent, that is, as Outer Mongolia. But whatever the form, the substance of the new dispensation in Korea would have to be wholly satisfactory to the Kremlin.

The United States, on the other hand, is seeking to establish its own decisive influence and control in Asia on terms which would suit American economic, political, and military requirements. At some line across northern Asia, still unfixed, the Americans must meet the Russians, balance precariously with them, and if they do not coalesce they must eventually collide.

Between two such titanic forces, the Koreans—like the Chinese and eventually the Japanese—will be squeezed and driven. There is no room in this baleful competition for such trivial things as the national independence or free growth of subject peoples.

Instead the Koreans are presented with the miserable alternatives of throwing in their lot with one power or the other, to try to measure the jockeying back and forth, and to find some spot in the midst of it that they can hold on to as their own. Many Koreans are soberly aware that any road open to them now is a blind alley. Through a long and uneasy armistice the country would be torn asunder, as it is being torn now. As a Russian satellite, it would become an object of American suspicion and hostility. As an American satellite, it would be under constant, paralyzing pressure from Russia. If the issue should come to Russian-American conflict, little Korea would be swallowed up in the holocaust. All Korean parties and groups demand the withdrawal of all foreign troops from their land, and—except for a few Communist Party zealots who would just as soon see the Red Army remain—they all mean it passionately. They all want some ground to stand on and call their own. So even old ultraconservative Syngman Rhee could speak with the voice of a whole people when he faced 50,000 of his countrymen in Seoul upon his return. It was a brilliant October afternoon and the sun played on the bright colors and waving banners and on the faces of the people crowding the streets. Syngman Rhee said: "Through the years of Japanese oppression we remained unconquered and undivided. We intend to remain so, even at the cost of our lives. The Allied Powers might as well know that now."

For Koreans the hysterical joy that followed Japan's collapse gave way to a bitter time of hope and fear, of aspiration and gnawing disillusion. Their land was not free. It was a little test tube for Russian and American power politics in Asia, a trial zone, an outpost, a boundary where mighty opponents eyed each other. Korea was a minor preliminary proving ground for Russian and American professions and Russian and American practices. Whichever way the tests came out, the future did not look bright for Korean freedom. Koreans are not sophisticated. Neither are they naïve. A Korean friend said to me: "We spent long hard years learning Japanese. Now we must learn English or Russian. When shall we be able to concentrate on learning Korean?"

5 SOUTHERN ASIA: THE WANING EMPIRES

Southern Asia is a vast belt of conquered and reconquered countries. It extends for more than 6,000 miles from the scorched hills of Baluchistan in far western India to the easternmost of the Indies in the lower Pacific. In these many lands and islands live half a billion people, nearly one-fourth of the world's population. They are a tremendous mass of human beings who live in primitive poverty. They are divided by their many races, their ancient religions, their multiple tongues. They are burdened by their past, by a way of life and toil in which they continue to multiply but never to thrive.

For all their differences, they hold one thing in common: with the single tiny nominal exception of the sixteen million Siamese, they are all subjects of foreign rulers.*

Here in southern Asia lies India, the crown jewel of the old British Empire; Burma and Malaya, its satellite gems; Indochina, the richest colony of France; Indonesia, the fabulous archipelago that belongs to tiny Holland. These are the great Asiatic empires, formed out of wars of conquest and wars between the conquerors going back more than three hundred years. Here out of cotton, jute, rubber, tin, oil, quinine, rice, and spices, power and profit waxed while colonies could still feed the expansion of the West. But here today, in our age of decline and smothered growth, empires are waning.

Here, in a futile, bloody, and costly challenge, Japan threatened briefly to appropriate the great wealth and power accumulated for centuries by the Western powers. Here, after the Japanese collapse, the British, French, and Dutch scrambled desperately to regain what they had lost. They met with solid and serious obstacles. For across the entire area people for so long subjected and frustrated were demanding and fighting for change. In varying degrees and by varying means, they attempted again to assert themselves, to determine

---

* The exception is nominal because Siam is wholly dominated by British capital and since the war it has become more than ever a virtual British protectorate.

their own fate, to make a fresh start of some kind in some kind of new world.

For these people the basic issue was simple: to submit no longer to any foreign rulers. They were intent upon becoming their own masters. Their determination cut across all the arguments and counterarguments, all the ifs and buts and howevers, all the slow mulling and all the inertia, all the brute force that lay behind entrenched foreign privilege. Whatever the real or fancied perils of freedom, these peoples insisted upon being free. Whatever the complexities of their internal problems, they were bent upon facing these problems, for better or worse, by themselves. After the spectacle the world has presented in the past decades, and in particular after the demonstration their masters gave of their inability to prevent war or to defend themselves, their subjects, or their lands, colonial submission was no longer possible. Subject peoples everywhere refused any longer to agree that anybody was more fit to rule them than they were themselves.

A young Annamite in Hanoi expressed this minimum program quite succinctly: "The Western powers have made enough of a mess of things. We are fighting for our right to make our own mess. We cannot do worse than they have done."

INDIA: THE BRITISH STAKE

Of all the colonies in southern Asia, India is the largest and the richest. No subject land has ever yielded greater returns to its conquerors. None has ever played a more crucial role in the building and maintaining of an empire. India is a vast, rich country. Its place in Asia is second to that of China only because it has been subjected more directly and for a much longer period. India is in fact more advanced than China in many aspects of its development. The loosening of its British bonds was unquestionably one of the major facts in Asia in the aftermath of the war.

Britain's past relation to India was strikingly illustrated by the fact that by a simple declaration and without consulting a single Indian, the British government could involve India in war, first against Germany and then against Japan. It was also illustrated by the fact that when the war came close to India itself, Britain had to imprison and keep imprisoned for the war's duration thousands of Indian political leaders, from Gandhi and Nehru down to the lowliest local committeemen of the Indian National Congress. It had to put down a major insurrection. It had to operate in India like an armed power in passively hostile territory. It was able again, as in 1914-1918, to draw on Indian manpower for military service and exploit some of India's resources for war purposes. But it never had the active support of the Indian people nor that of any of the important Indian leaders.

Nothing in Britain's relation to India gave the overwhelming mass of Indians any cause to feel that Britain's war was their war, that they had any stake at all in defending the British Empire against its enemies. On the contrary, everything in the development of this relationship over a period of more than three hundred years had given the Indian much greater cause to look upon Britain as his enemy above all enemies. Not even the shadow of Japanese conquest could alter this conviction. On the contrary, Subhas Chandra Bose, the onetime Congress president who threw in with the Japanese and organized an Indian National Army to invade India in cooperation with the Japanese, lost no credit with Congress nationalists for what he did. Many of them may have thought him unwise or ill-advised. But it never occurred to them to look upon him as a traitor. When Bose was reported killed in an air crash the week the war ended, he was nationally mourned in India. When the British tried to court-martial the men who had followed him and borne arms against the British, there was angry rioting in every major Indian city, and in the end the British had to give up the attempt. Most conscious Indians during the war simply refused to consider the threat of Japanese domination more serious than the fact of British domination. For too much of the misery in Indian life bore the stamp of British rule.

It would be oversimplifying a complex picture to suggest that all the evils that abound in India are the direct results of British rule. There was intense exploitation before the British came. There was extreme poverty and the gross weight of superstition, caste, and religion, bearing down upon the peoples of India long before the British conquered them. There are even a few respects in which Britain, in the broadest historic sense, served some useful purposes in India. It was an agency of change and transformation in an ancient and economically backward land. But the changes it wrought were for Britain's benefit, not India's. The process of British enrichment over the many decades was a process of deepening poverty in India. In establishing and entrenching its political power in the land, Britain aggravated all the internal divisions that existed, utilizing them with conscious and cynical deliberation for Britain's own political purposes. Once it was molded to a shape that suited British needs, the old Indian society was deliberately preserved with emphasis on its worst features. The consequences are hardly a matter of debate. They are a matter of fact. They are there in India for anyone to see. And for what is to be seen there, the British, after nearly two centuries of absolute rule, must surely bear the major responsibility.

What there is above all to see in India is poverty, staggering, appalling poverty. India is a crowded land, the second most populous on earth. It has 390 million people, three times as many as the United States, living in territory a little more than half as large as the United States. Of this great number the overwhelming bulk, about 90 per cent, live in India's 700,000 tiny villages. Most of the remainder live in the packed slums of its great cities. Their visible wretchedness almost defies detailed understanding. The first impact on the newcomer from the West is primarily a physical impact, and an emotional one. It takes in the unsmiling, unrelieved preoccupation with toil, desperately necessary toil. It takes in the strong sense of an absent vitality. It takes in the filth and the nakedness and the hunger, the visible disease and the prevalence of death. It takes in the rare glance of uncurious eyes, the remoteness and the distance and the indifference to almost everything but the simple and monstrous facts of a struggle for bare existence. It is easy to understand, standing on any non-European street of any Indian city or on any Indian country crossroad, why so many notions of human dignity in the religion and philosophy of India have had to dissolve in doctrines of the forgetfulness of self or else find refuge in glittering mythologies.

It has taken potent magic indeed to make men submit to such a lot as this.

There is no real measure in statistics for the depth of human degradation that this poverty implies. Nevertheless, statistics sometimes have their own peculiar kind of eloquence; and here are a few of them. Per capita income in India has been estimated at sums between $15 and $23 a year. This is about one-twentieth of the per capita income in the United States. But even this figure is something of an exaggeration because it is an average that includes the gem-glutted maharajah and the gauntest peasant. Indian economists have calculated that sixty per cent of India's people share among them only thirty per cent of the national income. So for this majority, the national per capita average has to be nearly halved to arrive at a more accurate picture of the real income received. Half of the national income comes from the land, which has to support more than three-quarters of the people. Agricultural productivity is held to abysmal levels by the medieval system of land tenure, by uneconomical strip farming, and by the almost total absence of modern methods or implements. The cultivated acreage in India is about the same size as that in the United States, but it has to support a farm population nearly ten times greater. Yet from a single acre the Indian farmer can produce little more than half as much wheat as the American farmer can, less than half as much rice, and only about one-third as much cotton. From his toil, the Indian farmer gets an average income officially estimated in 1929 at 42 rupees a year, or about $13. Of this sum the government, the landlords, and the money-lenders take about two-thirds, leaving the farmer with nothing but an accumulating debt.

The industrial worker is little better off. An official survey in 1929 (by the Royal Commission on Labor in India) reported the top wages being paid to skilled Bombay textile workers: $14 a month. Only a small minority received so much. The wages scale down to $7 a month for unskilled labor in Bombay, $5.50 a month for miners in Jharria; eighteen cents a day for men, twelve cents a day for women, and eight cents a day for children in Bengal, Bihar, and Orissa. The report of the Royal Commission said: "Workers as young as five years of age may be found working in some of these places, working without adequate meal intervals or weekly rest days and often for ten or twelve hours daily, for sums as low as two annas (four cents) in the case of those of tenderest years." Nor does this enslavement of children add sufficiently to the family livelihood. The commission found that in most of India's industrial centers up to two-thirds of the working people were in debt to money-lenders for sums equivalent to three months' earnings and often far more.

This scale of earnings is also reflected in living conditions. In Bombay in 1931, 74 per cent of the whole population of that great and rich city of commerce and industry lived in one-room tenements. The kind of living this afforded is illustrated by a single appalling figure: in those tenements in one year more than half of all babies died before they were one year old. The Indian who survives his infancy can expect to die by the time he is twenty-four years old. In four cases out of five, he will die of a preventable disease: cholera, plague, smallpox, dysentery, or "fevers," an inclusive term used in the official statistics to cover the deaths due to simple starvation and the multitudinous and unnamable diseases of poverty.

This poverty exists in a land that abounds with wealth. India's soil is rich, and there is a good deal of it. Acreage now under cultivation can be increased, it has been estimated, by at least a third. With the radical revision of the system of ownership and exploitation and with the introduction of scientific methods and modern implements, Indian agriculture can be made immensely more productive than it is now. India's industrial potential is even greater. A real attempt to exploit its possibilities could in a fair measure of time transform India into Asia's greatest center of production, capable of supporting many millions of its own population by its own industry and assuring to the rural population a higher standard of living. India's iron ore reserves are third in the world in quantity, and first in quality. It has large, though inferior-grade, reserves of coal. On the other hand it is second only to the United States in potential hydroelectric power resources, of which only a tiny fraction has been brought into employment by the British. India already mines a third of the world's supply of manganese ore. It has quantities of chrome, bauxite, tin, lead, gold, silver, and copper. It lacks petroleum, but large supplies are available in nearby Burma and Sumatra. India is in addition the world's second grower of cotton, has a virtual world monopoly in jute, and is a heavy producer of sugar cane and tea. With these resources and in a world capable of meshing them into its pattern of needs and production, India could be one of the most flourishing lands on earth. Instead it is one of the poorest. This fact is, surely, one of the gravest and most direct consequences of British rule.

It is no exaggeration to say that British wealth and might have been built out of Indian poverty. The initial period of plunder and conquest under the East India Company, which reached its height in the last half of the eighteenth century, brought to England vast stores of treasure. In its annual report for 1812, written as its power drew to a close, the East India Company defined very clearly the contribution it had made: "The importance of that vast empire [India] to this country [England] is to be estimated by the great annual addition it makes to the wealth and capital of the Kingdom rather than by any eminent advantage which the manufacturers can derive from the consumption of the natives of India."

This "great annual addition" in no small measure financed England's industrial revolution. It provided the primary accumulation of capital over a period of more than a century which enabled Britain to lead the world in changing over from simple mercantilism to industrial production. As British industry grew, the anarchic plundering methods of the East India Company had to be replaced by the more systematic exploitation of India as a source of agricultural raw materials and a market for English goods. The company's monopoly came to an end in 1813, and forty years later passed entirely from the scene. As British manufactured goods flowed into India in a thickening stream, they shattered India's extensive handicraft industries and nothing was allowed to take their place. Indian handicraft production centers, particularly in textiles, literally went back to the weeds and the artisans were driven into the crowded fields of agriculture.

Expanding British trade required the more efficient commercial penetration of India. This need called forth investments in the development of a railway system, roads, posts, telegraphic communications, and, somewhat later, a limited program for irrigation and hydroelectric power development. Money went into companies and installations, plantations, shipping and harbor facilities, and all the miscellaneous machinery built up to extract wealth from India. Most of the capital thus invested came from the profits of the rich Indian trade, from the exploitation of cheap Indian labor, and from direct tribute levied in various forms on India by the home government in London. This British investment in India rose to an estimated total, in 1933, of £1 billion, or about $5 billion, representing at that time approximately one-fourth of Great Britain's total foreign investment.* It produced a return which has been estimated at £150 million annually. Protection of this huge investment not only included the maintenance, up until recent years, of tariffs designed to favor the movement of British goods, but equally called for the active discouragement of the competitive development of Indian capital.

In the face of numerous obstacles, including complete British control of the modern banking and credit system in the country, Indian capital expanded only with the utmost difficulty. There was growth in spurts, as during the First World War, and immediately afterward when tariff concessions wrung from the British created more favorable conditions. An Indian textile industry grew up and a beginning was made in iron and steel production. But the total was small. Factory-type industry in India, up to the eve of the recent war, supported less than two per cent of the population.

Hand in hand with the stunting of Indian economic growth to serve British economic ends went the malforming of the political structure of the country to serve the ends of British power. Out of the pattern of conquest and out of the constant creation and shifting of internal levers of support, emerged a jigsaw puzzle of administrative machinery to which the British alone could hold the key. The country was divided into British India and a miscellaneous collection of no fewer than 562 nominally independent Indian states dotting the map like spattered random blotches. These states, occupying just under half of India's territory and with one hundred million people or one-fourth of the population, are ruled by compliant and usually

* For varying summaries and breakdowns, see *Foreign Policy Reports,* February 11, 1944.

decadent princes, maharajas and lesser noble lights under the firm "guidance" of British residents.

British India has been the scene of various pseudo-democratic reforms in recent years, but none of these ever affected the total autocratic power of the Viceroy. He remained the real ruler of the country. He has had under him a Council of State and a Legislative Assembly, both partly elective, the former by an electorate restricted to about 40,000 of the country's wealthiest individuals, the latter by an electorate of less than one and a half million, or less than one half of one per cent of the population of British India. Neither body ever had any real power. Whenever they voted contrary to the Viceroy's wishes he could, and did, override them. The provincial legislatures, open to election by some 34 million voters, or just about ten per cent of the population, hold the same impotent position in relation to the provincial governors, who are responsible not to the legislators but to the Viceroy. For the hundred million who live under the princes, there is no franchise at all.

This limited machinery of elections has been used by the British as an instrument of division, hardening and deepening the existing social cleavages within the country. For in the name of protecting the minorities, the British forty years ago introduced the system of communal electorates under which Moslems vote only for Moslems for a selected proportion of seats, Sikhs only for Sikhs, Anglo-Indians only for Anglo-Indians, and so on for a total of no fewer than thirteen sectional or communal groupings. The "general" seats open to the predominantly Hindu population, both in the central and provincial legislatures as set up by the reforms of 1919 and 1935, remained in the minority in relation to the whole representation.

The two largest groups in India are the 255 million Hindus and the 95 million Moslems. There are, to be sure, differences between them. But they are not racial differences, most Moslems being descendants of converted Hindus. They are by no means unbridgeable social differences, as the peaceful coexistence of Hindus and Moslems in thousands of Indian villages has long testified. There are no "natural" political differences, for there is a large Moslem group that supports the Congress—which has had Moslem presidents—and there have been provincial Moslem ministries much closer to the Congress than to the Moslem League. There are economic cleavages but these, as always, cross the lines of religion. In Bengal and the Punjab there is conflict between Moslem peasants and Hindu landlords and money-lenders. Elsewhere Hindu peasants are in conflict with Moslem land-lords and money-lenders. But religion has no more to do with such conflicts than, say, with the strike of Polish Catholic coal miners against Protestant mine owners in western Pennsylvania. The fact is that where religious fanaticism has become the source of friction, every British act in the past has been calculated to promote rather than allay it. The whipped-up fervor of "communal" conflict in India in recent decades has been only in a relatively minor degree inherent in Indian social relations. In its sharpened forms, it has been far more the product of a conscious and deliberate British policy aimed to insure British power over a divided people.*

The British have systematically applied the ancient and well tried principle of "divide and rule." They applied it widely and deeply and judiciously in their own interest. The British early supported the Hindus against the old Moslem aristocracy. Later they fostered the development of Moslem group consciousness and political action, in the words of the onetime Secretary of State for India, Lord Olivier, "as a makeweight against Hindu nationalism." The worst nightmare ever visited upon the British in India occurred during and after the First World War when Hindus and Moslems were joined in close-knit political unity. They managed to break up that unity and in the person of M. A. Jinnah they found with delight a fanatical Moslem politician who abandoned cooperation with the Hindus in favor of the most extreme and enormously exaggerated antagonism. Under Jinnah, Moslem politics eventually focused on the idea of Pakistan, a fantastic plan for the partition of the country into separate Hindu and Moslem nations, with the Moslem section occupying two widely separated areas in the west and in the east. Jinnah's intransigence has served the British interest by deepening and prolonging and largely even creating internal divisions. It has, the British now find, served them also too well. Seeking a greater degree of safe "stability" in

* A useful recent study of this problem, past and present, will be found in *The Communal Triangle in India*, by Asoka Mehta and Achyut Patwardhan (Allahabad, 1942).

India, they could wish that Jinnah's fanaticism were a little less genuine.

It cannot be said that British rule has been entirely without benefit to the Indian people. After nearly two centuries of conscientious effort in behalf of the poverty-stricken masses in India, the British Indian Government reached the point of spending four cents per capita per year on education, with the result that 88 per cent of the population still enjoys the bliss of illiteracy. On public health, according to a recent report, the government has spent from five to fifteen cents per capita per year, varying according to locality, with the result that misery for many millions is mercifully brought to an end by premature death.

Out of this soil Indian nationalism grew like a twisted vine, often stunted and clipped and sometimes almost smothered but forever nourished by the abundance of India's discontent. Originally encouraged by the British as a means for drawing off currents of rebellion, the Indian National Congress became the principal organ of Indian nationalism. It grew through the years to embrace a following of many millions, and for better or worse it has expressed the Indian will to win freedom from British rule.

The span of the Congress now has passed sixty years. The story of Indian national struggle is long and complicated and the subject of much history that has been written and much that still waits to be written. But the whole of it has followed a pattern clearly visible overlying the years: waves of popular struggle, bitter and brutal repressions, grudging and half-given reforms, intervals of uneasy truce, more struggle, more repression, more half-given reforms. Such was the course marked by the uprisings and repressions of 1919, the Swarajist revolts of 1921-22, the civil disobedience movement of 1930-32, the leaderless insurrection of 1942. One thing emerges plainly enough from the record: Indian nationalists have fought long and bitterly to gain little, and what they gained came with agonizing slowness. The reason for this was in part the British capacity for combining guile with force and the British ability to absorb pressure. But it was also a result of the leadership that the Indian nationalist movement has had in these eventful decades.

This history has been dominated for most of the last thirty years by Mohandas Gandhi, the wizened little man known as the Mahatma. Mixture of saint and schemer, mystic and politician, Gandhi is perhaps the most remarkable self-made enigma in modern politics. He is a reformed intellectual, an ex-lawyer turned preacher and healer, an ascetic and a soul-searcher who sometimes gives the impression that the whole vast struggle involving the fate of India's millions of people is only an incident in his own quest for salvation. And this, ironically enough, is the main source of his hold on the popular Indian imagination. It is Gandhi, the mystic and religious martyr, not Gandhi the politician, who holds the allegiance of the millions. More worldly Indian nationalists who try to cope with the facts of life are often confused, intimidated, and bemused by the little Mahatma who deals in the mistier things of the spirit.

Gandhi's saintly aura is a liberating thing for a man who is also a politician. He is serene in his many contradictions while others must struggle to give them coherence or find coherence in them. He is unconcerned with the apparent confusions in his thinking because he more often appears to be concerned with beatitude than with practical clarity. The morality of love and the purged soul are ill at ease amid the harsher realities of politics, but Gandhi manages to live and lead at both levels. Neither his friends nor his foes can ever be quite certain how the blend will apply in any given circumstance, and sometimes they have been shocked and hurt when they found out. Gandhi's peculiar virtue has possibly brought him some of the balm he has sought. Its effect on the cause of Indian nationalism, however, has been to make a hard road harder to follow.

It would be difficult to take all of Gandhi's premises and examine them as a whole because the manner in which they mesh into consistency is one of the secrets locked in Gandhi's breast. A mystic and a martyr does not have to be consistent; and Gandhi makes full use of his prerogative. Still, Gandhi has expressed himself on a host of quite material subjects and it is possible to examine some of his opinions at their face value. He has distinguished himself from other politicians by his fear of power. He seems to fear the fetters of poverty less than the chains of centralized control. In the complexities of industrialization he perceives the diseased germs of Western life from which he would spare himself and his country if he could. He sees in it the degrading ambition and violence which underlie the anarchy and brutality of the Western world. He may actually believe that Western man with his iceboxes and his sanitation has less chance of preserving his immortal soul than the sodden Indian peasant who has nothing but his belief that the world of the spirit must surely be easier to live in than the world of man. And Gandhi knows too how relatively few Western men have iceboxes and sanitation. So he fears the machine and the factory. He would see Indian society built around the land and the spinning wheel. He would restore some idyllic kind of rural balance in which simple physical well-being would interfere at the minimum with the business of cultivating purity. The glorified Indian village is for Gandhi the refuge from the madness and the hopeless sin of modern urban existence.

In political struggle, Gandhi has preached the doctrine of *satyagraha*, meaning "strength derived from truth." As a political weapon, it means non-violent civil disobedience. In Gandhi's sense this involves complete mastery of self, conquest by example, struggle that means taking upon oneself the maximum suffering rather than inflicting the maximum suffering upon the foe. Gandhi seriously believes that the cost implicit in this doctrine is still lighter than the cost extorted from the human race by the unabashed violence of Western political struggle. After all, political struggle in the West, which bears no resemblance to Gandhist doctrines and practices, has not exactly demonstrated its superiority. All political methods have been brought into question by the all-inclusive failure of our times to produce even a modicum of well-being for men. Gandhi's method therefore cannot be dismissed simply on the ground that it is difficult to practice, or that it is naïve and unrealistic. But the fact is that Gandhi's method has not worked either. Whatever the starting point or the method, the end result of political struggles in India as elsewhere has been determined by the relationship of force between the two opposing sides. In the measure of this relationship simple moral virtue has played small part.

To the extent that Gandhi has been successful in his program of non-violence, he has merely increased the relative weight of the violence opposed to his movement by the British. On the other hand, Gandhi has not been too successful. His non-violence has generated violence whenever it was applied. For saintliness, if Gandhi indeed be a saint, is distinctly a very individual matter and it is, happily or not, quite rare. It may command respect but not necessarily emulation. Generations in the West have found it easier to worship Jesus than to follow his precepts. In Gandhi similarly, great masses of Indians are led to glimpse and admire or revere what is for them the unattainable. He is still, in his role as saint, more engaged in trying to convert than in leading his own people.

But these are the less palpable aspects of Gandhi's leadership. There are other consequences of it which are much more readily subject to review because they have been written into history as objective facts. History, for a fact, has scant respect for the human soul; and Gandhi has been compelled to play a certain historic role. Into this role there have entered the quite corporeal factors of British power, the interests of Indian industrialists and landlords, the counter-interests of Indian workers and peasants. Every non-violent movement of any size initiated by Gandhi has passed over to violence or produced a violent reaction. British rule in India has not suffered so much from Gandhi's doctrine of non-violence as it has from violations of that doctrine by Gandhi's followers. These violations had a tendency to embroil more than the interests of British power. Aroused Indian masses would threaten entrenched Indian interests as well. And it is a matter of peculiar interest that whenever such unholy violence reached its most dangerous pitch, Gandhi, more effectively than British whips, truncheons, and guns, brought it to an end in a way that invariably served not the Indian cause but the British, not the revolting mass but the men of property.

Gandhi too has had a role to play in shaping the very relationship of force which he would abjure. In playing this role in repeated crises of recent Indian history, Gandhi overcame the misgivings of many other Indian leaders who might have acted otherwise but who bowed to him because as even the enlightened Nehru has put it: "The unknown stared at us through his eyes." The student of human history in our time will still have to determine whether Gandhi has best served India or himself.*

Gandhi's impress endowed Indian nationalism with the basically conservative weakness that for so long served Britain so well. The British have long boasted over the fact that they could rule huge, discontented India so easily with a handful of soldiers and civil servants. But this was possible for them only because Indian nationalism forswore force as a matter of inherent policy. Its program, diluted and confused by Gandhi's pacifism and his mystic ruralism, never acquired the dynamic character it needed to offer a positive challenge to British rule.

Indian nationalism also reflected the fear of the Indian propertied men for the unpropertied. It suited the Indian manufacturer and landlord, as well as the British overlord, that the movement under Gandhi's leadership remained a movement of passive protest. Whenever the logic of social struggle and human limitations drove it beyond these bounds, Gandhi and those who followed him always brought it back within the limits of safety. Without this assistance, British rule could not have sustained itself so long.

As it is, the British have been able to apply with great success the technique of yielding as little as possible as seldom as possible. They could combine frequent and drastic repressions with infrequent and mild reforms. They could find and use allies within the Indian nation, either in the form of religious groups or economic groups. The reforms they granted, always grandly hailed as prodigal acts of justice, were almost invariably designed to sharpen divisions between groups in India or bring one or more of them closer to the British Raj. And with these reforms the British took their own good time. It was not until 1917 that Britain acknowledged self-government as the ultimate aim for India, not until 1929 that it opened up for some dim future the prospect of Dominion status. Out of the con-

* Jawaharlal Nehru has written some illuminating passages describing the consternation and confusion and ruinous consequences following Gandhi's acts in arbitrarily terminating the great mass revolt in 1922 and again when he suddenly came to terms with the Viceroy, Lord Irwin, in 1931, at the height of the great civil disobedience campaign of that year. Nehru writes, with a curiously muted anguish, that he bowed to Gandhi's decision "not without great mental conflict and physical distress." Cf. Nehru, *Toward Freedom* (New York, 1942), pp. 79–84, 188–194.

stitutional reforms of 1919 and 1935 the Indian nationalists won no measure at all of self-government. They merely received the right to whisper meekly in the chambers of the all-powerful Viceroy.

In 1939 Britain again ordered India to war by simple fiat. Gandhi's reaction was one of sentimental pacifism. When Britain refused to commit itself to India's freedom, he led the Congress to dissociate itself formally from the British war effort in India. But in this form opposition turned out to be a matter of submission. Gandhi declared his unwillingness to "embarrass" the British in their great time of crisis in 1940. He ordained a limited program of individual acts of civil disobedience by leaders who were to inform the police in advance of their intentions. The British accepted this accommodation. By mid-1941 they had an estimated 20,000 Congress leaders behind bars.

When in 1942 the bastions of empire in Southeast Asia fell to the Japanese and the attackers stood on India's frontiers, Britain bid again for Indian support with the well known Cripps offer. The Indians were demanding a national government of their own. What Cripps brought with him was another offer to enlarge the Viceregal council. The Indians wanted power. The British offered them only a slightly louder voice at the Viceroy's elbow. The Congress declined. Gandhi, raising again the demand that Britain quit India at once, announced he would lead the country in offering to Japan, if it invaded, the same passive resistance it offered to Britain. The Congress Working Committee passed its famous "Quit India" resolution on August 8, 1942. The next day the British struck back with mass arrests, beginning with Gandhi himself.

The Indian answer to this came not from Gandhi but from the people. It was a spontaneous uprising that began with simple demonstrations of protest and grew into seizures of police stations and railway depots and the fighting of large pitched battles against police and troops. For weeks British rule ceased entirely to exist in numerous towns and districts. By the end of 1942, according to one extremely conservative estimate, 940 Indians had been killed, 1,630 wounded, and 60,000 arrested. The rising was scattered and leaderless. From his prison cell, Gandhi deplored it. The entire Congress leadership, also in jail, was impotent. Outside of prison there were only a handful of leaders who never succeeded in generalizing the struggle, even if, indeed, they ever actually dreamed of doing so.

British "order" was restored. India was yoked to the war. The princes supported the British. The Moslems, in return for a promise of a Moslem veto on any future solution that did not satisfy them, also rallied. The Indian wealthy, the military elements, stood with the rulers. And along with them, the Indian Communist Party. This party began giving its unreserved support to the British from the date of the German attack on Russia in June, 1941, when, as everyone knows, the recent war was abruptly transformed from an imperialist war into a crusade against Fascism. From the August uprising the Communists held themselves completely aloof and were in the main responsible for the failure of the Bombay textile workers to take part. For this among all the nationalists thereafter they were scorned as quislings and were so regarded throughout the war. The grateful British Raj, however, legalized the Communist Party and gave it ample quotas of paper to carry on its ardent propaganda in support of the war.

But such support from the people was never forthcoming. Articulate Indians, with a stubborn simplicity quite their own, did not see any reason to fight a totalitarian threat on the outside by first submitting to a totalitarian reality on the inside. It was not their war. Churchill had made that plain enough when he announced that the Atlantic Charter did not apply to India. It had been made plain enough by the manner in which the British filled India's prisons with nationalist dissidents. But the ferment died down. For the rest of the war period, amid the disorientation and confusion and dispersion, the Indian national struggle simmered low. Not even the monstrous Bengal famine in 1943 aroused it.

A mood of helplessness and a sense of lost initiative seemed to grip most of the Indian nationalists who could still be met during the war years. There seemed to be almost complete surrender to the feeling that the next move would have to come from the British. In preparation for it, efforts were made to achieve a greater measure of accord between the Congress and the Moslem League. Various studies were made and widely discussed in the press. A Gandhi-Jinnah meeting was finally arranged, but it produced no results. A period of uneasy waiting followed in which bitterness increased and strains tightened. The advent of the Labor government in England at the end of July, 1945, brought neither relief nor rosy anticipation. There was satisfaction over the passing of Churchill and the Conservatives, but no impulse to expect Labor's Attlee to serve British imperial interests any less actively than Churchill had. Indian nationalists knew British Labor governments of yore.

When the war ended abruptly in mid-August there was no echo of jubilation among the Indians. The war had been throughout a remote shadow to the great mass of the people. Its passing was hardly felt. The British in India's cities broke out their flags, but in the crowded streets the people went by unnoticing. They saw nothing for them to celebrate on the day of Britain's victory.

Still the war had worked vast changes for India. The steady attrition of British imperial power was working for Indian nationalism almost despite the Indian nationalists. The British had again been able to draw on Indian manpower and resources. But this drain, which caused such intense hardship among Indians in the form of shortened rations and local famines, was undermining the foundations of the Empire itself. Fighting for survival, the Empire was drawing heavily on its capital. Because they had to take so much from India and could give nothing in return, the British underwent a total transformation of their financial position from that of heavy creditor to that of far heavier debtor. With the goods and services it provided, India paid off its bonded indebtedness to Britain. This indebtedness included charges that went back to the days of the East India Company. It included charges levied on India for Britain's wars against Afghanistan and in the Levant in the last century. It included charges incurred by British troops in the suppression of the great mutiny of 1857. This entire debt, amounting to about £350 million, was liquidated. Beyond this, further credits accumulated on a steeply ascending scale. By the war's end Britain was in debt to India for about £1 billion. This means that if India were in a position to call in its credits it could bankrupt the United Kingdom, which is already in virtual receivership. Only by virtue of the fact that they hold India's sterling credits blocked in England do the British now prevent India from appearing on the world market as one of the heaviest buyers of capital and consumer goods. India, always before in the imperial credit column, is now one of the Empire's heaviest liabilities.

The war transformed not only the financial relationship between England and India, but the strategic relationship as well. Britain had nearly lost all it had because, as the events of the war showed, it could not rely on the support of any sizable part of the large populations under its rule in Asia. These events showed even the most obtuse of the British leaders, including Winston Churchill, that Britain had to make a radical shift that would transform India from a disaffected colony into a stable ally. To safeguard the surviving British investment—estimated at about £240 million—and to create a new strategic balance for British power in Asia, the British could no longer afford to stave off the Indian demand for independence. They had to adapt themselves to it. The old system was played out. Only American military might and the weaknesses of Indian nationalism have given Britain a chance to reshape the elements of its power in southern Asia.

Reacting automatically in the first months after the war's end, the British were still turning machine guns on impatient demonstrators in Calcutta, Madras, and Bombay. But these were acts of inertia. The signs of the times were too plain. Even the British hold on the Indian armed forces, long inoculated against the virus of nationalism, was breaking down, as the Indian naval mutiny in Bombay and other flareups among Indian troops patently showed. To find their way out of their impasse, the British had to find, in the war's aftermath, a way of stabilizing where formerly their object had always been to divide. The new Cripps-Pethick-Lawrence mission of 1946 had to find ways of circumventing the Moslem demands for Pakistan which had arisen originally out of British encouragement of Moslem separatism in Indian affairs. The British had to try to find the basis for a new and viable Indian régime in which the British economic and strategic position in southern Asia would find new safeguards. To accomplish this they had to seek to make in India the changes they had for so long been unwilling to grant.

Britain is not acting in India out of moral principle or new-found generosity. It is acting from dire necessity. Nor will it, of its own accord, yield any more than it has to. The British do not want matters to move too fast. They want a settlement which will allow them to continue exploiting every remaining advantage, every remaining interest. In India the numerous political and economic problems and the unaggressive character of the Indian nationalist leadership seemed to assure the slow pace of change the British would desire. It was from outside of India, rather, that disturbing threats and influences came, for in the neighboring colonies that belonged to France and Holland the people were far more militantly fighting for their immediate independence. Their early success, too quickly won, and the consequent elimination of foreign rule in these large and critical territories, would clearly have had enormous effects upon the attitude and psychology of Indian nationalists. That mainly is why Britain moved to retard the powerful pressure for independence which rose in French Indochina and the Dutch East Indies as Japan fell.

INDONESIA: "INDEPENDENCE OR DEATH!"

Across the walls and houses and public buildings of Batavia, the people had scrawled slogans to greet the arriving occupation troops. They thought the Americans were coming, so they used language that they thought Americans might understand:

"We are fighting for government for the people, by the people, of the people."

"We are fighting for our inalienable right to life, liberty, and the pursuit of happiness."

"Give us liberty or give us death!"

The occupying forces turned out to be British, but the effect was by no means wasted. A weary British officer irritatedly said: "Your damned American revolution is still giving us trouble."

It was, however, the Indonesian revolution that was providing a good deal of "trouble" for the Dutch. The Dutch thought they could return to power in the Indies unchallenged. The British thought it would be a simple matter to see the Dutch reinstalled. The trouble was that the Indonesians had developed some ideas of their own and had seized the opportunity to put their ideas in effect. They were summed up in the single word: *merdeka,* or independence.

In the week that Japan sued for peace, Indonesian delegates were arriving in Batavia from all parts of the East Indies. They had been summoned by the Japanese to form a Committee for the Preparation of Independence. For the Japanese, it was an act of desperation. Invasion of the islands was expected almost daily. The Japanese armies had long since been cut off from their communications with the rest of the empire farther north. Preparing to defend themselves against attack, they made a final bid for the political support of the Indonesians by giving them a stake in the outcome of the approaching battles. But it was too late. When the Committee met on August 14, 1945, it was to hear the news of Japan's surrender. Three days later, at four o'clock on the morning of August 17, the delegates took into their own hands the authority that had fallen away from the Japanese conquerors. They proclaimed and established the independent Republic of Indonesia.

By this simple declaration, made amid the same kind of uneasy quiet that prevails at the center of a storm, the little assembly announced the end of nearly 350 years of Dutch rule over the rich archipelago of the southern seas. In towns and cities along the slender stretch of Java, from Batavia through Semarang, Bandung, and eastward to Surabaya, local committees assumed power. Everywhere the Indonesian banner of red and white was raised. The insurgents restored to their capital city of Batavia its ancient name of Jakarta. They were attempting to regain the total independence they had not known since the days of the proud Sumatran and Javanese dynasties of more than three centuries before. Whatever happened now, it was at least clear that the Dutch would never again play the role of unchallenged lords in a realm of some seventy million people living in an island empire nearly sixty times the area of little Holland itself.

The Dutch long enjoyed an official reputation as "ideal" colonial administrators. Only their colonial subjects seem not to have shared in the general admiration for the way the Dutch ruled their rich possessions. The history of Dutch rule, in fact, parallels in rapacity and in some ways exceeds the record of British and French exploitation in neighboring colonial areas. The Dutch started, as the British did in

India, with nearly two centuries of armed conquest and outright looting. From 1602 to 1800, the Dutch East India Company paid recorded dividends at the rate of 18 per cent a year and reaped a golden harvest of hundreds of millions of guilders besides in unreported plunder. The Company, like its counterpart in British India, served the purpose of swelling the primary accumulation of capital at home. It also effectively destroyed native Javanese and Sumatran commerce, shipping, shipbuilding, and handicrafts and drove the entire population back to simple agricultural pursuits. Early in the nineteenth century, the Dutch introduced the "culture system," a program of forced cultivation of the most profitable export crops: sugar, coffee, and indigo. This system eventually resulted in a series of famines which reduced the population of some parts of Java by more than half. The "free" economy system which followed converted the islands into what the Dutch called a *wingewest,* or "exploitation-province." Monopolies, including spirits, tobacco, gambling, opium, and poll tax collections, yielded fat revenues to swell the profits from cultivation and trade. The *batigslot,* or "contribution" to home revenues from East Indian administrative profits, amounted to nearly a billion guilders between 1831 and 1877. The subsequent heavy capitalization of East Indian enterprises, the development of rubber, the expansion of tin and coal mining and the discovery of oil made the colony one of the richest in the world.

The system of preserving local customs and institutions, which won so much applause for the Dutch from admiring scholars and sentimentalists, was simply a means of using the village system as the basis of Dutch exploitation and converting village headmen into agents of the Dutch regime. The law against alienation of land, similarly admired, was a device aimed to prevent the enterprising Chinese from acquiring control of cash crop acreage. Political reforms in the Indies, even of the meagerest kind, began less than thirty years ago. Before then and since, Dutch colonial officials were vested with total power, as employers, police, governors, and judges, all rolled into one. The Dutch did not even admit missionaries into the Indies for the first two hundred years. It took even longer than that for them to inaugurate the scantiest kind of educational system for Indonesians. A Dutch commission in 1928 admitted that at the rate they were going, it would take 167 years to get all the eligible children of the country into primary schools. Not even the most kindly studies of Dutch history in the Indies have been able to gloss its ruthless and despotic character.*

This history has followed the familiar colonial pattern: an economy of wealth and ultra-comfort for a narrow segment of the people of the exploiting nation, and an economy of poverty, illiteracy, and backwardness for the colonial mass. Thus in 1936, Europeans in the Indies, comprising 0.5 per cent of the population, received 65 per cent of the total income. The Indonesians, 97.5 per cent of the population, received 20 per cent of the income. The rest went to the Chinese and other foreign Asiatic communities. Of the Indonesian adult population, 93 per cent were illiterate. More than four-fifths of them were wholly dependent upon agriculture. In 1939, after two years of a sudden forced spurt in industrialization, home industries employed 500,000 workers and modern-style powered factories only 300,000. The wealth and labor of the Indies provided direct and indirect support for about one-fifth of the home population in Holland. Dutch investments, estimated at about four billion guilders in 1938, yielded an annual return of just under 400,000,000 guilders, which did not include the 287,000,000 guilders received as income by Europeans living in the colony. The European community in Dutch India lived in conspicuous comfort amid all the profound poverty of their lush island empire. Its members built up a myth about the docility and contentment of their subjects that admitted little of the reality of the stolid and brutal repression and exploitation on which the entire regime rested. They were accordingly outraged and uncomprehending when the turn of events finally brought their whole structure tumbling down around their heads.

Indonesian nationalism stirred into organized life only forty years ago. The Dutch countered it with heavy-handed suppression, spaced by rare and limited concessions, of which the first came in 1918 in the form of a hand-picked and impotent "Volksraad" or People's Assembly. The nationalist movement reached its first peak in November, 1926, when a series of strikes culminated in an open insurrection

---

* Most of the facts cited here, for example, will be found in J. S. Furnivall, *Netherlands India* (New York), 1944.

of which the outside world heard little. It was put down by punitive action in which thousands of rebels were killed and many thousands more deported to prison camps on the outer islands. The Dutch were less successful, however, in withstanding assault from the outside. They relied almost entirely on British naval strength in the southern oceans for defense of their islands, but when the Japanese attack came, the British failed them. The collapse of the Dutch army in March, 1942, was so swift, so complete, that the Indonesians could forever laugh down with scorn the notion that "protection" of the islands was justification enough for Dutch rulership.

The Japanese were welcomed in Indonesia. Flowers were strewn in their path. They were hailed as conquering liberators. The pleasant spectacle of the defeat and humiliation of the Dutch and the Japanese pledges of equality for all Asiatics brought Indonesians flocking to the new banner. Nationalist leaders like Soekarno and Mohammed Hatta, long exiled and imprisoned by the Dutch, wholeheartedly threw in their lot with the Japanese. Shrewd, opportunist, politically supple, these leaders deliberately set out to reap maximum advantages for themselves and for the nationalist movement out of the new dispensation. The honeymoon of enthusiasm did not last long. The Japanese began to drain the country of its food and to suck out all other commodities and supplies to feed their war machine. They compelled forced sales of all exportable crops at fixed low prices. They heedlessly brought on serious famines. They laid a heavy repressive hand on the people to keep them within the rigid mold of Japan's concept of its new role as master in Asia. Officials and troops of the occupying forces acted with brutal contempt toward their new subjects. Assaults, beatings, arrests, killings, secret police operations became part of the regular order of things under the new dispensation as they had been under the old.

Nevertheless, the effects of Japanese conquest and occupation cut deeper, went farther, and produced more direct political consequences in Java than perhaps anywhere else in Japanese-conquered Asia. The Japanese wanted food, labor, auxiliary military forces. To gain these objectives, the conquerors gave the Indonesians more of a chance to organize their own affairs than they had ever had before. Laborers were grouped in new organizations. Village assemblies were transformed into functioning bodies. Indonesians were able to enter local, provincial, and island-wide government positions from which they had always been barred. They created an Indonesian police force and an Indonesian army. Young people were trained to fight. Even peasants in the hinterland were taught guerrilla warfare tactics and methods. All of this, scaled and controlled to fit Japanese objectives, nevertheless established a framework of Indonesian activity which had never before existed. And to knit it all together, to give it coherence and purpose, and equally, no doubt, to deflect popular feeling from the less savory aspects of the occupation, the Japanese sponsored intensive propaganda that went far and deep, reaching into the remotest villages. It was aimed against the British, the Americans, and the Dutch. It aroused and played upon the most fanatical racist ideas and emotions. It gave new shape and new content to thinking in places and among people who had long been insulated from such things by the careful watchfulness of the Dutch.

The Japanese maneuvered crudely with the idea of Indonesian independence. They usually withdrew with one hand what they proffered with the other. But there can hardly be any doubt that they helped create the conditions which made independence a practical possibility when Japanese power collapsed. The Indonesian leaders made no attempt to deny this or to apologize for it. President Soekarno quite simply declined to express, for the benefit of American and British correspondents, any regret over his role as a "collaborator." Mohammed Hatta, vice-president of the Republic, was even more explicit in a private conversation we had one evening at his home. "The Dutch say that the Japanese facilitated our movement for freedom," he said. "Do they mean this as an accusation against the Japanese? Or against us? When the Dutch say this, they merely accuse themselves. They, after all, never in three hundred years gave us any chance at all to win independence or even self-government!"

As a group, the Dutch in the Indies showed barely any sign of understanding what was going on around them. Some 7,000 Dutch soldiers emerged from prison camps. They were diseased and warped men, weak, and frightened and shaken. When arms were put in their hands, they turned on the insurgent Indonesians like savages, ruthlessly machine-gunning the *kampongs,* or native compounds, and inviting atrocity for atrocity by all their acts. In internment camps there were more than 50,000 Dutch women and children and a sprinkling of civilian men. They had been compelled to live for more than three years in huddled, crowded quarters with inadequate food, water, and sanitation, and under the constant strain of Japanese over-lordship. They had been reduced, in other words, to living precisely in the conditions that were the common and permanent lot of the overwhelming majority of Asiatics. The experience of these pin-neat, educated Dutch womenfolk, accustomed all their lives to the highest kind of living standard, proved that poverty, overcrowding, and lack of sanitation will produce about the same set of results for anybody subjected to them. I visited Tjideng, an internment camp in Batavia, as late as three months after the end of the war. The camp population had been reduced by better than half. But conditions were still appalling. Filth and foul smells pervaded the place. Garbage littered the yards and streets. The women were slovenly and seemed to have lost all vanity about their personal appearance. Half-naked children raced about like little animals. It looked like any one of a thousand miserable communities I had seen in the crowded towns and cities of Asia for years or like a slum in any big Western city. Only these internees had once been comfortable, well-to-do bourgeois folk. They were bitter over what seemed to them the ungrateful hostility of their former subjects and minions. They were even more outraged, however, by the slowness with which they were being evacuated. They knew that the internees' plight was being deliberately used by Dutch officials as a lever to secure more effective British military action in the Dutch behalf. "We cannot evacuate them all or let them go too fast," a high Dutch official frankly admitted to me. "It would look to the natives as though we were getting out of the Indies altogether."

The Dutch officials who came back with the British occupying forces refused to accept or admit the reality of Indonesian nationalism and Indonesian strength. Or if they did, they did it in whispers and looking over their shoulders for fear of being overheard. Almost all of them would insist with hysterical monotony that the whole affair was a Japanese plot, or the work of a handful of "extremists." Once these extremists were "rooted out like a cancer," the traditional docility of the population would surely return. This argument ran like a theme of a single melody that could be heard also among the British in Burma and the French in Indochina. Another popular theory was the notion that the Indonesians had simply gone mad. An analysis seriously drawn up by a Dutch doctor, complete with professional jargon, was actually issued by the Dutch in Batavia in the form of a news release under the title "Collective Amok in Java." It described the Indonesians as suffering from a bad case of "wish-fulfillment as regards Eastern superiority." He said that "a kind of dream life, a trance, a spiritual madness" had come upon the people, taking "the place of rationalism brought by Western education, yes, even in highly educated individuals." He went on: "The hordes live in a mystic world of makebelieve. . . . They carry on right in front of machine guns and beneath thundering planes. Still, the military answer is the only answer available to these hordes of fanatics."

Quizzical old Hadji Agus Salim, the "wise old man of Islam" in Batavia, commented: "So we are mad? If that is so, then the Dutch are acting like the people of medieval times who put madmen in chains and left them in deep pits to die. Enlightened people now use more enlightened methods. They do not use the ways of madmen to cure madmen. I fear this report shows that it is the Dutch who are much more seriously afflicted with the hysteria of which this doctor writes."

The Dutch for a long time did insist that force was, indeed, the only answer to the "hordes of fanatics." They refused to meet with or treat with the insurgent Indonesian leaders. For the failure to apply enough force quickly enough, they blamed the British. Dutch rancor against the British on this point was scarcely less intense than their bitterness toward their rebelling subjects. The Dutch could not, without grinding anger, face the fact that whatever they were or whatever they would be again in the Indies, they would owe to the British. For it was quite plain that the Dutch would never have been able to set foot again in their East Indian domain if it had not been for British military power.

The Dutch had previously been given signed assurances that they would be allowed to reassume control of civil administration in the East Indies as soon as they were reoccupied. When the islands still lay within the American military sphere, this assurance was written into an agreement signed by General MacArthur and Hubertus Van Mook at Tacloban, Leyte, on December 10, 1944. When the last-minute changes in Allied arrangements were made at the Potsdam Conference, the Indies were transferred to the British sphere. A similar agreement was thereupon signed by the British and Dutch governments on August 26, 1945. The British came to the Indies nominally to enforce the surrender terms, to disarm and repatriate the Japanese and to restore "order." What they did not advertise was that they also came explicitly committed to restore Dutch power.

There were bitter complaints from the Dutch, however, over the fact that it took the British five weeks to land their troops. In those five weeks following the Japanese surrender, the Dutch said, the Indonesian rebels were able to consolidate themselves, to "terrorize" the peaceful population, and above all—and this was quite true—to acquire considerable stocks of arms and ammunition from Japanese stores. As a matter of fact, in contrast to the situation of the Anna-mites in Indochina which will be described in the next chapter, the Indonesians were well entrenched, with an army of more than 100,000, with mass organizations, government machinery, and military formations set up, in part at least, during the years of the Japanese occupation. Against this power, the Dutch by themselves were utterly helpless. The British were, indeed, slow, and as usual, superficially ineffectual. But in the end, they accomplished their purpose.

The first British troops began landing on September 29. They were Indian troops, whom the British were still able to use everywhere against colonial nationalists despite the protests of the Indian nationalist movement in India itself. Batavia was quiet when they arrived. Not until a week later, when about 1,000 Dutch troops and Ambonese mercenaries landed from a British transport, did trouble start. Equipped with American weapons and wearing American uniforms, the trigger-happy Dutch and Ambonese were turned loose on the city. Shootings, clashes, incidents suddenly multiplied. The Indonesians had welcomed the British and accepted at face value the statement of the British commander that his mission was strictly nonpolitical. Now they began to wonder. They protested to the British against the Dutch landing and demanded immediate withdrawal of the offending troops. They received no satisfaction.

At Surabaya, on the eastern end of Java, British forces landed on October 10. There, too, quiet reigned for a week until the British commander indicated his intention to disarm the Indonesian forces in the city. That precipitated clashes that grew swiftly into a major battle. It involved a full British division, mostly of Indian troops, many days of shelling, numerous sorties by British fighting planes, 900 British and Indian casualties, 6,000 Indonesian casualties, and five weeks of fighting before "order" was restored.

The Surabaya events made plain enough what British "non-interference" really meant. "If the British had kept their word to us," said an Indonesian spokesman, "things could have been quite different. But now it seems clear that the idea is to restore Dutch power under British protection. So now we are all 'extremists' because none of us wants the Dutch to come back."

The British were disconcerted to discover how strong the Indonesians actually were. Their own strength was limited. In an effort to reduce the number of unwanted incidents, they temporarily halted plans to bring in thousands of additional Dutch troops, many of whom were already waiting at Singapore. They tried to impress upon the angry and uncomprehending Dutch that it would be necessary to negotiate and to make concessions. Meanwhile, they brought British strength up to two full divisions and they continued bringing in large numbers of Dutch civilian officials. Nominally these officials were confined to relief activities for the internees. In practice wherever they went they provoked bloody incidents because the Indonesians, quite rightly, regarded them as advance agents of returning Dutch sovereignty. Clashes led to clashes, atrocities to atrocities.

Japanese troops, kept under arms, were ordered into action against the insurgents. At Semarang and Bandung, where bitter battles were fought to take those cities away from the Indonesians, Japanese infantry and tanks carried the main brunt. In his official report on the fighting at Semarang at the end of November, the local British commander, a brigadier named Bethel, gave the late enemy his enthusiastic accolade: "The Japanese were magnificent!" he wired.

British fighter-bombers were constantly in action, using rockets and 500-pound bombs. The planes struck repeatedly at what the communiqués called "extremist concentrations." They bombed out the Indonesian radio stations at Jogjakarta and Surakarta, principal political centers in the interior. Attacks were called "reprisals" on the flimsiest pretexts. For an example, an Indonesian raid on an Allied convoy took place early in December on the road near a town called Tjibadak. The next day, according to a Royal Air Force announcement on December 10, six Mosquitos and six lend-lease P-47s strafed and rocket-bombed Tjibadak and wiped it off the map. The planes, the announcement said, "dived low, sending their missiles ripping through dozens of buildings lining the main streets. . . . Roofs were tossed into the air, walls collapsed, and only skeletons of many houses remained when the fighter-bombers struck with their guns, making five attacks." The R.A.F., according to an official communiqué, flew 148 such sorties in the month of November alone.

The Indonesians lacked bombs and rockets but in the least of their villages they owned knives. When they had a chance to retaliate they did not do so with the same gentlemanly methods of the restorers of order who came in from the air. When a lend-lease C-47 troop-carrying transport made a forced landing near a town called Bekassi, the local people seized crew and passengers, killed them, hacked their bodies to pieces. The British promptly replied by adding Bekassi to the long list of Javanese Lidices.

The Indonesian nationalists appealed, by radio and by direct messages, to Truman, to Attlee, to Stalin. They received no replies. They appealed to the United Nations. They received no sign of recognition. They appealed to the conscience of the world. Nothing happened to halt the undeclared war in Java. They protested to Washington over the British use of American weapons and equipment in Java. Washington promptly asked the British if they would not please remove the American insignia and the initials "USA" from their fighting gear. Neither did that stalwart action in the spirit of the Atlantic Charter halt the war in Java. The Indonesians waited for the Four Freedoms to manifest themselves, by a miracle or by a sign. But they waited in vain. They finally had to stop scanning the skies for the harbingers that never came.

They had to count on their own strength alone when they finally sat down to negotiate a compromise with the equally reluctant Dutch. It would take long months. It could not result in all they had hoped for and all that their strength really warranted. For however it came out, the Dutch were back. There would be months of talk and bargaining and debate. Meanwhile Dutch troops would keep coming in, reaching ultimately a strength of 50,000. There would be Dutch concessions of an administrative character. There would be gains of a kind for the Indonesians but something far, far less than the independence they had held within their grasp. For in any case the Dutch were back, shoe-horned into their place by British might. A thousand miles to the north, the French were getting back into Indochina in precisely the same way.

6 INDOCHINA: THE STRUGGLE FOR FREEDOM

PEACE COMES TO SAÏGON

The little women hovered there like frightened birds. They peered timidly down the long alley through the gates of the Sûreté. At the far end prisoners were filing out of a cell block into a small yard. The women craned for a glimpse of their men. I walked through the gate. The police guard made half a restraining gesture, then drew back. Like all Frenchmen at this time in Indochina, he was unsure of himself except when facing Annamites with overwhelming force. It was feeding time. The prisoners filed out, small brown men of all ages. Some were old and haggard and bent. Some were boys. They came out and formed lines, crouching on their toes in close rows, twelve to a row and thirty rows by the time they were done. Ragged, tired-looking women came after, twenty-two of them. They huddled against the wall to one side.

A short, gray-haired Frenchman hovered obsequiously around me, worried. "You must have the authorization of the commandant to remain here," he said.

"I'm not remaining," I said.

"But it is not permitted," he repeated anxiously.

"You worry yourself too much," I said. "Are they all politicals?"

"But certainly," he replied. "Taken with arms in hand."

I looked across the rows of quiet brown faces and small brown bodies. Most of them stared passively forward. With a few, eyes locked and spoke their own silent syllables.

"And the women?"

"Oh, the women," with a deprecating wave. "They were caught carrying grenades in their rice baskets."

A few of the women were very old, a few very young. They kept their eyes on the ground.

"What do Americans think of this movement here?" the guard asked.

134

"I don't know. I suppose they know it is a movement of Annamites who do not want the French back in their country."

He jumped up and down with excitement. "But no, that is not at all exact, not at all exact," he cried. "These people were all paid by the Japanese, armed by the Japanese, instigated by the Japanese."

"You think so?"

"But yes. It is a Japanese movement against the Allies, nothing else but that. Without the Japanese, it wouldn't be possible."

"You think so?"

The prisoners were almost all in the yard by now. Some were bent half over. Some limped. Some showed scars. Some had ugly sores and unbandaged bruises.

"They all look in good health, don't you think?" the guard asked eagerly.

They began to hand out the food. Three at a time the prisoners came forward to the big basket filled with rice and big black chunky crusts. It was ladled out, a small bowlful to each. Some prisoners took it in their hands, some in torn old hats. A few had tin cans. Most of them took it in rags taken off their backs. Grains of rice would fall to the ground and the prisoner would stoop to retrieve them, but he was usually pushed forward to get his fish. This consisted entirely of heads and tails of some very small kind of fish, handed out of a foul heap in a flat pannier.

"How the Annamites love fish!" exclaimed the short French guard.

One of the women was handed a fish tail. She held it out mutely. It was very small. The guard—a *métis* or halfcaste (these are always the most brutal)—pushed her roughly away. The little guard glanced my way, saw me looking on. He hesitated an instant, then shouted a sudden peremptory phrase in Annamite. The woman was called back and handed another piece of fish head.

A little boy, no more than ten, was in the line. The guard gestured at my question. "Him? Oh, he's here seeing his brother," he said.

"What happens to these prisoners?" I asked.

"They are held for court-martial," the guard answered.

They were going back into the cell block. A *métis* jailer shouted

angrily at some laggards. I turned and walked back down the alley
and out of the gate. A few of the little women were still there.

With its buff-colored homes with their red-slate roofs bordering
quiet tree-lined streets, Saïgon might have been almost any drowsy,
southern French provincial town. But this was a city, eight weeks
after the war's end, half dead under siege. A general strike of the
Annamites had stripped the shops, hotels, and homes of all their
helpers, clerks, servants. No trams were running nor any other kind
of public transportation. The Annamite population had almost entirely melted away. This city, built by Frenchmen for Frenchmen,
had been abandoned by its hewers of wood and drawers of water,
and nothing in the world is emptier than a city in the Orient where
only Europeans are to be seen. Downtown, evenings, the streets
would fill with French soldiers and sailors and civilians, Indian
soldiers, a few British tommies, a scattering of Chinese. French or
métisse girls would pair off with the troops, walking arm in arm, or
sitting across tables at the few open bars and cafés. Armed French
civilians walked self-consciously on patrol. Housewives, carrying
their children with them, would comb the few open markets where
fruit and vegetables could be had from Chinese vendors. When the
occasional straggling lines of manacled or trussed-up Annamite
prisoners would pass, French men and women would stop to glare.
When newly arriving French troops marched up Rue Catinat from
the river, the civilians would gather at the curb and applaud and
cheer. This was power returning. This would restore the golden yes-
teryear. "It is really nothing," said a Frenchman watching. "Some
agitators bought by the Japanese. We'll kill them off." He nodded
at the marching singing soldiers. "It won't take long. Then the rest
of the people will come back."

But it would take time. The Frenchman was only now occupying
a small foothold, thanks to the British and the Japanese. Not even
Saïgon was as yet his. Long before curfew its streets were dead except
when bands of drunk French soldiers and sailors split the warm,
somber darkness with song and except when in the later hours the
night was shaken by the sounds of gunfire and explosions right in
the city or out toward the environs. Or the sky would glow where
a gasoline dump went up in fire or a barracks was set ablaze. The

perimeter began only a few thousand yards from Saïgon's center. Out there along the roads and waterways French and British and Indian and Japanese troops were fighting off guerrilla attacks along narrow fingers of communication. Beyond the first visible row of rice paddies all the hinterland was hostile. There the sweeps and searches were being made. There the thatch of Annamite villages was going up in smoke every day and the people flushed out by this means were coming into Saïgon in those long straggling lines of prisoners.

I stopped in the cathedral square to ask a *métis* policeman the way to what the French call the Palais de Justice. He told me.

"Where are all the Annamites?" I asked.

"They've run away." He shrugged contemptuously. "They're afraid."

Of course he wanted the French back, he explained. "Under the Annamites I'd be worse off than under the Japanese!" Under the Japanese he had been put to pushing barrows through the streets. Now he was a *policier* again, with a rifle slung over his shoulder. A pretty *métisse* went by. She smiled a greeting. *"Voulez-vous vous amuser?"* he asked; "it would be very easy . . ." He was a pimp too.

The French officer on duty in the lobby of the Palais de Justice was an expert on the habits and habitat of Indochina's most beautiful women.

"Ah, in Hué," he said, "in Hué before the war, that was the time and place to sit at a sidewalk café in the evening and watch them go by." He shook his head reminiscently. "Not too bad here either," he went on. "It's a pity for you they're all gone now. But they'll be back. It might take two years." He shook his head again. "Two years of killing. But they'll be back!"

A double line of half-naked manacled prisoners came up the steps herded by burly French guards with unslung rifles and fixed bayonets. The officer nodded at them.

"Voilà," he said, *"voilà des spécimens de la race jaune!"*

I looked at him and at the French guard. *Voilà,* I thought, *voilà des spécimens de la race blanche.*

The court-martial sat in a gloomy, second-floor room. Along the corridor outside, with windows giving on the bright green sunlit park, crouched the manacled men, stripped to denim shorts and barefooted. Inside, the accused stood before their judges, five French army officers sitting under the tricolor. The president of the court was a Colonel Rougier, a tall, gaunt, nervous man who kept putting on and taking off his glasses, shrieking irascibly at prisoners who did not give right answers or did not seem to understand what was asked of them. The interpreter, a *métis*, echoed his tone, his manner. His voice would take on the same edge of hysteria as it rose. The prisoners, for their part, spoke in whispers and could barely be heard.

No trial took long. For by the rules of this court no witnesses were heard, no testimony taken, no cross-examination made. The charge was read out in French, and no one bothered to translate for the prisoner's benefit. The questioning by the court was on the basis of statements supposedly made during the preliminary investigation. The prosecutor, an army officer, would speak briefly, for conviction. The defender, a civilian attorney, would make his ingratiating plea, for mercy. "Next!" the president would bark. The average time for the first five cases was eight minutes each.

The first accused was a 27-year old Annamite named Pham van Sat. He was charged with being a member of a group which had engaged in looting and attacked a French patrol. He denied everything.

Judge (waving a sheet of paper in front of him): "Then what about this declaration you made?"

Prisoner: "I have no knowledge of it."

Judge: "Then why do you think you were arrested?"

Prisoner: "I don't know."

That was all. The prosecutor asked conviction. The defender asked leniency.

"Next!" shouted Colonel Rougier.

Next was a small man with a tiny beard. His name was Nguyen van Ty. He was 29, he said, was married and had two children. The charge: distributing inflammatory leaflets. Colonel Rougier pulled a piece of paper out of a heap in front of him.

Judge: "It says here you 'wanted to aid justice by punishing the leaders of a régime of terror.' What is meant by that?"

Prisoner: "During the interrogation I was beaten. I don't know what I said."

Judge (angrily rereading sentence): "My question was, What did you mean by that?"

Prisoner: "I don't know anything about it."

The pleas followed. "Next!" shouted Colonel Rougier.

Before the court came two boys, Tham van Tam, eighteen years old, and Tran duy Gian, nineteen. They were accused of distributing leaflets. They stood straight and spoke plainly. One of them, Tran, spoke French quite well and he made his own answers, ignoring the interpreter. Both admitted belonging to a "shock troop" of propagandists. Both admitted distributing the leaflets. The judge stared down at them, then put on his glasses and read from a leaflet.

Judge: "It says here: 'You are not to fight British or Indians or Japanese unless they attack you.' [Waving the paper angrily in front of him and removing his glasses] "What about the French, *hein*, what do you do about them?"

Tran: "I don't know. My order was to distribute leaflets. That's what I did."

Judge: "But you said you belonged to a 'shock troop.' That means fighting, doesn't it? And if you were not to fight British, or Indians, or Japanese, who were you to fight, eh? [screaming] Who were you to fight?"

Tran: "What I did was to distribute leaflets."

The prosecutor was even briefer than usual. They had admitted the charge. They were obviously guilty. The defender was more eloquent than usual. He appealed on the grounds of youth and the bad influences they would meet in prison. The colonel listened, tapping his glasses on the desk. When the lawyer finished, he rose and the court rose with him.

I spoke to the defending counsel, a local Frenchman. "Do you consider that justice is being done here?" I asked.

He shrugged. "No. As a lawyer, I am not in favor of this procedure. But as a Frenchman, I can understand it. We have to make a demonstration. We have to show them that France is strong."

The court returned in fifteen minutes. All the prisoners were sentenced to five years' hard labor except young Tran. He was sentenced to seven years' hard labor. The prisoners were manacled and led out.

"Next!" shouted Colonel Rougier impatiently.

These were light sentences, the lawyer explained in a whisper. He was quite gratified. Out of ninety-three previous cases, there had been four death sentences and sixty-nine sentences ranging from ten to thirty years of hard labor and imprisonment. These terms would be served at Poulo-Condor, a penal island off the coast of Indochina.

"And you think it will help France to reestablish its power here this way?" I asked.

He shrugged again. "Without the French, there would be no Indochina. It is not fit or ripe to be independent. If we left, somebody else would take it, China, or Russia, or America, or Britain. We have interests here. Do you think we can abandon them? We have brought French culture to this country. We cannot ignore our obligations."

Out in the corridor the guard removed manacles from three more prisoners and pushed them into the courtroom. The clerk droned out the next charge. Colonel Rougier looked at his watch, took off his glasses, and tapped them on the desk in front of him.

THE FRENCH

The Colonel Rougiers of France were engaged after Japan's collapse in an attempt to regain a valuable piece of property they had lost during the war. It consisted of nearly three-quarters of a million square kilometers of rich real estate located at the southeastern tip of the continent of Asia. It produced rice and coal and rubber and silk and pepper and a host of foods and minerals, all in profitable quantities. It was inhabited by nearly twenty-four million people* who toiled mainly for the profit and comfort of Frenchmen and the rest of the time grubbed in the earth for a bare sustenance for them-

---

* Of these more than seventeen million were Annamites, and the remainder Cambodians, Laotians, and lesser tribes. These peoples come partly from indigenous tribes of the region and partly from blends with the neighboring Chinese, Siamese, and other races which in their time migrated across the Indochinese peninsula.

selves. The Rougiers were trying to recapture a colony which even with the limited and inefficient exploitation carried out by the French had yielded about a quarter of a billion dollars in export surpluses over three decades, huge profits from opium and alcohol monopolies, and a fine living for several generations of French colonial officials, soldiers, policemen, placeholders, planters, ship owners, and priests.

To many of these Frenchmen it was incredible that the Annamites should desire to reject French rule. With intolerable ingratitude, a handful of malefactors had conspired with the Japanese against the French. The insurgents, one heard endlessly from Frenchmen in high place and low, were nothing but a handful of agitators and paid terrorists, tools of the Japanese who stood momentarily between the benevolent French and the great mass of the people who yearned only to have the French return and desired only to till their lands in the peace assured by French rule. Some of the older French residents were bewildered, like the aging dentist's wife in Saïgon who rocked back and forth on her chair and said: "The Annamites astound me! What more could we have ever done for them than we did? Why, do you know we organized a municipal council here in which they were to have half the seats! Imagine, half the seats! What more could they want?" She was in dead earnest. "All the seats," I replied. She looked at me aghast. Others, usually officials, liked to refer to the *mission civilisatrice* of France overseas. It appeared that France had in reality conferred an immense cultural boon on the naked and ignorant Indochinese and had done so, what's more, at considerable sacrifice. "Where would this country be if we hadn't worked so long and so hard to develop it?" they would ask. "What do you think would happen to it if we left now?"

Yet the fact was that many Frenchmen were thinking of leaving. They thought of little else. In their homes, in the cafés and hotels, the most pervasive topic of conversation was emigration, of going back to France, or to Australia, or to the United States, to anywhere out from under the slings and arrows of outrageous fortune. Not even the constant arrivals of fresh troops, with their efficient-looking American weapons and equipment, helped much to restore the shattered self-confidence of Frenchmen in Indochina. It had been so

long since they could play the master role with any of the old assurance. Theirs had been a history of defeat at home and servile
capitulation in the colony. They had lost to the Germans and knuckled
under to the Japanese. For their return to power, they had to depend upon the British and upon Japanese assistance. In the north
they were subject to the control of the Chinese. The Annamite rising
against them was the overflow in their cup of sorrow and humiliation.
Morose and defensive, Frenchmen in the colony in these first months
of Allied "victory" were thinking only of escape or of savage retalia-
tion against any opponent who of a surety was weak. This was in
the anger and the hysteria of the Colonel Rougiers. This was in the
hypnotic belief that only the Japanese were responsible for all their
woes. This was in the angry and monotonous insistence upon the
truth and glory of France's cultural and civilizing mission and the
justification for the blood and terror wreaked on people benighted
enough not to want to be civilized. Only rarely did one meet relatively refreshing characters like the seamed old ex-master mariner
who observed with honest Gallic wit: "There are two kinds of people in the world: people who work and people who make others
work for them. When you are engaged in making other people work
for you, surely"—with a deprecatory shrug—"surely, you do not tell
them the truth!"

The truth, of course, had nothing to do with civilization or culture, at least not in the sense that Frenchmen in Indochina were using
those words. The French took Indochina by force of arms. Their
conquest began in the classic manner, with the first arrival of missionaries nearly three hundred years ago. Being hardheaded folk
even then, the French did not bother with the proprieties of divided
labor as other expanding nations did. French priests did double and
triple duty. They were also traders. They were also soldiers. They
brought cargoes with them, and shipped cargoes back. They com-
manded military expeditions from time to time whenever the native
people balked at trading in the currency of man or the virtues of
religion. This tradition the French carry forward to this day, for
the French High Commissioner, Thierry d'Argenlieu, is at the same
time an admiral in the French navy and major-superior of the
Carmelite Order in France. For nearly two centuries the French

alternately used force and guile, clashing intermittently with the rival Dutch, British, and Portuguese. The Indochinese resisted when they could, yielded when they had to, for such was the common fate of all peoples of the East who fell in the path of Western expansion. "These [French] men, akin to sheep and dogs by their manners, cannot be persuaded by the language of reason," said a memorial to the emperor of Cochinchina in 1848. "Reason to them is the voice of the cannon and in the art of making the cannon speak, they are extremely clever!" Ten years later, the Frenchmen made their cannon speak more loudly and more eloquently than ever before. In a fully mounted campaign they not only battered down the feeble resistance of the Indochinese, but also fought a war with China, which had tried to assert its distant suzerainty over the provinces of Annam and Tonkin. Campaigns followed treaties and treaties followed campaigns. The final conquest and "pacification" took twenty years of fighting. By a treaty signed in 1885, China finally yielded up its claims. Complete French mastery over all of Indochina (including Tonkin and Annam, Cochinchina, Cambodia, and Laos) was finally attained in the closing years of the century. The conquerors built on the old divisions, setting up a complicated pattern of protectorates and outright colonies administered by various means. They preserved little puppet kingdoms and ruled through Residents in some cases; in others they dispensed with these trimmings and governed directly. In either case, the rule was absolute. The country was kept in pieces, but all the pieces were tightly held by the same hand. Exploitation of Indochinese rice, and later of rubber and coal and other products, became an integral and profitable, and in some periods, even a sustaining sector of French imperial economy. The colony supported a top-heavy and heavy-handed colonial bureaucracy. Its garrisons, composed of Foreign Legion units, Senegalese, and other colonial levies, were engaged almost constantly in punitive expeditions against the dissident and the rebellious. Long before the days of Hitler, they employed the method of wiping out whole villages and towns in reprisal for the acts of individuals.

The cultural and civilizing mission of the French in Indochina is measurable by a few notable statistics, all based on official French records. The Indochina budget, for example, provided a sum of 15

million piasters for some 30,000 Annamite employes and functionaries of the government. The same budget provided 40 million
piasters for 5,000 French functionaries. In 1943, the colonial government spent 30,000 piasters for libraries, 71,000 piasters for hospitals,
748,000 piasters for schools . . . and 4,473,000 piasters for the purchase of opium distributed in the country through the official opium
monopoly. In their time, the French built thirty-one hospitals in the
colony and eighty-one prisons, not including concentration camps.
In the prewar years, the manual laborer in the colony earned an
average of 50 piasters a month. The rare Annamite able to go
through the polytechnical school and graduate as a modestly equipped
engineer could earn 400 piasters a month. The French concierge of
the University of Hanoi—a slightly glorified sort of janitor—earned
1,404 piasters per month. With great generosity and effort, the
French conferred the benefits of education on the people of their
colony. Forty years after the conquest, there was elementary education of a crude kind available for two per cent of the population and
secondary education available for one-half of one per cent. Three
libraries and one so-called "university" were established in the
country.

Over the years, Indochinese who did not appreciate these benefits
were imprisoned, or executed, or bombed and machine-gunned from
the air. In 1930, for example, more than a decade before Lidice,
a group of fleeing Annamite rebels took refuge in the village of
Co-am, in the province of Haiduong. Five French planes bombed
the village and strafed it afterward at low altitude, pursuing the
people who fled along the near-by roads. A few days later the
Resident Superior of the province circularized all local officials,
saying: "The village of Co-am has been bombarded by the Hanoi
squadron. I request that you give utmost publicity to this, and add
that any village which places itself in a similar situation will without
pity meet the same fate." *

The ability of the French to enjoy the advantages of superior
force—and the record is full of it right up to 1940—was the real

---

* This citation, with date and source, and many similar ones, will be found in
Témoignages et Documents Relatifs à la Colonization Française au Viet Nam (published by the Association Culturelle pour le Salut de Viet Nam, Hanoi, 1945).

measure of French rule in Indochina. It could be employed with all the desired effect against the Indochinese but proved to be a little less than adequate when Japan's powerful drive for continental conquest reached southward into the French domain. At home, the French régime in 1940 collapsed under Hitler's blows. In Indochina that year the colonial administration yielded without resistance to the Japanese. In return for being permitted to retain administrative authority, the colonial government under Admiral Decoux allied itself actively with the cause of Japanese expansion. It placed Indochinese rice and Indochinese labor at the disposal of the new masters and employed its widespread and efficient police organization to ferret out anti-Japanese underground fighters as well as Allied agents. Indochina served as the jumping-off place and principal operational base for the southward push of the Japanese in 1941 into Malaya, Burma, and the Indies, and served thereafter as the principal supply depot and replacement center for Japanese armies dispersed throughout Southeast Asia. Despite all French efforts to satisfy Japanese requirements, however, the Japanese were unwilling to rely any longer on the French when they came, in 1945, under the threat of direct Allied counterattack. They took over administration of the colony in a sudden coup on March 9, 1945. The coup was almost entirely bloodless. The French capitulated without a struggle. Only in the north, where there was a chance to escape across the Chinese border, a small French detachment, numbering 1,000 men, fought a slight rearguard action to cover their flight. The Japanese, belatedly trying to rally Annamite support to themselves, parceled out local administration to small groups of Annamites drawn from the oldest and most reactionary religious political sects. But there was neither time nor means to set up anything but the feeblest interim puppet régimes. For Annamite nationalism had been gathering strength and the coming Japanese collapse was to prove its prime opportunity.

THE ANNAMITES

Nguyen van Ba was a grizzled man of perhaps forty-five. He had gone as a youth to France to study, was briefly a teacher, then wandered around the world as a sailor on French merchant ships. He spoke familiarly, with long-cherished memories, of glimpses he had of New York and London and New Orleans and Hamburg, and of his years in France. "In France I liked the French," he said. "They were *chic* and generous, and we had many friends among them. I have happy memories of Frenchmen in France. But Frenchmen here?" He leaned across the table. "I hate them," he said slowly. "We all hate them with a hatred that must be inconceivable to you, for you have not known what it is to live as a slave under a foreign master."

This hatred of the Annamites for the French was a living, leaping thing in the land. You read it in the faces of the ordinary people, in the faces I saw in the yard of the Saïgon Sûreté. You heard it in the voices of the educated Annamites, speaking impeccable French. I even found it in the bearing of a rich and timid Annamite businessman who mortally feared the "anarchy" of a nationalism that had become too popular. He wanted protection against it, anybody's protection but that of the French. It was like a social disease of the subjected, this passionate loathing. Whole generations had been infected with it, by the vermin in French prisons or by the slower poison of an enforced inferiority haunting every step of their lives from cradle to grave.

This was a hatred compounded of many things. The dull and weary sense of unrepaid toil was part of it; and so was chronic injustice never articulately understood. There was also the nettle of racialism in it, for the masters were white and the least of them was greater than the greatest of the land's own sons. Racialism, where it does not impose dumb submission, outrages manhood and breeds violence. The French in their own country are not a people who practice the American kind of Jim Crowism. But freedom is not among the exports of any imperial nation. The great French libertarian tradition was never carried by Frenchmen east of Suez, because it is not a commodity from which profits can be made. Only the small number of Annamites who were sent to France for higher schooling encountered it when they reached the homeland of their masters. The France of the great classic revolutionary tradition, of free thinkers and free livers, was a new France to them. They had seen no trace of it in the physiognomy of France overseas. In Paris they discovered at least the roots of the freedom they were denied in their own land. The result, in most cases, was that their French schooling did not train them, as was intended, to become pliant adornments of the colonial régime but to become rebels against it and leaders of rebels when they came back home. "This is a movement led against France," an Annamite told me, "by intellectuals who were all educated in France. Almost all who went to France returned as revolutionists. That is why so many Frenchmen here regret having provided any education at all for any Annamites. There was a governor general of Cochinchina named Cognac about twenty years ago who said: 'We want no intellectuals in Indochina. They are a misfortune for the country.'" And it was indeed a fact that almost every Annamite graduate of a French lycée or university took his postgraduate degree in French colonial culture at any of a score of prisons, at Sonla or Banmethuot, or on the island penal colony of Poulo-Condor.

Annamite nationalism has a history as long as the history of French rule. The line of French priests and conquerors and colonial governors is matched by a line, no less long, of Indochinese fighters and martyrs and leaders of the people. But Annamite nationalism had long been a scattered, dispersed, underground movement, cleft in many segments. It had burst into violence sometimes out of sheer circumstance and without benefit of any prepared organization. It was for many a mood rather than a movement, a condition rather than a program. So isolated uprisings, like those in Vinh province in 1930 and 1931, could be drenched in the blood of the rebels and the rest of the world was little the wiser. By the time of the next big flareup, in Cochinchina in 1941, all the currents of Annamite nationalism had begun to flow into a single, widening stream under the banner of the Viet Minh.

"Viet Minh" is the popular contraction of Viet Nam Doc Lap Dong Minh, the League for the Independence of Viet Nam. Viet Nam, meaning Land of the South, is the ancient name of this ancient country. The Viet Minh was first formed in 1939 as a coalition of various groups, democrats, socialists, communists, and other less well defined sections of the independence movement. They agreed primarily on a program of common struggle for independence and a social program based on the idea of a democratic republic. Clashes and incidents in Mytho province of Cochinchina grew into an open revolt under the Viet Minh banner in December, 1940. The French at that time were already under the pressure of Japanese penetration and were being attacked by the Siamese in the west. They were unable or unwilling to oppose effectively either the Japanese or the Siamese, but they turned with ruthless cruelty on the revolting Annamites. During the repressions, some 6,000 were killed or wounded and thousands more arrested. French courts-martial for months afterward were grinding out condemnations to long years of penal servitude or to death.

During the long years of the Japanese occupation, the Viet Minh carried on increasingly strong underground activity under the slogan: "Neither the French nor the Japanese as masters! For the Independence of Viet Nam!" The French and Japanese joined in an equally persistent but unsuccessful attempt to stamp out the movement. Early in 1943 when Viet Minh partisans contacted certain French officials and offered collaboration in an anti-Japanese underground, they received the reply: "You want arms now to use against the Japanese. But later you will use them against us. Nothing doing!" After the Japanese coup against the French on March 9, 1945, the Viet Minh gathered forces with increasing strength and boldness. The Japanese never had the time to develop a police apparatus in the colony as efficient as the French had, and their Annamite puppets were few, weak, incompetent, and somewhat affected themselves by the nationalist upsurge. Many an Annamite patriot joined the puppet militia only to get his hands on a rifle and then to melt away into the hinterland to join the Viet Minh partisans. After March 9, Viet Minh guerrilla activity took on major proportions in the north. They secured arms from abandoned French stores, from attacks on isolated Japanese detachments and supply depots, and at long last arms began to filter across the Chinese frontier from American army sources. A small quantity of tommyguns, automatics, radios, and other supplies was parachuted to the partisan bands and was soon followed by teams of American officers who entered Indochinese territory and joined the partisan bands in operations against the Japanese. Between March and August the Viet Minh guerrillas cleared large sections of five of the northernmost provinces of Tonkin and engaged the full attention of the bulk of the Japanese 21st Division. In the city of Hanoi, principal center in the north, the Japanese imprisoned 2,000 Viet Minh followers but they never, by their own means or through their monarchist puppets, brought the movement under control. In the south there was partisan activity on a smaller scale, raids on Japanese communications and supply dumps. Then the war suddenly ended. "Too suddenly," ruefully smiled Pham Ngoc Thach, one of the Viet Minh leaders. "We were doing so well!" But the Japanese collapse was the Viet Minh opportunity. The puppet régimes in Saïgon and Hanoi all but collapsed at the same time. The Viet Minh moved in to take over.

A Viet Minh congress was held at Caobang, near the Chinese border, the week the Japanese surrendered. A provisional government was formed. On August 19, after a few scattered clashes with Japanese troops and puppet militia, this government took power in Hanoi. Bao Dai, for twenty years the puppet king of Annam under the French and briefly under the Japanese, wearily and gladly laid down his scepter. In a remarkable document, the puppet ruler abdicated, saying: "We cannot but regret the thought of our twenty years' reign during which it was impossible for us to render any appreciable service to our country. . . . We have known much bitterness. Hereafter we shall be happy to be a free citizen in an independent country. Long live the independence of Viet Nam! Long live the democratic republic!" The new government gave him his wish and even appointed him, as plain M. Nguyen vinh Thuym, a counsellor of state in the new régime. Even Bao Dai, from his early boyhood educated in France for his puppet role, proved to be a "misfortune" for the French.

The new government quickly restored quiet in Hanoi. The new banner of the republic, a yellow star on a red field, fluttered throughout the city, in Annamite hands now for the first time since Francis Garnier conquered it for the French in 1873. In the south, at Saïgon, the Viet Minh on August 25 called for a popular demonstration. A throng estimated at more than 100,000 turned out and marched, amid perfect order, past the Cochinchina government buildings under banners proclaiming the new power of the Viet Nam Republic. The monarchist puppets had already largely melted away. The Viet Minh

People's Committee, announcing itself as a subordinate arm of the provisional government in Hanoi, took power the next day. There were a few clashes, with Japanese at nearby Tyninh and Thudaumot and with a puppet group in the Saïgon suburbs. But fighting quickly ended. The Viet Minh was solidly in power in the north and south. In Hanoi on September 2 the new leaders issued a declaration of independence in which they said:

They have deprived us of all liberties. They have imposed upon us inhuman laws. . . .
They have built more prisons than schools. . . . They have despoiled our ricelands, our mines, our forests. . . .
They have drowned our revolutions in blood. . . .
For these reasons we, members of the Provisional Government, representing the entire population of Viet Nam, declare that we shall henceforth have no connection with imperialist France; that we cancel all treaties which France has signed on the subject of Viet Nam; that we abolish all the privileges which the French have arrogated to themselves on our territory. . . .
We solemnly proclaim to the entire world: Viet Nam has the right to be free and independent, and in fact has become free and independent.

Thus the Republic of Viet Nam came into being, while the occupying Japanese army stood by, awaiting its fate, and thousands of unmolested but unarmed Frenchmen looked helplessly on. The new régime took swift hold. In the cities and the countryside there was order. Markets thrived, utilities and public services continued to function. In government bureaus Annamites set about the exciting business of creating a government of their own. There were scarcely any incidents. In all the month of August, by subsequent official French acknowledgment, only one Frenchman was killed in a street clash. The Viet Nam government opened wide the prison gates. Thousands of political prisoners çame blinking into the light from the sordid dungeons of Saïgon and Hué and Hanoi and other cities. A fleet of seagoing junks was hastily mobilized and sent off to the island penal colony of Poulo-Condor to rescue the victims of French and Japanese justice held there.

It seemed indeed, for a breathless interval, that the new dispensation had come. The Annamites believed that what they had won for themselves, the victorious Allies would never take away. "We are convinced," they said in their declaration of independence, "that the Allies who recognized the principles of equality at the conferences of Teheran and San Francisco cannot fail to recognize the independence of Viet Nam." That they believed. But the Viet Minh ruled in Saïgon for only one month. By the time the prisoners of Poulo-Condor approached the coast in their fleet of junks with their brown-patched sails, they landed, not to join a freely functioning republic but to enter a harshly renewed struggle to be free.

PAX BRITANNICA

By agreements made at the Big Three Potsdam Conference just as the war ended, all of southeastern Asia was acknowledged to be within the sphere of British influence and control. Here, in the form of responsibility for enforcing the surrender terms and "restoring law and order," the British were given a free hand to pick up the broken pieces of empire. In Indochina, however, owing to special circumstances, they had to divide this opportunity with the Chinese. For occupation purposes, the French colony was cut in half at the 16th parallel. North of that line was the Chinese zone, south of it the British. The French, sidetracked by events and quite powerless at the moment, were given no choice. The Chinese and British received identical mandates: to concentrate, disarm, and repatriate the defeated Japanese armies. But events in the two zones soon showed how the special interests of the occupying powers could produce different interpretations of this mandate. In the north the Chinese, for their own reasons, interpreted "law and order" to mean recognition of the insurgent Annamite régime as the de facto government. In the south the British, for their own reasons, interpreted "law and order" to mean the overthrow of the Annamite régime and the restoration of the French to power.

The first British representatives arrived in Saïgon during the last days of August to set up the headquarters of the Allied commission. The Annamites covered the city with Allied flags in welcome. The Viet Minh People's Committee called a demonstration for September 2, both as a welcoming gesture and as a show of Viet Minh strength. Several hundred thousand people turned out that afternoon, paraded through the city for three hours, listened to speeches by their leaders, and began to disperse, quite peacefully, just before five o'clock. Suddenly, on the fringes of the crowd, shooting started. The Viet Minh later charged that French provocateurs had used drunken liberated prisoners of war to provoke disorders. The French version was that Annamites, inflamed by the day's speeches, had begun attacking Europeans. The Annamites scornfully rejected this charge, pointing out in correspondence with the British headquarters that there had been Europeans in the watching crowd all afternoon without incident. The Annamites, moreover, had every interest in maintaining order. The French had every interest in fomenting disorder. In any case, the shooting occurred. Initial French and British claims that 100 Europeans had been killed boiled down eventually to the officially acknowledged fact that the afternoon's dead totaled three. The angry Annamites that evening rounded up and arrested nearly 200 Frenchmen, but most of these were released at the request of the small American team that had arrived to take care of American war prisoners.

This was the beginning, and it set the tone for all that followed. The British refused to treat directly with the Viet Minh Government. They insisted it was a creature of the Japanese, the product of Japanese plotting and intrigue against the Allies. So they communicated with the local Viet Minh authorities only through the Japanese army headquarters. Pham Ngoc Thach, the young foreign affairs secretary of the committee, patiently wrote the British commander day after day, requesting direct contact and offering fullest Viet Minh assistance in the task of concentrating and disarming the 70,000 Japanese in the southern zone. His letters were ignored. The British ordered the Japanese to keep their troops in full war kit, to sit tight where they were, retaining all arms and holding all garrisoned points until Allied forces could take them over.

The British had come to "restore" order, and they began by promptly disrupting the order they found prevailing throughout their zone. They declared martial law. They suppressed Annamite newspapers. They rearmed the bulk of 5,000 French troops who had been under Japanese internment. They ordered the disarmament of Viet Minh militia and police. As their own troops—almost all

Indian—began arriving on September 12, they moved even more directly against the local régime. They evicted it from the Cochinchina government building and sent troops to take over from Viet Minh police most of the important police stations in the city. Viet Minh representatives were evicted from the Bank of Indochina and the Treasury. Annamites in general were excluded from arrangements made for bank withdrawals and rationing scarce commodities. Each one of these acts was formally protested by the Viet Minh Committee, with warnings that they would lead to conflict for which only the occupying authority could be held responsible. These protests were ignored. The British were proceeding upon a deliberate course and with a deliberate object in view. The ranking French officer in the city, a Colonel Cedile, regrouped the French soldiers who had been rearmed and joined them to the small force of about 150 commandos whom he had brought in with him. With these forces, he prepared to seize power.

This was accomplished by a coup d'état, carried out with armed stealth in the early morning hours of September 23. With Cedile personally commanding, the French troops moved against the Hotel de Ville, the new seat of the Viet Minh government. They attacked the post office and the Sûreté. Annamite sentries were shot down. Occupants of the building were either killed or taken prisoner. Records were seized and scattered. Scores of Annamites were trussed up and marched off. Foreign eyewitnesses that morning saw blood flow, saw bound men beaten. They saw French colonial culture being restored to Saïgon. There was a house-to-house roundup in which many more prisoners were taken, but the principal Annamite leaders, warned in time, made good their escape into the near-by countryside. By 9 o'clock that morning the tricolor again flew over Saïgon. In the city and in neighboring Cholon, the large Chinese quarter, Annamite resistance immediately began. There was street fighting. Grenades were thrown. And as these first battles began, Major General Douglas Gracey, the British commander, issued an invitation to Viet Minh leaders to come in for negotiations with the French around his table.

"But why," Gracey's chief political spokesman was asked, "why would you not talk with the Viet Minh before the shooting started?"

"Because you cannot negotiate when a pistol is held at your head," the British official replied.

"You mean you can negotiate only when you hold a pistol at the other party's head?"

He shrugged.

Saïgon was swiftly paralyzed by a general strike of all Annamites. Shops and markets closed. Trams stopped running. Rickshas disappeared from the streets. The city was dead except when it rippled with gunfire at night or with the thudding explosions of grenades. An uneasy truce began on October 3 when the Viet Minh leaders, at Gracey's repeated invitation, finally came in to parley. The French offered negotiations on the basis of an extremely limited autonomy in which French control was assured. The Annamites demanded recognition of their independence, restoration of their position in Saïgon, and disarmament of the French. There was, of course, no agreement. The truce, already broken by minor clashes and largely ineffective in the countryside where Japanese and British Indian troops were skirmishing with Viet Minh partisans, came to an end. The only thing gained was six days' steaming time for the French cruiser *Gloire* coming up the coast with the first contingent of French reinforcements. On October 12 the British and French, with Japanese troops assisting, opened a formal campaign to widen the perimeter around Saïgon. Five days later the Annamites counterattacked in the city itself, and the fighting came to within a few blocks of the French and British headquarters. That was the last major Annamite challenge in Saïgon itself. After that the fighting spread across the swampy flatlands of the Saïgon River delta. By grace of the British, and with the aid of the Japanese, the French had regained a toehold in Indochina.

As this spectacle of armed reconquest unfolded, the main Anglo-French justification was the charge, repeated with insistent monotony, that the Annamite insurgents were nothing but Japanese tools and the Viet Minh government the creature of a Japanese conspiracy.

"*The Japanese created the Viet Minh,*" it was said, "*and put it in power.*" This was a comforting thought for the French, but it did not happen to be true. The Viet Minh itself had come into being long before the Japanese appeared on the scene, and the organizations which composed it had a history of decades of nationalist resistance to French rule. In Indochina the Japanese had never, until the last moment, attempted to apply their program of "Asia for the Asiatics" which resulted in factitious grants of "independence" in Burma, the Philippines, and Indonesia. On the contrary, they had found it a good deal more efficient and convenient to work instead with the compliant French régime in the colony, which gave them every possible practical assistance. Their decision, in the face of threatened Allied invasion, to dispense with the French and rely instead on Annamite puppets, came late, much too late. The only Annamites they found as collaborators were small sects of monarchists known as the Caodaoists in the south and the Viet Dai in the north, both of them ancient, arch-reactionary organizations. When the war's end came, the Japanese in Indochina were certainly not averse to seeing the turmoil gather to discomfit the returning "victors." They contributed to it by flooding the country with counterfeit bank notes and lifting all controls on the economic life of the country, throwing it into currency chaos and black-market disorganization. But politically, the initiative was no longer theirs. During the spring and summer of 1945 they tried to resist the growth of the Viet Minh. When it became plain, finally, the end was near, they simply stood aside and let events take their course. When the Viet Minh came to power, it had a consistent record of opposition to the Japanese. I have looked over great heaps of Viet Minh anti-Japanese propaganda leaflets and other publications dated from 1940 to the last weeks of the war. This was more than the French could show, with their record of four years of ignominious submission and collaboration.

"*Japanese soldiers deserted to the Viet Minh and are the backbone of the Viet Minh resistance.*" Frenchmen in Saïgon, many of whom had acted as police agents, stooges and worse for the Japanese throughout the occupation, tried to give foreign observers in Saïgon the impression that every Viet Minh partisan band fighting in the countryside had been formed by the Japanese, armed by the Japanese, officered by the Japanese, and their ranks swelled by Japanese soldiers encouraged to desert. There were, to be sure, some Japanese desertions, acts of individual despair following the surrender, or in rare cases possibly acts of conscious solidarity with the Annamite nationalists. But the total number was small. The American intelligence team in Saïgon arrived at a top estimate of 2,000 Japanese deserters out of the total force of 70,000. This estimate was admitted by these observers to be high. Very few of these, moreover, had by all available evidence actually joined the Annamites. They roved the countryside in small groups, preying like bandits on Europeans and Annamites alike. The remaining bulk of the Japanese army and navy forces in the southern zone acted with complete and docile discipline, much to the outspoken admiration of the British staff. Under British orders, they retained their arms and fought the Annamites wherever required on the scattered small battlefields of the Saïgon delta.

"The Japanese supplied arms to the Viet Minh." This, unfortunately for the Viet Minh, was not true enough. The Annamites tried by every means to get arms from the Japanese. In a few cases, by bribes or threats applied to individuals, they managed to get a few weapons. The total secured in this manner came to 300 rifles and revolvers. "It was our greatest failure," one of the Viet Minh leaders ruefully told me. "I wish half the French claims about this arms business were true. We tried our best, but we didn't succeed. We got only a dribble. If we were half as well armed as the French say we are, they wouldn't dare send a single soldier out into the countryside." Some arms came to the Viet Minh via the Annamite puppets or from raids on ill-guarded stocks of French arms held by the Japanese. The chief Japanese liaison officer in the north told me that he estimated Viet Minh armament, from all sources, at not more than 20,000 rifles. In the south, the fact was that a check made by the British accounted fully for the overwhelming bulk of the French and Japanese arms known to be in the country. The only rearming going on was British rearming of the French. A British lieutenant colonel in charge of this task took me to a block of warehouses facing the Saïgon River and showed me the piled stocks from which the French were drawing their weapons. They were almost all French weapons, since few Japanese arms had as yet been taken. He showed me his correspondence and receipts. In less than two weeks' time, the French had already received 12,000 automatic weapons, eight million rounds of ammunition, French and Japanese; 70,000 hand

grenades, all Japanese; and a quantity of Japanese mortars with ammunition and stocks of explosives. "And there's lots more still,"
he said. "It's a filthy business. I can tell by simple count that the
Viet Minh could have gotten very little. The French are getting the
lot. For my part, I wish it had been the other way around. I didn't
put in five years in this damned war to end up in a filthy deal like
this."

If the Japanese had wanted to arm the insurgent Annamites, they
had nearly a month in which to do so. If they had done so, the Viet
Minh would not have been desperately supplying its partisans with
ancient muzzle-loaders made by hill tribesmen, or manufacturing
home-made grenades out of discarded Japanese cigarette and food
tins. Its fighters in the Saïgon delta would have had something more
lethal in their hands than the bows and arrows often captured by
the scourging British, French, and Japanese patrols.

But let it be assumed for a moment that the charges were true.
Let it be assumed that the charge of Annamite collaboration with the
Japanese was as well founded and fully established as the charge of
French collaboration with the Japanese. Let it be assumed that the
charge of Japanese armament of the Viet Minh was as true and as
well established as the fact of Anglo-French use of Japanese troops
and weapons against the Annamites. Any Annamite could, in effect,
ask: "So what? To whom, precisely, are we beholden for anything?
To whom do we owe anything? What claim did any power have
upon us in this great bloody war for mastery in Asia? We are
simply the people who do not want to be mastered by anybody.
The circumstances of the Japanese defeat gave us the chance to
strike a blow for our independence. Should we have waited passively? For what? For the French and the Allies to keep their
promises? Should we have waited on their good will? Or for the
heavens to open? No. We are learning now what all the talk about
self-determination amounts to. We will get just as much freedom
as we are strong enough to fight for. The French will give us as
much as they are forced to yield to us. We had no obligations to
the Japanese, nor any obligations to the French or British, or to anybody but ourselves. We are the victims and we would be quite justi-

fied in taking any opportunity that would be to our advantage. We want no foreign masters of any kind. For better or worse, we intend to run our own affairs."

There was no secret about the use of Japanese troops against the Annamites. The British command did make it quite difficult for correspondents to get firsthand information on this subject, and they forbade Japanese officers to talk to newsmen. However, due recognition to Japanese assistance was given in official communiqués issued by British mission headquarters. A sample on October 22: "Japanese troops supported by armored cars manned by troops of the 16th (Indian) Cavalry extended the perimeter west of Cholon against slight opposition." Again, the same week, the Japanese "repelled an attack" on the RAF petrol dumps at the Saïgon airfield. These dumps, incidentally, went up in flames two weeks later when the Annamites tried again and succeeded. At Cap St. Jacques, downriver, Japanese naval contingents repelled an Annamite attack on gun positions there. The British spokesman announced on October 18 that the headquarters had thanked General Terauchi, the Japanese commander, "with highest praise" for his cooperation. The British were delighted with the discipline shown by the late enemy and were often warmly admiring, in the best playing-field tradition, of their fine military qualities. It was all very comradely.

Some Japanese garrisons which had prematurely stacked their arms, expecting to be disarmed, were ordered back on their wartime footing. The Japanese garrisons at Dalat and Nhatreng and other outlying points were specifically ordered to hold their areas against the Annamites. When it was inadvertently revealed at one of the daily briefings at headquarters that Japanese patrols were operating far outside the positions shown for them on the map, the British brigadier patiently explained: "But of course. They are holding defensive positions. But that does not mean you sit and wait until you are attacked. You go out and patrol your perimeter, and you go beyond it to flush out any hostile elements that might be preparing to attack you. Best defense is offense, you know," he added with a smile. For weeks the British refused to release any casualty figures or to announce how many prisoners had been taken. We all knew, from the long lines of bound men and women we saw coming into the city every day, that the number was large. Only in one week was a figure given, when it was announced that 1,000 prisoners taken by the Allied forces had been turned over to the French for trial. The French claimed they had released most of them. But the prisons were full and the courts-martial ground out their daily budget of prison terms.

Both the British and the French made extensive use of other Japanese facilities and personnel. The Japanese air force in Indochina was converted into a transport service for the Allies. During the first month of operations against the Annamites (October-November), the British officially revealed that Japanese planes operating with Japanese crews under British orders had flown 100,000 miles, carried 45,000 pounds of supplies, ferried 1,000 French and Indian troops over road-blocked areas. French troop movements down the delta waterways toward Mytho and other towns were made in American lend-lease landing craft manned by British naval crews, but all food and supply convoys moving along the rivers were Japanese-manned. All supply lines, all roads and outlying installations were guarded by Japanese soldiers.

As time passed, it became slightly bad form ever to remind the British that their announced mission in Indochina was the disarmament of the Japanese. Only unmannerly correspondents would raise the matter and insist upon progress reports. Eight weeks after the British arrived, General Gracey acknowledged that "less than five per cent" of the Japanese had been disarmed. On November 13, when the perimeter zone—announced as an area for concentrating the Japanese—had been extended in fingers stretching approximately forty kilometers out from Saïgon, the British announced with a flourish that disarmament of the Japanese "will now begin." A week later dissatisfied correspondents who had been denied all detailed information finally faced a Colonel Ritchie, who was operations officer for the 20th Indian Division.

"The number of Japanese specifically disarmed so far is not large," said Colonel Ritchie.

"How large?" he was asked.

"I can't say."

"How many are still being used in operations?"

"They are still being used for patrolling and guard duty," the colonel replied.

"How many?"

"I can't say."

"How many have been concentrated and are awaiting disarmament?"

"I can't say."

"How many are still in outlying garrisons?"

"I can't say."

The colonel grew more and more exasperated, and finally began to abuse his questioners. The session ended in a general exchange of insults. That afternoon all the non-French correspondents in Saïgon sent a formal protest to Admiral Mountbatten charging that news was being concealed at the source in Saïgon. The next day the headquarters produced a brigadier with better manners but without much more disclosable information. He located the Japanese units for us on the map, and apologetically agreed that no disarmament to speak of had yet taken place. "But it is beginning," he said, "and will proceed as quickly as possible."

Later that day I saw a truck convoy loaded with fully armed Japanese soldiers heading out to the fighting zone. That night when we drove to the scene of a fire set by Annamites at a petrol dump on the city's outskirts, we were saluted at intervals by Japanese guards patrolling the road and solemnly presenting arms as the headlights picked them out.

This was a bizarre and bitter little war, filled with irony as well as terror. The British force consisted of the 20th Indian Division, which was ten per cent British and the rest composed of Hyderabads, Punjabis, Rajputs, Gurkhas, and others. Most of the tommies and not a few of the British officers were thoroughly fed up. Away from home, most of them, for more than five years, their anger cut deep. "Why," a British soldier asked me, "why is this our job? Can't the French do their own damned dirty work? We could have disarmed the Nips and been out of here in a few weeks. Instead we get ourselves into another war. As far as I'm concerned, I've had it." There was, curiously, a good deal more of this feeling among the British of lower ranks than I ever discovered among the Indians, who were doing most of the fighting and suffering most of the casualties in this war against the freedom of a fellow subject race. Back in India the Congress Party was protesting the use of Indian troops here as well as in Java, but the Indians on the spot were professional soldiers, men whom the British had taught so well to fight for them so unquestioningly. I never met or heard of one of them who saw any paradox, or showed any reluctance or any sympathy for the Annamite cause. On the contrary they were fierce and ruthless, especially the Gurkhas. An Indian correspondent went among them and found not a glimmer of what he sought. We talked once to a tall Rajput rifleman who when he spoke used the pronoun "we"—and by it he meant the British. "We have come here to disarm the Japanese," he said, "and the Annamites are interfering with us. They shoot at us, and that gets us angry. So long as they shoot at us, we'll kill them, that's all. I don't mind doing it, not at all."

"But how about their cause, their fight for independence?"

"I suppose," he replied, "that if they want their independence, that's all right. But shooting and throwing grenades is no way to go about it. They ought to stay quiet. Then everything would be all right."

The British were very proud of the "loyalty" of these Indian troops. Only Indians like my fellow correspondent and a few of the Indian officers were ashamed of them. And they had to keep silent.

Meanwhile French troops were arriving, thousands every week, first in French transports and then in a long succession of American ships, flying the American flag and manned by American crews. They came ashore in their American uniforms, with their American lend-lease weapons, tanks, trucks, jeeps. They marched past cheering crowds of relieved French civilians and moved out almost immediately to the flat ricelands of the peninsula to restore French order. A young French soldier, newly arrived, swore because there was fighting to do. "The colonel told us we were coming out to rest," he said. "Do you believe then the Annamites should have their freedom?" I asked. He stared at me. "I think we must be firm," he said, and turned away.

The French slowly gathered enough strength to be firm. Before Christmas there were about 50,000 French troops in the southern zone, and the British prepared to withdraw. "We have done our best for the French," General Gracey told me. "They are our allies, and we have discharged our obligation to them. Now it's up to them to carry on." The French were soon left alone to complete, by force and by guile, the job of "pacification." They had been restored in the south by the British and had brought overwhelmingly superior forces to the spot. They could pacify Cochinchina now, if it meant leveling every village in it. In the west, in Cambodia, they were successful in signing an agreement with the Cambodian court, and that province—"land of the lotus-eaters," the Annamites called it—was safely in their hands. There remained the north, where the Chinese were in control and where the Viet Minh still ruled.

NORTH OF THE 16TH PARALLEL

The seat of the provisional government of the Viet Nam Republic was in Hanoi. It is a pleasant city lying quietly in the sun on the Red River plain in northern Tonkin, not far from the Chinese frontier. Like most cities in the colonial east, it has its spacious foreign quarter, built here in the familiar French provincial style with its broad avenues and comfortable, ugly homes. Back of these avenues are the seamed, crowded alleys where the Annamites and the Chinese live. But when I drove into Hanoi from the airfield in the sleepy warmth of that mid-November afternoon, many evidences of great change flickered past on the walls and on the shop fronts. The Viet Nam flag flew everywhere. Across every open surface there were slogans chalked or painted or printed: *"Doc lap hay chet!"* ("Independence or death!"); *"Nuoc Viet Nam sua nguh Viet Nam!"* ("Viet Nam to the Viet Namese!"); *"Tha chet cou hon trelaine le!"* ("Death rather than return to slavery!").

All the French street signs were gone, and in their places were Annamite names. On inquiry I found that Boulevard Henri Rivière, Rue Amiral Courbet, Rue Miribel, all named for French conquerors, had become Dailo Phan Boi, after a famous Annamite revolutionist, Duong Lethaite, after a fifteenth century king of Annam, and Duong

Nhan Ton, after the first king of Viet Nam ever to call a popular assembly, sometime in the fourteenth century. The street names, the old and the new across the entire city, were like chapter headings in two histories, one of conquest, the other of resistance. There was no question about who was writing the current chapter. It showed in the boarded-up fronts of the slick French shops on the main avenues, on the banners waving over the crowded, busy, streaming Pipe Street, Cotton Street, Wood Street, and Copper Street, in the flags and signs draped over the tramcars traveling their appointed routes, or bobbing from rickshas, or flying proudly from flagstaffs in what used to be the government quarters of the ruling French.

When I saw his picture painted on a huge banner on one of the main streets, I was fairly certain. When he walked into the sitting room on the second floor of the Résidence Supérieure and held out his hand smiling, I knew he was indeed my Shanghai friend of long ago.

"You have changed," he said, looking me over with cocked head. —"So have you," I replied.—"You used to have black hair and you were thinner," he said; "and I? How have I changed?"

Ho Chi-minh had become an old man in these twelve years. His hair had turned gray. He wore now a scraggly little moustache and a beard of thin long strands. His cheeks were deep hollows, his skin like old paper. His brown eyes shone with a quizzical brightness. He wore a faded khaki jacket and trousers, a white shirt and old slippers.

"And now," he said, "I'm president of the provisional government of the Republic of Viet Nam. They call me 'Excellency.' Funny, eh?"

He spoke much better English than I remembered him speaking. As he told me of what had passed with him in these years, I understood his painful thinness and the two teeth missing, fallen from the front of his mouth. He had gotten to Europe, then returned to Hong Kong. He made his way to the Indochinese frontier region, where for years he lived the life of a wanderer in the mountains, meeting friends, tortuously keeping contact with his fellows farther south, slipping into Indochina again and again and making good his escape. There was a long siege in Chinese prisons. "All the way up to

Liuchow and Kweilin," he grinned. "It was at Kweilin that my teeth began to fall out. I looked at myself once and then tried never to look again. I was skin on bones, and covered with rotten sores. I guess I was pretty sick." The Chinese held him as, of all things, a French spy!

Clear finally of his Chinese jailers, he returned to the border region, began organizing guerrillas in the mountains that rim southern Kwangsi and the Tonkin frontier. In March he crossed over and was the leader of the bands which made contact with the Americans, received arms and training and direction from American officers, and succeeded in three months in liberating large areas in the northern provinces. When the Viet Minh congress met at Coabang just as the Japanese surrendered, they named him president of the provisional government. He entered Hanoi and was riotously greeted in streets jammed with demonstrators.

Ho Chi-minh put on a battered old cork helmet and picked up a bamboo cane. "Come on," he said, "you will have dinner with the president of the Republic!" Out in the corridor smart young Viet Minh guards snapped to attention and saluted. Two of them, very businesslike-looking youngsters with Sam Browne belts and holstered revolvers, got into the car with us. He chuckled, "How funny life is!" he said. "When I was in prison in China, I was let out for fifteen minutes in the morning and fifteen minutes in the evening for exercise. And while I took my exercise in the yard, there were always two armed guards standing right over me with their guns. Now I'm president of the Viet Nam Republic, and whenever I leave this place there are two armed guards right over me, with their guns."

Later we sat in the home of our host, a soft-spoken Annamite professor. Around us crowded the professor's children, ranging from three to the teens. Old Ho Chi-minh was awkwardly embarrassed when the six-year-old brought him a packet of his drawings, covered by an elaborately designed dedicatory page addressed to him. "I'm all alone," he said afterward. "No family, nothing. . . . I did have a wife once . . ." but he left it at that.

The French identified Ho Chi-minh as Nguyen Ai Quoc, the most persistent, canny, and dangerous of all the revolutionary nationalists in Indochina. He never once fell into their hands, although he had often been within reach. If they had ever caught him, he would have been given short shrift. Nguyen Ai Quoc shipped to France as a laborer during the last war. There, like so many other Asiatic laborers —Chinese, Korean, Indian—he caught a glimpse of what it was not to be a slave. He became a Communist. He wrote eloquent articles and pamphlets. He became an international figure, the representative of his country's struggle for liberation from the French. In the years that followed his name became universally known throughout Tonkin, Annam and Cochinchina. It became synonymous with the most dogged and persevering attempts to create and keep alive kernels of resistance to French rule. Nguyen Ai Quoc was like a shadow across French mastery in Indochina. His presence was reported everywhere. His name was spoken in whispers. His influence stirred young people in the villages and towns.

Ho Chi-minh was born in the province of Vinh, in northern Annam. "The home of revolutionists," the Annamites call that place with its sparse hills and valleys, its thickly crowded population. From out of that mass grubbing in the soil to live has come a peculiarly large proportion of Indochina's greatest national leaders. As a boy of twelve, Ho began his revolutionary career as a courier, carrying messages from village to village for his conspiring elders. Today, at fifty-five, he likes to think of himself as a man who has cast aside parties and programs. He speaks not in class political terms but in nationalist terms. "My party is my country," he liked to say; "my program is independence." In long discussions we had of the problems of the nationalist movement in general and in Indochina in particular, he would impatiently wave aside all misgivings. "Independence is the thing," he said. "What follows will follow. But independence must come first if there is to be anything to follow at all later on."

Ho Chi-minh, however, was under no illusions about the difficulties faced by the newborn republic. It stood alone and no one in the world seemed interested in its fate. It had the powerful support of its own people, but it faced far more powerful and hostile forces with almost empty hands. The French return to power in the south had been a blow. The Annamites would organize partisan war. They would fight and keep on fighting, "and our children will keep on fighting if need be," Ho said. In the north they were at the mercy of the Chinese, and while the Chinese were being momentarily friendly —at least not unfriendly—no one in the Viet Minh government, least of all Ho Chi-minh, could mistake the rapacious Kuomintang militarists for apostles of freedom.

The Chinese were in northern Indochina by a fluke of interpower politics. There is an ancient and well established Chinese institution known in pidgin English as *cumshaw*, which roughly translated means a tip, an extra cut, a slight premium, an additional reward, or in current American parlance: gravy. Temporary occupation of northern Indochina was *cumshaw* handed out to the Chinese by the Big Three at Potsdam. It was an easy piece of Anglo-American-Russian generosity, at French expense. The French, having been pushed well down to the lower rungs of international authority, were in no position to protest. Their status as a Great Power, like that of China, was purely complimentary, subject to change without notice. The Chinese had been heavily bilked at the Yalta conference. They were due to suffer heavily from the grants made to Russia in Manchuria. It seemed only fair, by Big Three standards, to give them some slight compensation in the south. Accordingly the authority to occupy Indochina down to the 16th parallel and there to enforce the surrender terms was given to Chiang Kai-shek as commander of the China theater of operations.

The Kuomintang government had certain outstanding issues to settle with the French. There was French extraterritoriality in China and the concessions, which had been yielded by the other powers in 1943. There were French holdings in the Yunnan railway. China wanted to recover these and, reversing the historic process, wanted certain privileges for herself in northern Indochina. Many Chinese militarists and politicians in adjacent southern Chinese provinces had long looked covetously across the border at the wealth of Tonkin. There were half a million Chinese in the French colony, most of them merchants and traders, who suffered under legal disabilities and discriminations. There was, in the language of the powers, a Chinese "interest" in Indochina. The occupation, it was understood, would be temporary, but it would last long enough to be profitable. So when

Chinese troops poured in great numbers across the frontier, there was no Chinese desire at all for any early return of French power.

The Chinese military authorities promptly recognized the de facto authority of the Viet Minh government at Hanoi. The 3,500 French troops they found in Hanoi without arms were kept without arms and were held in semi-internment at the Hanoi citadel. Some 1,000 French soldiers who had escaped across the Chinese border in March were not permitted to return. As a result, in sharp contrast to conditions in the south, perfect order reigned in the north and the disarmament of the Japanese was carried out quietly and with relative speed. In Hanoi, correct though wary relations were established with Ho Chi-minh and the insurgent Annamite régime. There was no great mutual trust—the Annamites suspected Chinese designs, and the Chinese suspected Annamite radicalism—but protocol was observed by both sides. Viet Nam and Chinese flags were entwined on many a ceremonial arch, and leaders of both sides wined and dined each other amid much formal cordiality. The Chinese military guaranteed "law and order," but most of the policing and all administration was left in the hands of the Viet Minh government. Toward the French, the Chinese adopted a highly satisfying attitude of authority. The French mission was kept cooped up in a small residence over which they dared not fly the tricolor. French officers arriving from the south were frisked for arms, at aggravating length, before they were allowed to leave the airfield.

For there was much anomalous irony in this Chinese penetration of foreign territory, especially territory that had once owed distant allegiance to the Chinese emperor and had been wrested from Chinese control by a treaty exacted at the cannon's mouth. Here the Chinese could taste the unfamiliar fruits of conquest. Here the European had lost face immeasurably and the Chinese was master. He could keep French troops under humiliating restrictions. Here all his orders had to be obeyed by deliciously reluctant Frenchmen. Here, for a change, the Chinese kept "order" to which the European had to submit. He could demand, requisition, seize, pre-empt, in the time-honored style of Europeans in China, and he could not be denied. And here, most importantly of all, there was rich territory to exploit, fabulous profits to be swiftly gained. This was a heady draught indeed for the Chinese militarists and politicians in on the deal and, on a lesser scale, for the Chinese soldiery for whom, in turn, there was the *cumshaw* of selective looting.

One item of the payoff was the cost of the occupation, which by the terms of the arrangement was to be covered by the French. The Chinese promptly let it be known that they had 150,000 troops in the area. This was only transiently true. Haiphong, the chief northern port, was being used for transshipping Chinese troops to the north. Whole armies were being moved across northern Indochina in transit and they were all counted in, although the permanent garrison was about 50,000. The larger figure, however, enabled the Chinese to bill the French for 350,000,000 Indochinese piasters (roughly $23,000,000 by the current military rate of exchange) as an initial payment. They also pressured the French into shipping rice from the south at one piaster per kilogram, compared to a market price of seven piasters, and in return grandly allowed the French to ship some Tonkinese coal needed in the south. But all this was small change. The principal instrument of profit-taking and economic penetration was the debased Chinese currency.

By proclamation of the Chinese commander, General Lu Han,* Chinese currency was made legal tender in the northern occupation zone. The rate of exchange was arbitrarily fixed at 1½ piasters to one Chinese customs "gold" unit—$20 in Chinese national currency. This was roughly ten times the value of the Chinese money on the black markets in Kunming and other near-by Chinese cities. Fantastic black-market money manipulation resulted, with profits of 1,000 per cent easily and quickly made. Merchants in the zone, Chinese and Annamite alike, were caught in the squeeze between the two currencies. A ruinous inflation set in. Prices rocketed more than 200 per cent. Foodstuffs and commodities, always scarce, rose far beyond the purchasing power of ordinary working people, and Chinese controls functioned only to favor the Chinese black-market operators, the

---

* The Indochina deal was in every way a felicitous one for Chiang Kai-shek, even serving his domestic political purposes. As the occupying force he sent in the best units of the Yunnan provincial armies controlled by Governor Lung Yun, Lu Han's brother-in-law. Then Chiang Kai-shek knocked over Governor Lung in a swift coup at Kunming and acquired full control, for the first time, of Yunnan Province.

largest of whom were nothing but agents for the high Chinese command and a chain of profit-taking officials which stretched all the way back to Chungking. Favored by all these conditions, the Chinese moved in on French-owned property. Only a few weeks after their arrival, when I was in Hanoi, they had already bought up the leading hotels, cinemas, shops, and many residences. They had varied means of frightening Frenchmen into selling, and Frenchmen were not hard to frighten at that time. The two leading Chinese banks, the Bank of China and Central Bank of China, were preparing to open Hanoi branches and companies were being formed for the purpose of acquiring French interests in mines, factories, utilities, and port installations.

For however long it lasted—and as things turned out it lasted more than four months—the Chinese occupation of northern Indochina was a profitable foray long to be remembered by all, French, Chinese, and Annamite alike. For the French it was painful and costly, and for the Chinese merchants long established in the area it was an unhappy interlude. But for the Annamites it was a grievous additional burden laid on the already heavy load of the threatening famine. The previous year nearly two million people had died in Tonkin, it was said, because the French had taken the bulk of the rice crop to satisfy Japanese demands. In addition Tonkin ricelands—never sufficient to feed the area, which had to import additional supplies from the south—were taken out of rice production and cultivation of castor beans was ordered, because the Japanese wanted the oil. The Japanese coup in March and the subsequent war conditions in Tonkin had resulted in neglect of the irrigation system controlling the turbulent waters of the great Red River that comes down from the Chinese mountains across the Tonkinese plain to the sea. The river overflowed the crumbling dikes. When the Viet Minh took power in Hanoi, the ricelands of eight provinces were under water, all the crops ruined. When the Chinese came in, they did nothing about it and even took for their own use the meager rice supplies still available. The Hanoi government was desperately trying to apply emergency measures and to stem the spread of the flood, but its resources were few and the outlook was grim. The Chinese, the French, and all the greater powers of the outside world, and even the more malignant forces of nature itself were all conspiring, it seemed, to throttle the newborn Republic of the Viet Namese.

THE PROBLEM OF SURVIVAL

The tiny Viet Nam Republic stood very feeble and very alone in the world. It had nothing but the will of its people behind it and a profound moral conviction of the justice of its cause. These were assets that could buy little on the world political markets after the end of the great war.

The Annamite government knew it could not stand long alone. Its leaders were quite aware that existence depended on what adjustment they could make to the stronger forces surrounding them and beyond them. It was a grim and characteristic paradox of the times: the millions of the rest of the world, especially the peoples of America and Russia, were scarcely aware of the struggles in Indochina, hardly aware the country even existed. Yet for the Indochinese this indifference was a matter of life and death because their fate depended on how much people elsewhere cared if they were free.

Internally, the Viet Nam Republic could count on relative cohesiveness. The dangers of internal conflict were small. The different states of French Indochina—Cambodia, Cochinchina, Laos, Annam, and Tonkin—had known historic rivalries but had also always managed somehow to federate their common interests. Once the divisive influence of the French were removed there would be no obstacles in the way of union. Within the numerically dominant Annamite population there was negligible class differentiation. Under the all-embracing power of the French, all the people shared the bond of subjection. The real ruling class of the country consisted of the 45,000 Frenchmen who lived in it as the administrators and representatives and defenders of French capital. The merchants and traders of the country, as elsewhere in Indochina, were largely Chinese. The Chinese, to be sure, represented a particular problem as an important minority, and they were essentially a conservative factor as well as a disturbing one. But the Chinese too suffered severe restrictions under the French and stood to profit from Annamite independence. In Cholon they gave shelter to Annamite insurgents and they suffered, along with the

Annamites, the wanton burning of their shops and homes carried out as acts of reprisal by the British. So much so, that the entire Chinese community staged a four-day strike in the midst of the fighting around Saïgon, threatening to throttle the city entirely. "Officially we're neutral," a leader of the Chinese community told me. "In fact, we sympathize fully with the Annamites."

Among the Annamites themselves, the only group with any share in the exploitation of the country was a small one, roughly estimated to number no more than 10,000. They were landlords, with relatively small holdings, a few minor industrialists, a larger group of agents and functionaries of the French régime and of French business. This group would always be a menace to Annamite nationalism, but only when it was umbilically attached to the French. Cut adrift and left to their own resources, these Annamites were weak, their grasp on wealth too feeble, their impact on the nation too light. Quite a few among them sympathized, a little fearfully, with the Viet Minh nationalists. Many others, chiefly the landlords who feared the radicalization of the peasantry, stood passively aside and waited on events. There was not much they could do when the people moved, and the overwhelming bulk of the people were peasants and fishermen, tenant workers of the land and seasonal workers on the plantations. And it was among these people, with the least to lose, that the Viet Minh found its greatest support. The Viet Minh program was mild, limited to land reforms and guarantees of living wages and working conditions. So long as the people believed the Viet Minh would live up to these promises of greater security, the régime was in small danger from the Annamite wealthy. The inevitable process of differentiation could come only when the French were removed from the scene and interplay of Annamite class interests would begin to assert itself. But for now, the few wealthy Annamites who toadied to the French were no threat. The rest, who prayed that some other power or powers would rescue them from the anarchy of the mass, were helpless. On this score, the Viet Nam Republic was secure enough.

This, in effect, was the reasoning of Ho Chi-minh and other Viet Minh leaders in Hanoi when they impatiently brushed aside references to the history of the Chinese nationalist movement and the way in which it was crushed when the rich landlords and bankers and militarists seized control. "Such conflict cannot arise among us," Ho said, "at least not for a long time to come. Our country is too backward and its wealth is too overwhelmingly in the hands of the French. Remember that in China the imperialists controlled the outlets of Chinese wealth. Here the French own it all outright. That is why independence is the prime issue, the only real issue."

But independence, he also recognized, would not be enough. It would not sustain Viet Nam by itself. Viet Nam would need outside help, it would have to be integrated into a world which would allow it to profit from its rice and rubber and coal and labor and to begin reorganizing the exploitation of its resources in terms of its own needs. Did such a world exist? If not a world, then a friend upon whom they could count among the mighty?

Upon whom could they count? Certainly not now upon the Chinese. China was so immensely larger than the little Republic of Viet Nam—and perhaps there would come a day when China would have realized her capacities and assumed her place as the leader of Asia. On that day Viet Nam would profit, perhaps, from being China's neighbor. But China now was weak and assailed, rent by internal struggles and external pressures. It was ruled by the kind of men who were in northern Indochina now, sucking at the land like leeches. Because they held the French at arm's length, they were temporarily helpful. But that could not last. The Chinese were already negotiating their settlement with the French and would be interested only in gaining their own immediate ends. From those ends, Annamite nationalism had little enough to gain.

What of the Russians? Would they bring any strong political support to the Annamite cause? I met no Annamite who thought so; and I spoke to many Annamite Communists. The Annamite Communists, like all their fellow nationalists, suffered from a terrifying sense of their isolation. They were unusually frank and cynical about the Russians. Even the most orthodox among them, like shaggy-haired Dran van Giau, the partisan organizer, granted that the Russians went in for "an excess of ideological compromise," and said he expected no help from that quarter, no matter how distant or verbal it might be. "The Russians are nationalists for Russia first and above all," another Annamite Communist said with some bitterness. "They would be interested in us only if we served some purpose of theirs. Right now, unfortunately, we do not seem to serve any such purpose."

"How about the French Communists?" I asked. He snorted with disgust. "The French Communists," he said, "are Frenchmen and colonialists first and Communists after. In principle they are for us, but in practice? Oho, that is quite another thing!" One of the top-ranking Annamite Communists spoke contemptuously of Thorez, who in a Paris speech had said he was in favor of the Annamites "finally arriving at their independence." He laughed sourly. "A fine rubber phrase, is it not? You can stretch it into any shape or any meaning. No, I am afraid we cannot depend on these fine gentlemen. They are the dominant party in France now. And look what Frenchmen are doing now in Indochina."

From the small handful of French Communists in Indochina, the Annamite comrades learned a remarkable lesson in their kind of politics. There were only twenty in the French Communist group in Saïgon. "Of these only one," said my Annamite Communist companion, "*only one* solidarized with us. The rest stood aside." The French group prepared a document for the Indochinese Communist Party which bore the date of September 25—two days after the French had seized power in the city. I was able to read the document, but not to copy it, so the notes I made immediately afterward are not verbatim. But the substance was as follows: It advised the Annamite Communists to be sure, before they acted too rashly, that their struggle "meets the requirements of Soviet policy." It warned that any "premature adventures" in Annamite independence might "not be in line with Soviet perspectives." These perspectives might well include France as a firm ally of the U.S.S.R. in Europe, in which case the Annamite independence movement would be an embarrassment. Therefore it urged upon the Annamite comrades a policy of "patience." It advised them in particular to wait upon the results of the French elections, coming up the following month, in October, when additional Communist strength might assure the Annamites a better settlement. In the meantime it baldly proposed that an emissary be sent not only to contact the French Communist Party but also the

Russians "in order to acquaint yourselves with the perspectives of coming events."

This document displayed with remarkable and unusual bluntness the Communist Party's notion of the relation between a revolutionary movement and Soviet foreign policy. It apparently came as a shock to the Annamite Communists ,who were thrown into considerable confusion by it. There was a sharp internal argument within the party which ended in a decision to dissolve the party entirely, to cease functioning within the Viet Minh as a distinct unit but to work in it purely as individuals. In this way the party apparently figured on avoiding any responsibility at a time when its responsibility was the heaviest. I do not know what the internal development was in any detail, but I do know that the Annamite Communists I met were men bitten deeply with the bitterness of having been abandoned by their ideological comrades overseas. They had consequently taken refuge in a pure and simple nationalism. Ho Chi-minh was making no idle phrase when he said: "My party is my country." They were oppressed, in common with all the non-Communist Annamite nationalist leaders, by a fearful sense of loneliness. There seemed to be support for them against the French nowhere, none from the Chinese they could count on, none that could be anticipated from the Russians, none from the French Communists, who did gain enormous strength in those October elections without effecting any noticeable change in Indochinese affairs. What then of the United States?

Annamite nationalists spoke of the United States as men speak of a hope they know is forlorn but to which they desperately cling all the same. Could all the fine phrases of the Atlantic Charter, of the United Nations pact, of President Roosevelt and his successor, really have meant nothing at all? Nothing? All right, let us make allowances for expediency, for big-power politics, for all the shabby realities. Would not the United States still find it wiser for the sake of its position in the Far East to win support among the people rather than to cling to the rotten imperial system of the past? It seemed not. For the only indication the Annamites had of America's role in their struggle came in the form of lend-lease weapons and equipment being used against them by the French and British, and the stunning announcement of an American deal with France for the purchase of

$160,000,000 worth of vehicles and miscellaneous industrial equipment for the French in Indochina. To the Annamites this looked like American underwriting of the French reconquest. The Americans were democrats in words but no help in fact, just as the Russians were communists in words but no help in fact. "We apparently stand quite alone," said Ho Chi-minh simply. "We shall have to depend on ourselves."

This left them to consider the possible terms of compromise with the French. In relation to the French, the Annamites did not feel weak. They could mount and were mounting an extensive guerrilla war that was frightening the French badly in the south and forcing them to seek for their own part the terms of a less costly deal. The Annamites could threaten—and their words were not empty—to destroy everything the French owned in the land, to burn down their houses, destroy their railways, ruin their plantations. Colonel Cedile himself went on an expedition up the waterways of the Saïgon delta late in that November; and every time his gunboat approached a town, flames and smoke rose above it as Annamite partisans wielded torches in the French quarters before retreating in front of what they thought was an attack. "We will make Indochina uninhabitable for the French," Dran van Giau said. "They will fight their way. We will fight our way. If we have to, we'll destroy everything the French have built in order to make our own beginnings."

But still, under the pressure of their isolation, the Viet Minh offered a great deal to the French. Ho Chi-minh told me he was prepared to negotiate Viet Minh recognition of the whole French economic position in the colony in return for French recognition of Viet Nam independence. "Why not?" he demanded, defensively. "We've been paying out our life's blood for decades. Suppose it costs us a few hundred million more piasters to buy our freedom?" If there was not to be a world in which Viet Nam could exist wholly free, then at least they would force upon the French a compromise in which the Annamites were somewhat freer than they had been before. This was the argument, and nobody who looked at the shoddy, slack, bloody face of the postwar world could quarrel with it.

Four months after I left Hanoi, the Viet Nam government found itself—as its leaders had foreseen they would be—squeezed by a deal between the Chinese and the French. In payment for withdrawal of its troops, Kuomintang China won French surrender of extraterritoriality, railroad rights in Yunnan, and free passage for Chinese goods along the rails to the port of Haiphong. The same week, the French negotiated a convention with the Viet Nam government at Hanoi in which it recognized the Viet Nam Republic "as part of the Indochinese Federation and the French Union." The French agreed to withdraw all garrisons within five years. The Chinese had gotten what they wanted. The French regained something of a hold on the colony they had so nearly lost. What the Annamites gained remains to be seen.

There was no way of knowing, from thousands of miles away, what pressures—Chinese, French, or Annamite—were effective in the final parleys. There was no way of knowing how the Annamite leaders felt or whether the agreement meant what it said or to see clearly what would result from it. There was no way of knowing whether it satisfied in any degree the passionate will to freedom that surged through so many of the young people and caused so many tillers in the fields to raise their heads. Or whether it matched the expectations of the youthful Annamites I was with one night when they packed the ornate empire-style French theater in Hanoi to listen to reports by young partisans newly arrived from the south. They crowded the stalls and boxes, young taut men and women, an unlikely audience in this setting built by Frenchmen for Frenchmen. The young man from the south spoke alone on a platform against a simple backdrop of a huge Viet Nam flag. He told of clashes and exploits around Saïgon, making his words glow with that fine inspiration that comes only when men see things by their own inner light. On the enemy he poured scorn. "We are inferior to the French in the matter of arms," he said. He paused a long instant and then added: "Also in the matter of cowardice!" The youthful audience roared. "Blood will flow across our country," he soberly concluded. "In this blood we must write the words: 'an independent Viet Nam'!"

There were songs sung like a litany, and then the young people poured down the steps and across the marble lobby and out into the night, where lights shone on the cornice of the building, adorned at ten-foot intervals with clusters of Viet Nam flags.

THE NEW PATTERN OF POWER

THE NEW PATTERN OF POWER

7 POWER, NOT PEACE

Out of the war everyone hoped for some kind of peace. But there has been no peace. Instead there were the small wars of the aftermath, the many shadows of more and greater wars to come. The wartime alliances dissolved at once and the victors jockeyed avidly across the ruins of a weary world for new positions, new strategic boundaries. All the moods and conflicting interests of nationalism were aggravated rather than lessened. The world lay shattered in fragments and seemed farther than ever from finding its way to any new wholeness. The war's end brought the beginning of a new pattern, not of peace, but of power.

This is no problem of good will or moral purpose. There is a great deal of good will and even of moral purpose among a great many people, but these are factors which have seldom interfered seriously with the course of human history. It may even be that the present rulers of our world are all honorable men. Perhaps, like the late Franklin D. Roosevelt, they even hate war and want peace. But the trouble is that in their separate national entities they want peace on their own terms, and these terms are the terms of power. Their politics is power politics. And power politics is the politics of war. They responded to the need for a new international unity by setting up the United Nations organization. But like the League before it, this new body was designed not as an instrument for leveling national antagonisms but as a stage on which they could find political expression, a gathering place for the national factions, a mirror in which the real world could find itself remotely and fuzzily reflected. In this real world, in Asia and in Europe, the principal postwar activity of the ruling politicians has been the carving out of spheres of influence or decisive control, the cynical buffeting of peoples, governments, territories, in the interests of broad and conflicting patterns of power.

The object of all this, the peoples are told, is security. Security against whom? Against what? Sometimes the polite answer to this is:

179

security against a renascent Japanese or German militarism. But who after the first few months of "peace" took this answer seriously? Japan and Germany were crushed in a fashion unduplicated in history since the days of the Huns and Genghiz Khan. Their cities were razed, their empires stripped away, their economic power harshly reduced. Even were we to assume that new world conditions will give them the chance to rebuild and that in such rebuilding they will regain their war-making capacities, it is obvious that they could do so only as the pawns or instruments of this or that Great Power. Tendencies in this direction have, indeed, already grown quite visible in the wrangling over occupation policies both in Germany and Japan. But even under such patronage, the process would require many years, possibly decades. As direct military threats, Germany and Japan have been eliminated for a long time to come. The victor powers are not menaced by Germany and Japan. They are menaced by each other.

The war of 1939–45 brought to an apocalyptic climax the German drive to master all Europe and the Japanese program for the conquest of all Asia. Both of these dynamic twentieth-century imperialisms came close to achieving their aims. Close, but not close enough. The Anglo-American combination and the new Russian supernationalist state, brought into a common struggle for survival against Hitler's Reich, prevailed in the end in Europe. In Asia, where Japan's fifty-year march of conquest had led it inexorably into collision with the United States, superior American resources successfully repelled the Japanese threat and established American primacy. In both hemispheres, the military victories ushered in a new epoch dominated by the two great surviving power blocs, the Russian and the American, with the waning British Empire in the main reduced to the role of adjunct and satellite—and sometimes mentor—of the American colossus. The entrenched wealth and position of Britain and the United States passed under the pressure of their new and powerful and more dangerous rival, the totalitarian, imperialist, quasi-communist Russia.

The so-called "security zone" extended by Russia across eastern and central Europe, across the plains of Manchuria, and out to the Kuriles in the northern Pacific, bulges outward until it meets the rival "security" zones coveted or defended by Britain and the United

States. The American pressure for a string of Pacific bases, for decisive control in East China through the Kuomintang government, for transformation of Japan into a docile puppet, for creation of secure and friendly Asiatic outposts, similarly extends until it reaches the gray and uncertain border areas where American interests confront Russian interests. The diplomatic and political conflicts that developed right out of the war's end had to do with the more precise fixing of these boundaries. These conflicts represented the push and pull, the advances and retreats, the diplomatic reconnaissance patrols, the whole maneuvering competition to gain the last possible mile of territory, the furthest possible extension of control over strategic position, over sources of oil, coal, food, manpower which each side needed either to swell its own power or to keep from swelling the power of its rival. It was, in sum, the search for a modus vivendi capable of lasting two or five or ten years, a new and precarious balance of power permanent only in its instability, secure only in the certainty of future collision.

This competition for place and power governed every act of the victor powers at the war's end and in the aftermath. Their representatives in the many postwar parleys acted not like men building peace but like men who accepted as absolutely inevitable the prospect of future war. Throughout the premise has been the clash of their conflicting interests. The keynote has been hostility. The theme has been the dynamic advance of the new Russian imperialism and the active defense of the entrenched Anglo-American positions. The struggle has gone on in the cynical discussions of the United Nations Security Council, in angry parleys and conferences, in open meetings and secret meetings, in the use of food to serve political ends in a starving world, in the play and counterplay of occupation policies in the defeated countries, in the direct or indirect support of rival factions in France, Greece, Iran, China, or Manchuria. They meet, they argue, they play brutally with the fate of nations and peoples. They insist, they yield, they demand, they accede, they shift ground or they give ground or they take ground, all in accordance with their respective efforts to establish, to maintain, or to extend their positions of power in the world.

As they confronted one another repeatedly in the first year after the war, with their alternating "tough" policies and "soft" policies, their meetings would be reported in the press like sporting competitions. This side would win or lose, make small gains, suffer small losses. In the American press box James Byrnes would be hailed or damned according to his seesawing batting average against the pitching of Molotov. In Britain, Ernest Bevin would become a public hero because he went the whole length with Vishinsky, trading blow for blow and winning, if not a decision, at least a draw. The issue of power lying between them was so deep, the hostility so plain, that they could not through long months of wrangling even write peace treaties covering the smaller satellite victims of the war. They could not decide amicably on how to divide up the remnants of the Italian fleet, or agree on Yugoslavia's share in Italian reparations. They could not agree on what to do about little Korea or on who should have Trieste. They barely averted blows over the division of Iranian oil. They could not even approach the problem of what to do about Germany. And all the issues simmering in the Far East still remained on the upcoming agenda.

There was nothing in all this of the building of any peace. It was leading instead to the openly acknowledged splitting of the world into two hostile camps. They were maneuvering tactically in preparation for coming battles, engaging in the first phases of vast logistical movements for collisions they all feared and could not avert. As one Paris correspondent, during an abortive conference of the foreign ministers, wrote in a cynically witty paraphrase of Clausewitz: "Nowadays, peace is the continuation of war by other means."

Overhanging the whole course of this conflict was the menace of the new weapons of atomic war. While plans and counterplans for "control" of the new weapon were discussed and debated in public, the fervid, feverish, anxious and largely silent race went on to maintain or achieve leadership in this new and baleful means of destruction. The Americans went on making atomic bombs and the Russians were straining every means they had to make bombs of their own. At Bikini the Americans staged a demonstrative test of the new weapon, both as an act of warning of present American power and as a test that would fix the character and development of future American armament. In their scientific journals the Russians indicated that before too long they would be able to match bomb for bomb, disinte-grated atom for disintegrated atom, warning for warning. And clearly, the atomic bombs of Hiroshima, Nagasaki, and Bikini were only the beginning. Research was already yielding a host of new weapons that would entirely transform the conduct of warfare. The conquest of atomic energy, and the conquests obviously to follow, has given an even more apocalyptic character to the prospect of another war on this planet.

When we consider the destructive possibilities now open to us, a few miles of territory more or less, a few dotted islands more or less in the vast oceans, seem to acquire an immense irrelevance. Even now, at the threshold of the atomic age, we are told of guided missiles that go seventy-five miles high, travel twelve thousand miles in twelve minutes, and descend upon predestined targets, searing all human and material existence over large areas in single, conclusive explosions of atomic force. If such is the shape of things to come, it would seem superfluous to worry about whether the national security zone extends beyond the frontiers a few hundred miles more or less or whether the last island outpost is one or two or even four thousand miles away. The advent of atomic weapons, we are told, means that massed armies, air and sea fleets as we knew them in the recent war have been superseded. Atomic logistics will bear no resemblance to the logistics that defeated Germany and Japan. A few guided missiles, traveling a good deal faster than the speed of sound, will do the work of a dozen fleets, of a thousand bombing planes. We are asked by the experts to contemplate the fact that future wars may not be decided by the huge lumbering movement of millions of men across great distances wielding millions of tons of steel and explosives, but by a few dozen or a few hundred such atomic missiles launched by a few men at push buttons half a world away from their targets. In such a war it will indeed be of small importance who has Trieste, who con-trols Poland, or Manchuria, or Iran.

Yet this prospect does not transform the immediate situation as much as one might think it would. It is not entirely simple cultural lag which keeps the new great rival powers in the world arguing over Trieste, Manchuria, or Iran. To begin with, the development of new weapons does not at a single blow transform all the war maps of the world. It does eventually, but it takes a little time, even in our accelerated age. Many a man was killed by pikes and arrows long after the introduction of gunpowder in Europe in the late thirteenth century. Nearly a hundred years passed before the revolutionary conceptions of the *Monitor* and *Merrimac* grew up into the vast battle fleets that swept the Japanese from the Pacific. It took half a century for the first frail craft of the Wright brothers to grow up into the B-29 and the Flying Wing. To be sure, the intervals grow shorter and the capacity of industrial production grows greater. But so do the intervals between wars grow shorter. The powers that rule the world today can still figure that foreseeable conflicts will require a combination of the old and new modes of warfare, just as in the recent conflict the "obsolete" battleship was bracketed with air power. No matter how swift the generalized development of atomic weapons, the onset of the next conflict may be swifter. At least our rulers, in their chronic uncertainty, must count on that possibility and prepare accordingly.

Moreover even in our times big wars do not spring suddenly out of the blue. They emerge, with all their accumulated force, out of a succession of small wars and preliminary skirmishes. The war of 1914–18 was preceded by the conflicts in the Balkans. The war of 1939–45 was heralded by the Japanese war in China, the Italian attack on Ethiopia, and the civil war in Spain. Today there is already a sputtering of such small conflicts, particularly in Asia, which are part aftermath, part portent. And these wars in the next few years will certainly not be fought with atomic weapons. The admirals and generals can still bank on an active future for their armies and navies. The politicians must still meet the need for distant bases, for strategic territory, for spheres of control. If anything, the control of decisive raw materials is even more crucial from a military standpoint in the atomic age than it ever was before. The explosion of the next atomic bomb launched with hostile intent will undoubtedly come as a shock to its victims—but it will not be a surprise. It will come not out of the bright blue but out of an atmosphere long prepared for it. There was nothing surprising, remember, about the outbreak of the American-Japanese war. It was only the incident at Pearl Harbor that was unexpected.

In any case, if ultimate decisions rest with the weapons of the future, the issues will still be the unsolved issues of the past. Atomic power politics will simply be more explosive, more cataclysmic in its consequences than pre-atomic power politics. If TNT killed its tens of millions, split atoms will kill their hundreds of millions. We may measure our advance over the age of yesterday by the difference between the two-ton blockbuster and the atomic bomb. We may contemplate as a social gain the marvels of science that will substitute for the slow attrition of mankind the wholesale and speedy extermination promised by new developments in electronic, chemical, and bacteriological warfare combined in some efficient pattern with the use of atomic energy. The prospect is not particularly inspiring. But neither horror nor fear nor human suffering, as we have again so lately learned, can turn the forces of history from their course. A world organized on the basis of rival balanced powers is a world committed to war; and war requires the use of force carried to its utmost logical conclusion. If Hiroshima did indeed usher in the dark days of extinction, then the problem that faces us would seem to be not the abolition or "control" of the new atomic weapons but the abolition, even at this late date, of the roots of war in our society.

Whether this can be done and how it can be done is a matter we must urgently explore. But one thing is certain: this is not what the politicians of the United States, Great Britain, and Russia are engaged in doing right now. They are, on the contrary, committed to acts and policies that assume the inevitability of war. They did not, for more than a year, even bother, as the powers did after 1918, to offer lip service to the idea of general disarmament. They still quite frankly acknowledge and even insist upon the necessity for maintaining and developing their armed power. They were even careful to write into their United Nations charter a power veto which raises any of the Great Powers above the censure or opposition of any of the rest of the world. They made ludicrously certain, at the very outset, that their future resort to force would be wholly "legal."

It comes down to this: out of the war came survival for the victors, submersion for the defeated, and immediate preparation for further conflict. This was no turning point, no radical ending, no radical beginning, no relief for the very weary peoples of the earth. It was simply the passage into the next descending curve of the historical spiral. With their periodic eliminations and renewals and comebacks, their shifting alignments and dogged struggle for hegemony, the powers could only resume the old cycle of self-defeating self-interest in national terms. Peoples everywhere were caught in the writhing postures of perpetual conflict. Asia, like all the world, remained a battleground on which power, not peace, was the stake.

8 JAPAN

Defeat drove Japan from the foreground of Asiatic affairs. It marked the end of one of the most remarkable episodes in modern history: the rise and fall of a grandiose imperial dream by a country so weak in basic resources that it had to import or conquer the foundations of its power. An enclosed medieval realm only seventy-five years ago, Japan rose to challenge all the powers of the West for the mastery of Asia; and it came astonishingly close to its goal.

Japan achieved its Great Power status in the first place by defeating Russia in 1905. It lost that status finally by being defeated by the United States in 1945. Stripped of its conquests, its cities in ruins, its people drained and starving, Japanese imperialism lies prostrate. But it is by no means dead. The elimination of Japan as a dynamic factor in Asia left the field of mutually hostile ambitions to the United States and Russia. Japan's future lies in the role it may yet play, in the Russian camp, in the American camp, or strategically and precariously suspended between the two.

There is a good deal worth recapitulating, therefore, about the rise and fall of Japanese imperial power. Japan's fifty-year march of conquest will probably go down in history as the greatest shoestring operation of all time. There is a Lilliputian quality about Japan which is difficult to reconcile with the scope and consequences of the power it came to yield. The Japanese archipelago extends for about 2,000 miles, curving like the blade of a scimitar against the coast of northern Asia. All its islands together, however, occupy an area only a shade larger than the state of Montana. Nearly seventy million people crowd this small territory, of whom about half, even at the height of Japan's power, were poverty-ridden farmers (compared to one-fourth rural population in the United States, less than one-third in Germany and about one-tenth in England). There were only about two million industrial workers, in the Western sense of that term, or less than three per cent of the population (compared—prewar—to 30 per cent

187

in Germany, 27 per cent in England, and 28 per cent in the United States).

There are some striking resemblances between Japan and England. Both are small, crowded island countries hard off the edges of the great continental land masses. Both have been dependent upon the external markets they could conquer or control, on maritime trade, on a vast and teeming flow of goods across the seas. Both developed a doctrine of implicit, even divine, justice in their right to rule lesser peoples. Both enjoyed considerable freedom from scruples about the way they established and maintained such rule. But here the superficial similarities end. There was, first, the great difference in time. England entered the world picture early. Its conquering advance around the globe began in the seventeenth century. It subdued weaker peoples, fought off feebler rivals, carved out its colonies and its holdings as the first-comer in a newly opened world. It was able to spend nearly two hundred years consolidating and entrenching its gains during a great historic epoch of economic growth, transformation, and expansion. Japan, on the other hand, entered the world picture late. It began its march of conquest only fifty years ago. Its bid for expanding power was made in a contracting world, already parceled out, already strangling in the grip of the competition of rival titans. Britain rose in the dawn of capitalist society, Japan in its twilight. Japan was a sudden blaze amid the waning embers of empire.

There was an even greater difference in the sources of expanding power. England, building outward from its own coal and its own iron, was the pioneer of the industrial revolution. Japan's latter-day industrialization was a hasty and desperate graft on a land which itself yielded only negligible quantities of the fuels and minerals which are the source of industrial strength. Japan built its empire and made its near-successful challenge for continental mastery in Asia on the basis of a national industry created from nothing in little more than three decades. For this industry it had to import 48 per cent of its pig iron, 62 per cent of its zinc, 69 per cent of its iron ore, 87 per cent of its oil, 88 per cent of its lead, 95 per cent of its aluminum, 100 per cent of its wool, 100 per cent of its cotton. By its ruthless use of virtual slave labor at home, by its well timed economic onslaughts, its shrewdly spaced military conquests, Japanese imperialism built up its machine. It achieved, before its final war, a production worth about five billion dollars a year, and on the angry and crowded marts of foreign trade a predepression peak of imports and exports totaling annually two and a half billion dollars. By American standards this was still quite puny. Still it was on this basis that Japan, in a period of acute world decline, embarked upon a great war of conquest and managed to bring under its control or nearly under its control the greater part of eastern and southeastern Asia with a total population of 300 million people.

This historic tour de force began in 1868 when a section of the Japanese feudal aristocracy, through the Meiji restoration, began the deliberate transformation of the country. Their object was first to acquire strength to resist the penetration of the Westerners, second to match and if possible overtake the intrusive barbarians who were already at that time across the Yellow Sea battering China into submission. A unique military-financial oligarchy was superimposed upon the medievalism of old Japan. The peasants remained helots. Japan's economic transformation was not based upon the building of an internal market but was based from the beginning upon calculations for conquest. Finance capital and modern militarism were wedded in Japan from the cradle. They began their joint career early. First blow was the attack on China in 1894 which brought them Formosa and the Pescadores, and a foothold in Manchuria, which latter the Western powers, led by Russia, forced them to disgorge. Russia was the obstacle that stood in the way of Japan's reach for the coal and iron and the other rich resources of Korea and Manchuria. Russia was also Britain's prime rival. Hence the Anglo-Japanese Alliance of 1902 and Japan's sudden attack on Russia two years after that. Japan, to the astonishment of the other Western powers and the roused delight of Asiatics everywhere, swiftly defeated the lumbering Czarist giant. Korea passed under Japanese control and then was annexed. The "special position" enjoyed by Russia in South Manchuria was passed on to Japan, along with the oil of southern Sakhalin.

The outbreak of war in Europe in 1914 was a glittering opportunity for Japan. Its industries waxed under wartime demands. Japan, moreover, promptly seized its military opportunity. Declaring war on Germany, the Japanese attacked and captured German islands in the South Pacific and the German-controlled port of Tsingtao on China's Shantung coast. In 1915, Japan served on China the famous Twenty-one Demands in an audacious attempt to reduce China at a single blow to the position of a helpless vassal. The Chinese government at Peking capitulated. But this high pressure boomeranged. When at Versailles in 1919 President Wilson bowed to Japan's demands that its Shantung gains be recognized, the effect in China was a swift and tumultuous rising of nationalist feeling before which the Japanese had to retreat.

The Japanese were also checkmated when American pressure was again brought to bear on her after the war's end. The Japanese attempt to gain a foothold in Maritime Siberia by intervening against the Bolsheviks had failed when all White Russian opposition to the new revolutionary régime collapsed. At the Washington Conference in 1922, Japan had to agree not only to liquidate the Siberian adventure but to give up some of its gains in Shantung as well. American pressure likewise forced Japanese acceptance of a 5-5-3 naval ratio and secured Japanese signature to the nine-power treaty guaranteeing China's territorial and administrative integrity. Thus checked, Japan entered its "liberal" period. The cue passed from the militarists to the diplomats, financiers, and traders. For the next decade Japan pressed as hard as it could, as far as it could, in an economic offensive. It achieved remarkable success against the numerous quotas, restrictions, and other defenses set up by its rivals in Far Eastern trade, invading the markets not only of China but of all southern Asia. But these successes were insufficient. The onset of the world crisis in 1930–31 threatened to cripple Japan fatally unless it established new continental footholds. The result was a new resort to arms, in September, 1931, with the seizure of Mukden and the advance into Manchuria. Once again Japan had calculated shrewdly and well on China's weakness and on the reactions of its rival powers. America and Europe were profoundly preoccupied with the effects of the economic crisis. Moreover Britain and France, with negligible interests in Manchuria, saw in Japan's advance there a contribution to their own *cordon sanitaire* policy toward the Soviet Union. So when China came before the League of Nations to plead its case against Japanese aggression, it found that the British and French were more inclined to be advocates than critics of Japan's acts. The League, a simple creature of Anglo-French diplomacy, confined itself to leisurely examination and finally, after long delays, to moral censure. The Japanese contemptuously walked out. American diplomacy, anxious to check Japan but powerless to do so, could find outlet only in testy notes written for the record. The Japanese drive in China, secure from serious outside interference, went on for nearly ten years.

But conquest had its own logic and exacted its own cost. Once launched, it had to continue. Successful in Manchuria, the Japanese moved across the Great Wall into China Proper. By alternating military and political pressures, they won control of the northern provinces. To consolidate there, they had to go on. In 1937 they launched their all-out war for the conquest of all China. Step by step, with fateful and unerring precision, the pattern of conflict extended. When the war in China meshed into the greater war that grew out of other, similar roots in Europe, Japan finally had to commit itself all the way. The stunning initial victories, the blunting of American naval power at Pearl Harbor and the incredibly easy first conquests in southeastern Asia seemed to confirm beyond all expectation the wildest visions of Japanese grandeur. Japan now had only to knit the sinews of this swiftly won empire. It was a dazzling opportunity. But it was an opportunity Japan was incapable of exploiting.

Japanese imperialism had built its strength on weakness, and in the end this weakness was decisive. It was able to expand only so long as it expanded in a vacuum: the vacuum in Asia forty years ago created by Anglo-Russian rivalry and thirty years ago by the preoccupations of the First World War; the vacuum created in China by the disintegration of Chinese nationalism under the Kuomintang; the world vacuum of the great depression of the nineteen-thirties; the vacuums of the rotting colonial régimes in southeastern Asia; the vacuum in the Pacific created by American military complacency and national isolationism. All of Japan's victories through the course of its expansion had been victories based upon its superior timing and upon the transitory weakness of its enemies. But Japan came too late upon the scene to conquer its greatest enemy: its own permanent weakness. Because of it, Japan could not establish and maintain a Pax Japonica in Asia.

Because its resources were limited, Japanese capitalism built its power on light industry. It had to expand by finding, establishing, invading, and controlling markets for the products of this light industry and sources of raw material to feed it. Textiles alone, for example, employed more than 40 per cent of Japan's factory workers, and of the textiles they produced more than 60 per cent was for export. Japanese capitalist economy was deliberately designed not to thrive upon an expanding domestic market but on the contrary to develop on the basis of enforced poverty in the home population. It was oriented to an extraordinary degree upon the conquest of foreign markets and foreign sources of raw materials. Japan's fifty-year effort to dominate China was designed to win unimpeded sale of its cheap consumer products. Its gradual expansion, its acquisition of Manchurian and Korean coal and iron and Sakhalin oil, contributed to the building of its heavy industry, its steel plants and shipyards. These resources as well as the converted proceeds of its profitable foreign trade were, however, almost exclusively devoted to the building of Japan's war machine and formed part of Japan's preparations for continental and Pacific war. Japan's economy in modern times was never anything but a war economy.

The object of Japanese expansion was not only to ensure control of markets and raw materials but to eliminate competition. Japan's whole effort in China was to bolster its own frail economy by enjoying direct and undivided exploitation of the Chinese market, Chinese labor, Chinese resources. In this effort it not only collided with the rival interests of Britain and the United States, but could not tolerate even a relative growth of competing Chinese industry. Japan's margin was too narrow to leave much room for native exploiters. Thus whenever Japanese armies descended upon Chinese cities, a principal object was always the systematic destruction of Chinese factories. By bombing in 1932 the Japanese damaged many plants in Shanghai, and when they finally occupied that city five years later they openly wrecked or removed most of the Chinese industrial machinery not already destroyed by shells and bombs. The best of the facilities they took for themselves. The rest they scrapped.

In other words Japan was attempting, in the mid-twentieth century, to duplicate the process by which Britain, France, and Holland, many decades earlier, had molded their colonies into wholly dependent adjuncts to the imperial economy. Rigid control in behalf of a basically mercantile interest was all that Japan could offer. Its "co-prosperity" program in reality offered no chance of prosperity at all to the native holders of wealth in the countries it sought to dominate.

In this lay the crucial difference between the Japanese and American positions with regard to Asia. Simple trade was by no means the core of the American interest, particularly in China. The basic American interest lay in the possibility of supplying Chinese economy with capital goods, with the products of America's swelling heavy industries. American capital investment looked—or could look—toward an industrialized China whose factories, transportation systems, power plants, and industrialized agriculture could form an immensely profitable basis of financial and economic operations over a long term of years. This was, at any rate, the persistent dream. It was blocked by the mutual rivalries among the powers and by the stifling of independent Chinese economic development under the system of foreign control in the country. But it has always been, and still is, the American perspective in China. And this perspective offered to budding Chinese bankers, industrialists, and businessmen a most attractive future. It offered them position as shareholders, co-owners, managers, agents. Japan would reduce them all to foremen, stooges, and serfs. That is why would-be Chinese industrialists have always preferred to see themselves as the future vassals of New York rather than of Tokyo. In the period of their domination in eastern China, which lasted for nearly a decade, the Japanese found plenty of puppets to govern for them. They won the support of a whole section— and an important section—of the Kuomintang bureaucracy. But they could sink no new roots into the country. They could bring to it nothing that would grow. They could only destroy and loot. In the long and bitter Chinese experience with the Western powers, Japan had a tremendous asset to exploit. But Japan, coming late, could only attempt to imitate, with crude brutality, those other invaders who had come earlier.

In Southeast Asia, the Japanese opportunity was even more marked. In swift, easy blows, they pushed over the decomposing colonial régimes of the Western powers. Whereas in China the Japanese met from the beginning the stubborn resistance of important sections of the people, in southeastern Asia the local populations stood passively by, delighted at the rout of their foreign masters. Except on a small scale in the Philippines, no resistance was offered in support of the old rulers. On the contrary, the first impulse everywhere was to welcome the Japanese as liberators, and help sprang up from the rice paddies to hasten the expulsion of the hated Westerners. There was rejoicing over the humiliation of the white men for whom they had so long carried such great burdens. There was respect for the apparent invincibility of the victors, and there was ample and willing and enthusiastic collaboration. It is a little staggering to consider what might have been the result if the Japanese had been strong enough and acute enough to exploit this immense advantage. Their slogan "Asia for the Asiatics" struck a deeply responsive note in southern Asia. If they had meant it and had been able to act on it, it could well have proved hopelessly impossible ever to dislodge them from the empires they had won.

But instead of fostering genuine national independence for these colonial countries, the Japanese offered the colonial nationalists only puppet roles. Instead of entering into a serious and mutually profitable partnership in the business of driving the Westerners out and keeping them out forever, the Japanese almost everywhere terrorized and despoiled the countries they had overrun. "Asia for the Asiatics" really meant "Asia for the Japanese," and it did not take the Japanese very long to demonstrate this fact. In their haste to feed their basically feeble war machine, to build up their stock piles against the day of the counteroffensive, they stripped these countries of food, raw materials, and machinery. They could not integrate Southeast Asia into their ephemeral "co-prosperity sphere." Instead they simply looted and requisitioned, flooded local markets with worthless paper currency, and plunged all of that vast area into an economic morass from which it will not emerge for a long time to come. They dissipated quite quickly most of the support they had initially won. They retained the services of many a colonial stooge. They had the support of many who believed that the new dispensation would, for better or worse, have to be carved out of this seemingly permanent Japanese conquest. But most nationalists and the mass of ordinary people who had to suffer the brunt of Japanese depredations turned away from the new conquerors. It had looked for a while like a chance to win new freedom. It turned out to be simply an exchange of new masters for old. When Japan's collapse came, there were none to regret the passing of Japanese power. Japan had proved the bankruptcy of the old rulers and in turn demonstrated its own.

Japan's defeat, however, came not in China nor in the colonies of southern Asia, but in the Western Pacific under the direct blows of American power. Japan's geographic advantages and political advantages, its preparation, its master timing, its sudden offensives, brought sweeping victories at the outset. In the end its basic weakness told. It lacked the means to sustain what it had won. In the showdown, it was the difference between Japan's ten-million-ton steel capacity and the United States' hundred-million-ton steel capacity which decided the issue. The Japanese era as would-be master in Asia came to its fated end on the decks of the U.S.S. *Missouri* in Tokyo Bay on September 2, 1945. Neither the last-minute Russian entry into the war nor the dropping of atomic bombs on Hiroshima and Nagasaki determined the final conclusion, though they may have slightly advanced the date. Japanese production had already been roughly halved by destruction from the air. The Japanese stock pile of steel was said to be down to 180,000 tons, the store of liquid fuels down to 15,000 tons. Fanatical, suicidal struggle was all right for Japanese soldiers trapped on remote islands. The owners of what was left of Japan's wealth did not carry the Bushido code too far. They decided to take their loss. Japan's shoestring challenge had simply petered out.

Imperial Japan survived its defeat. The empire was lost, industries crippled, cities laid waste, but the social régime still stood. No groundswell rose from amongst the people to topple it. No anger rising among its millions of victims at home shook its foundations. This was, by far, the most striking fact about Japan as its armies laid down their arms and the American occupation began.

In the sudden ebb of defeat, the people seemed drugged and numb, resigned beyond comprehension to the blows of fate. In the ruined towns even the little people would tell you, with real tears in their eyes, that they had been prepared to die and had been re-prieved by the Emperor and that they would be forever grateful to him for his benevolence. Now they were prepared to starve, to freeze, to submit to the rigors of defeat as they had submitted to the rigors of war. This was torpor or hypnosis or the dullness of sustained shock. Or it was tribute to the effects of brutal terror and "thought control" pervasively practiced by a totalitarian police régime for generations. Whatever it was, it was the absence of hope or protest except in the breasts, perhaps, of a tiny minority without impact upon the people as a whole. New currents would sooner or later have to begin to flow, in one direction or another, but for now very clearly there was neither the thought nor the impulse to assail the régime that had brought such utter catastrophe upon the land. "The trouble was," said a mild little housewife in a small town north of Tokyo, "that the newspapers lied to us. They let us believe we had a stronger army and navy and air force than we really had." That was all. These were a people still held morally, mentally, and physically enthralled. So long as they submitted passively, the whole system which vic-timized them would remain intact, from the medievally enslaved peasant at the bottom to the puppetlike Emperor at the top. Drastic adjustments would have to be made, surely, but the power to make them would remain in the hands of the old rulers. And in those first months of the occupation it was plain enough that the con-quering Americans were quite content to have it so.

The more obvious "war criminals" among the Japanese leaders committed suicide or attempted to do so. The rest submitted to trial. The military caste in general simply retired from the scene, seeking patient obscurity wherever it could be found. For the first ten weeks the business of cushioning the régime against the shock of defeat was left in the hands of the little group of prime manipulators around the throne, led by Prince Konoye. Cabinet ministers ac-ceptable to the Americans were pulled out of the back drawers of

Japanese politics. A new constitution was drafted and beneficently bestowed upon the people by the Emperor. Decree after decree came out of General MacArthur's headquarters, but they left the basic institutions of Japan essentially untouched.

The divinity of the Emperor was dutifully renounced, but the imperial institution remained. The *zaibatsu,* the leaders of the great trusts and combines controlling all of Japanese economic life, were ordered to dissolve their economic empires. They complied, but economic power remained in the same hands nonetheless. The politicians thinned their ranks in accordance with purge directives, but political power remained in the hands of stooges of the same fraternal order of owners of the land and the wealth of the country. General MacArthur gave the vote to women, but women remained degraded in the unbroken grooves of an entrenched social system. He even "ordered" the abolition of prostitution, but the little prostitutes who heard of his order did not know what to make of it.

The MacArthur revolution by directive was hardly a substitute for social change arising out of the will of a rebelling people. None of these bolts from the Macarthurian heights could open the sluices for new currents in the ebb and flow of Japanese life. The financiers, the politicians, the bureaucrats soon realized that they had to jump through enough hoops to satisfy the new ringmaster. After their first fright and uncertainty, they soon realized that the results would not be as ruinous as they had feared. In the realm of political power they had to clip a little of the divinity off the edges of the imperial myth, but otherwise they could preserve the essence of their social and political system. In the economic realm they had to suffer the costs of defeat, of wartime destruction, and all that the loss of overseas markets would mean to Japanese economy. But their property rights were unassailed. If their holdings were sharply reduced, they could still pass on the costs to the people. If anywhere from one-third to two-thirds of Japanese urban real estate was completely devastated, they still owned what was left. They could regroup their assets. They could still live off the sweat of the peasants, whose land they still owned. They could wait as passively as need be for better times to come while the great mass of people paid in defeat as they had paid in victory. And all over Japan this price was fearfully heavy, in homelessness, starvation, and total dislocation of all economic life.

No challenge rose out of the debris of defeat. "New" political parties came into being, but they were in the main re-formed cliques of politicians of the old school. Largest was the "Liberal" Party, led by a politician named Hatoyama who was seriously considered by MacArthur as candidate for premier until correspondents dug out his wartime panegyrics for Hitler and Mussolini. The Japanese "Socialist" Party was led by the Christian leader Kagawa, who had lent his support to the wartime régime and who in the peace evidenced no desire to assail the basic institutions of the country. A handful of surviving Communists emerged from ten, fifteen, and twenty years of immolation in Japanese prisons. They had been sustained by a radical political virility that withstood all the tortures of the Japanese police régime but would hardly withstand the emasculating effect of party policies dictated by Russian foreign policy. There was no reason to believe, considering the evidence right across the face of the postwar world, that this influence would be any more progressive in its effects than the American influence wielded through the old-line politicians and their newly humanized little Emperor.

The great imponderable remained. No one could know how and when the workers in Japanese factories and the peasants on Japanese land and all the little people in Japanese towns and cities would throw off their numbness and torpor and begin to intervene in their own affairs in their own way. Until they did so, Japan's old régime would sustain itself by one means or another, and Japan's old leaders would continue to rely upon the conservative support of the American conquerors. For the long time being, the power and the initiative, as the first elections under MacArthur quickly confirmed, would remain in the hands of the old régime's politicians and bureaucratic stooges.

What, in such hands and amid present conditions and prospects, can Japan's future be?

In a world newly integrating itself, Japan would surely find a fruitful place. It is physically one of the most beautiful lands on earth and its people are a numerous, virile, and productive race.

Freed of their bonds, they could make a great contribution to any future world confederation of peoples which assured them their needs from beyond their island home.

But the prospect in Asia is no such world, no such integration, no such assurance. Instead Japan's power-politicians will still have ample opportunity to play power politics in relation to the new American-Russian duel for power. In power-political terms, Japan occupies the same place in relation to the Asiatic continent that England does in relation to Europe. There always has been and there still is an important school of thought among American rulers and military and naval men, which has regarded Japan as a defensive base against a potentially hostile continent. This was the basis of America's support of Japan, in Theodore Roosevelt's time, against Russia. Unfortunately for the United States, Japan wanted to dominate the continent by itself and thus, after a long and painful history of invasions and wars, had finally to be subjugated. But rendered now docile and pliant, Japan can still be adapted to its ordained strategic role in the American sphere in Asia, either in conjunction with an American-dominated China or, even more urgently, in the event that through the Chinese Communists Russian influence in China should become paramount.

This is not presented here as scholastic speculation. This is a line of thought one hears expressed in some circles in Washington and even more violently espoused in top circles around MacArthur in Tokyo. I heard it advanced, by the officer in charge of MacArthur's economic policies in Japan, as the prime reason for not going too far with the break-up of the Japanese domestic economic empires. Every correspondent in Tokyo heard officers of general rank describe Japan as "the staging area for the next operation."

The issues involved, both implicitly and explicitly, are similar to those in the dispute over the role of Germany, which Russia seeks to dominate as its chief buffer against the West, and which the Anglo-Americans wish to dominate in reverse as their bulwark against the East. The same premises govern now that governed in the past; for it should not be too readily forgotten that when Japan embarked upon its continental program forty years ago, it had the support of the British in the form of the Anglo-Japanese alliance of 1902, directed against Czarist Russia, and in its war against Russia likewise enjoyed the support of the United States. Again, when Japan invaded Manchuria in 1931, it had the explicit and implicit support of Britain and France, who looked upon Japan as a bulwark against Russian Bolshevism in the Far East. These motives, these arguments, these power-political necessities and calculations still exist and have become all the more pressing since Russia has emerged as one of the two major powers in the world.

What defeat did for Japan was to reduce it from the role of principal contender to the role of incidental tool. Both sides in the new conflict will attempt to use it. Failing to secure a direct hand in the occupation, the Russians will in their own good time make their influence felt through the Japanese Communists. The Americans, for their part, will try to see to it that Japan becomes and remains an American outpost. Amid such forces, the old-line Japanese politicians can well afford to bide their time. The turning wheels and the shifting cycles of power, as they now move, can be depended upon to lift them sooner or later from the low estate into which their defeat has now plunged them.

9 GREAT BRITAIN

With broad, heavy strokes, the war revised the standing of the British Empire in Asia. For the British the years of the war and the war's aftermath have been years of deepening eclipse. Only a scant twenty years ago, Britain was still the greatest of the imperial powers in Asia. It held the premier position in China. It ruled or dominated the richest territory on the rest of the continent. Its investments were the heaviest, its trade the most pervasive, its naval and maritime power paramount. But all of it was suffering the steady attrition of a lengthening history of decline. The events of the war showed how far Britain's powers of resistance had been whittled down. Folding under the swift, crippling blows of Japan, Britain came close to losing all that it had and held in Asia. Rescued only by the ultimate weakness of Japan and the ultimate strength of the United States, Britain emerged enfeebled and shaken. Out of the American victory, the British won the chance to pick up the broken pieces of empire. But there is little left either of the reality or the illusion of grandeur. The British know they are fighting a rearguard action in defense of their disappearing greatness.

In the new pattern of power that emerges from the war in the Far East, Britain is reduced to a secondary place. In the game of power politics it is something less than a junior partner and little more than a pensioner of the United States. In return for a free hand in recovering and reshaping what it could of its immense stake in southern Asia, Britain yielded to the United States what it would in any case never regain: its prime position in China. It held on with desperation only to Hong Kong, the heart and nerve center of Britain's billion dollar Chinese stake. The bulk of British assets in the treaty ports and in the rest of China was for the immediately foreseeable future beyond reach, certainly beyond early profit, and perhaps beyond all recovery. Britain, it was sure, would never again occupy the special position it held in China by virtue of the fact that

201

it was the first to wrest privileges, the first to build a large trade, the first to make heavy investments, the first to draw from them fabulous profits during a century of almost unimpeded exploitation.

As the most heavily entrenched of the powers in China for so many decades, Britain was the principal target of the modern Chinese nationalist movement. It was the spearhead and the leader of the resistance to Chinese efforts to regain national and economic independence. It was the most stubborn defender of the system of special foreign privilege. It was perhaps the most malign of the forces that kept China divided and prostrate and thereby helpless in the face of Japan's invasion. The British first regarded the Japanese drive on the Asiatic mainland with complacent calm. They thought it would usher in a new period of dismemberment in China which would establish Japan in the north and at the same time reinforce Britain's hold on the Yangtze Valley and the south. They also thought Japan would serve British policies aimed at Russia. But these calculations, like so many others in the years of the long armistice, were rudely upset. The advance of the Japanese into China Proper, the taking of Shanghai, Tientsin, and Hankow, directly assailed Britain itself in China. In the end, when the war spread to the southern ocean, the Japanese advance overran all of the British Empire in Asia except India itself. When the Japanese wave receded, Britain and its satellite imperial neighbors, France, and Holland, were left facing grim and hostile facts: (1) that the entire past strategic concept of defense of their Asiatic empires had been exploded and would have to be drastically revised; (2) that the old colonial system that had yielded such great profit for centuries had petered out and could no longer profitably work in their interests; (3) that colonial nationalism could no longer be countered with simple repression alone; (4) that the long era of Asiatic submission to Western rule was at an end.

This was no sudden or radical result of the war. The war simply accelerated a process long under way. During the two and a half decades between the world wars, political and economic strains on the British Empire in Asia had grown faster than Britain's capacity to absorb them. The British were under the constant though often inchoate and faltering pressure of Indian nationalism, always checkmated but never defeated. In Burma and Malaya the old methods of direct British rule and unhindered British exploitation were challenged with growing force. Despite its many failures, nationalism in southern Asia had on the whole grown stronger and Britain weaker.

Economically, Britain's position had been declining ever since the end of the nineteenth century when its many rivals began to overtake it. The Empire sustained the shock of the first German challenge in 1914–18, but never wholly recovered from it. In Asia it then had to meet the powerful assault of the Japanese. The British had to cede ground not only in China, where Japanese pressure was the greatest, but in its own colonies as well. The British actually lost to Japan first place in Indian imports of textile goods, so vital to the interests of Lancashire. The British share of these imports dropped from 97.1 per cent in 1913–14 to 43 per cent in 1936–37, while the Japanese share rose in the same period from .3 per cent to 54.6 per cent. In rich Malaya, Japan drove its share of all imports up from 21 per cent in 1929 to 68 per cent in 1933. The British and their smaller imperial neighbors were faced in these years with a widespread, expertly generaled, and remarkably successful Japanese offensive on all the markets of Southeast Asia. They tried to resist it with tariffs and quotas and restrictions but never wholly succeeded. It was, however, clearly only a question of time before the Japanese economic attack would be transformed into military attack, before Japanese economic competition would develop into an attempt at outright seizure of the disputed markets.

When this attack finally came, the British, French, and Dutch, to an even greater extent than the Americans in the Philippines,* proved even more inept in military defense than they had been in economic defense. They proved incapable of holding their colonies against the powerfully expanding Japanese. They were unable to put up, even by their own standards, a respectable resistance before yielding. The French made terms with the Japanese without resisting at all. The British, after bootless attempts to stave off attack by sporadic acts of appeasement, were swiftly and ignominiously defeated amid utter confusion and breakdown in Malaya and Burma.

---

* The Philippines, while part of Southern Asia, belong in the American political and economic and strategic sphere in the Western Pacific. Reference to them will be found in the following chapter.

The Dutch offered scant and demoralized resistance for a few days in Java before surrendering in their turn. The American showing in the Philippines was a little better, but it did not halt the sweep of the Japanese victory. In 100 days the Japanese took all of southeastern Asia from the Western powers, halting only at the frontiers of India. It was a remarkable tour de force by the Japanese. It was also a remarkable revelation of the dry rot of foreign rule in these vast regions. The readiness of the colonial subjects everywhere to welcome the Japanese as liberators needs no elaboration. The literature on the fall of Singapore, on the debacle in Burma and the Indies is already copious—and it all confirms the obvious fact that the Japanese pushed over a structure so organically rotten that only inertia kept it standing up to the time of the Japanese attack.

These humiliating defeats inspired a good deal of breast-beating among the ousted colonial rulers. The air was filled with self-criticism which was, however, rarely too harsh, and the record was filled with promises which were, however, seldom too precise. A month after the collapse in Malaya, the London *Economist* wrote:

> There can be no return to the old system once Japan has been defeated. . . . The need is for entirely new principles, or rather the consistent application of principles to which lip service has long been paid. For the colonies, Malaya, Indochina, Netherlands India, there can be only one goal, the creation of independent nations, linked economically, socially, and culturally with the old mother country, but learning to stand firmly on their own feet.

This type of acknowledgment was more easily converted into propaganda than into serious intentions. It helped divert some Americans in high places who toyed with the idea of involving themselves in some kind of colonial new deal. It provided material, albeit reedy and unconvincing, for broadcasts aimed at the people brought under Japanese control. But even in those days of the war's lowest ebb when they had been stripped of power, prestige, and even their own kind of self-respect, the colonial rulers were scarcely ready to yield any of the real perquisites of their vanished empires. The best the British could produce in 1942 was the Cripps offer to India. The Dutch government, in a declaration by Queen Wilhelmina in December, 1942, announced it would create a commonwealth after the war in which the home country and the principal colonies would assume equal status "with complete self-reliance and freedom of conduct for each part regarding *internal* affairs." General de Gaulle, first from his outposts at Brazzeville and later after his return to France, promised Indochina a new dispensation in the form of a French Union in which the Indochina Federation would enjoy "freedom consonant with its degree of development and its capacities." *

For American consumption in particular, the British made much informal ado over a plan for regionalizing the great colonial areas of the world, for setting up international councils with power to oversee such matters as health and welfare and education but without, of course, modifying the administrative and political sovereignty of the ruling state. At unofficial conferences of well intentioned "experts," this proposal was put forward by minor ex-colonial administrators like Lord Hailey. In the columns of *Life* magazine it was even outlined in great detail by as august a personage as Jan Christian Smuts. But less was heard even of this plan as the war years passed and Churchill discovered that Franklin Roosevelt had in reality nothing but satisfactory intentions as far as the British Empire was concerned. Intent itself upon winning full control of new Pacific bases, the United States showed no strong inclination to challenge the colonial position of the British or anybody else. The regional council idea dissolved into the trusteeship scheme, which in turn was altogether divorced from the old established colonies. At the San Francisco conference, the colonial problem was disposed of in a platitudinous pledge by the colonial powers to foster in their colonies "the progressive development of their free political institutions." Embarrassing attempts by the Russian, Chinese, and Philippine delegations to establish independence as the goal for all subjected countries were sidetracked by joint Anglo-American efforts.

It was not at San Francisco but at Cairo, Teheran, Yalta, and finally at Potsdam that the real shape of things to come in colonial Asia was seriously outlined. In the broad drawing of spheres of influence which took place at those conferences, Roosevelt acceded to

---

* Speech of Queen Wilhelmina, December 6, 1942. Déclaration du conseil des ministres, le 23 mars 1945. *Notes documentaires et études*, No. 115, Ministère d'Information, Paris.

Stalin in the north of Asia and to Churchill in the south. This was formally implemented at Potsdam where, as the war ended, all of southern Asia was placed under British military control. The British were given the mandate to concentrate and disarm the Japanese armies, and to restore "order" in all the reconquered territories. It was with this authority that the British moved into Indochina and Indonesia and there gave the world its first practical postwar demonstration of what the Atlantic Charter meant by "self-determination."

In their wartime propaganda the British and French and Dutch had tried to make their promises of a new dispensation in Asia sound like sacrificial offerings on the altar of human freedom. Yet it seems that the subject peoples concerned had remained unconvinced. They remained stubbornly ungrateful and unreceptive. But the British and French and Dutch were just as stubbornly determined to be self-sacrificing, so much so that they proceeded to force their solutions upon their subjects with all the armed weight that lend-lease weapons and supplies could muster.

In Southeast Asia, except in Burma, the Japanese armies had never even been engaged. The British, after endless bumbling delays, were teetering on the edge of a takeoff for the invasion of Malaya on the very day that Japan surrendered. Some of their invasion convoys were already at sea. Thus not even the war's end could restore any glory to British arms. It caught them in the slightly ridiculous position of being poised for attack and having the enemy suddenly bow before them because he had been kicked in the rear by somebody else. The British had to convert their invasion into an occupation at the last moment, and the change threw them into ludicrous confusion. The manner of their regaining their lost territory proved to be as embarrassing as their manner of losing it. They had looked forward to refurbishing their tarnished military prestige by winning sure-thing victories against an enemy whose supply lines had long since been cut. Instead, after considerable delay, they stumbled ashore on the Malayan beaches and could not even muster an appearance of decisive efficiency as they did so.

British headquarters was finally reestablished in Singapore. It was all a little bit like a flashback in an old, and very bad, moving pic-

ture. The old faces and the old manner returned to the terrace bar of
the Raffles Hotel each evening, and after eight weeks of earnest effort
the British Military Administration delightedly announced the early
resumption of horse-racing. From the Raffles terrace, all seemed again
for the best in the best of possible restored worlds. But only the faces
at the Raffles were the same. The pieces of empire so rudely torn
apart by the Japanese did not easily fit together again. The Japanese
left behind them a legacy of confusion and change. They left economic prostration, currency chaos, disrupted food distribution and
drained supplies, ruined transport, and factories and mines in an
almost hopeless state of disrepair. Even more difficult and frustrating
for the British were the political changes that had taken place during
the Japanese flood and were taking place now in the Japanese ebb.

The Japanese had made formal grants or promises of "independence" in Burma, Malaya, and Indonesia. They had actively sponsored
or complacently allowed widespread propaganda against the Western
colonial powers. This activity went far and deep and touched layers
of the people hitherto insulated by the vigilant controls of their old
rulers. Under Japanese occupation the nationalist movements which
the Japanese tried to use as puppets underwent genuine growth. The
Japanese believed they were creating instruments useful only to themselves, but when Japanese power abruptly ended, the new nationalist
currents continued to flow forward, powerfully and swiftly and out
of roots and with a logic all their own. In the momentary vacuum
created by Japan's defeat, they reached out for the opportunity it
offered to have done with Western *and* Japanese rule and to establish,
for the first time, a power of their own. New groups, political and
military, had taken shape and the returning Western powers, led by
Britain, had to meet their challenge.

Wherever the Japanese had allowed it, there had been a flocking
into anti-British, anti-Allied armies. Subhas Chandra Bose, former
president of the Indian National Congress, formed the Indian National Army out of disorganized units of Indian troops caught in
conquered Malaya. At the head of this army, Bose actually attempted
to invade India, together with the Japanese, early in 1944. That
attempt failed, by a narrow margin. Still, in India, Bose and his
soldiers were looked upon as honest patriots. Bose, in the Indian view,

had simply made the mistake of gambling on an Axis victory in the war. He had gone first to Berlin and after Pearl Harbor had placed himself at the disposal of the Japanese. When he was reported killed in an accident the week the war ended, all of Congress India publicly mourned him. When later, as already noted, the British tried to court-martial his followers as traitors, there were bloody riots all over India as people rose in their defense. In the end the British dropped the trials altogether.

In Burma, the nationalist leader Aung San formed the Burma National Army in cooperation with the Japanese, using as his original cadres the nationalist bands which had assisted the Japanese in their invasion in 1942. When in the spring of 1945 it became plain that the Japanese were doomed in Burma and everywhere else, Aung San blandly switched sides and helped the British in the final stages of the mopping-up campaign which drove the Japanese out of the country. When the British began restoring their administration in Burma, it was Aung San they had to deal with as the most powerful spokesman of Burmese nationalism. Months after the war's end, the world suddenly learned, through interpellations in the House of Commons, that Burma was in turmoil, with gangs of "bandits" infesting the hill country and making the return of "normal" administration difficult if not entirely impossible.

In Malaya, where the British-made jigsaw puzzle of state organization had long served to keep anti-British nationalism satisfactorily feeble, the British had to deal with Chinese-Malayan guerrilla armies, not all of whom quietly accepted the order to disarm. There was fighting in the hinterland of which the world never heard in the first months after the Japanese surrender. The British announced new plans for reorganizing the administration of the Malay states. Even here, where resistance to British rule had always been the weakest of any place in all of southern Asia, the British had to consider drastic revisions and had to act to prevent dissident peoples from imposing revisions all their own.

The sharpest and most serious dislocations occurred, as we have seen, in French Indochina and the Dutch East Indies, where powerful nationalist movements challenged the return of foreign rule with arms in hand. Here the nationalists had actually seized the power that dropped from the hands of the defeated Japanese, had proclaimed their own independence, set up their own governments, promulgated constitutions, organized armies, and announced they would defend their right to go now their own respective ways. This was an open, sweeping challenge to the colonial system as such, and the British could not ignore it. Unsettled and nearly unseated by the war, they had to impose a slower tempo on the rate of change. So when they moved in to restore "order," their mission turned out to be an attempt to compel the nationalists to accept the return of their old masters. This attempt brought on the hostilities described earlier in these pages.

Many conflicting elements entered into the British involvement in these bitter, cynical, brutal little wars. There were the broad considerations of British foreign policy, described by Prime Minister Attlee and Foreign Secretary Bevin as Britain's "obligations" to her French and Dutch allies. The "obligation" to the French included the obligation to keep the French from passing into the Soviet sphere in western Europe. The "obligations" to the Dutch were not unrelated to the heavy British investments in Sumatra and the closely interrelated economies of the Indies and Malaya in rubber and tin. The British had to consider the psychological effect on India and Burma of successful independence movements in neighboring Indochina and Indonesia. They also had to consider the ultimate effects of the rancor and hatred they were sowing for themselves among the Annamites and the Javanese. They had to weigh the effect of their acts in Java and Indochina on their own promises of autonomy, self-determination, or even lesser reforms, in their own colonies. In Indochina and Java they were revealing the measure of their own good will. Wading through these cross-currents, the British on the spot in southeastern Asia were for the most part in a state of fuming confusion, while in London the leaders of the new Labor government stoutly defended and justified every successive blow at the rebelling nationalists.

The British were determined to hold on to every shred of profit-making property they could regain or restore. Attlee and Bevin had fully reassured Churchill and Eden that neither did they desire to preside over the liquidation of the British Empire. At the war's end,

British naval forces in the Pacific made a mad dash for Hong Kong. By their action, carried out with American endorsement, they averted for the time being the Chinese attempt to regain control of that rich, strategically located south China port. They used the circumstances of the war's end to lay a heavy hand on little Siam. They moved troops into the country at paralyzingly heavy cost to the Siamese. They presented to the Siamese government a group of twenty-one demands, most of them bearing a striking resemblance to that other famous set of twenty-one demands served on China by Japan in 1915. Their acceptance would have converted Siam into a British colony. American frowns at this procedure brought some slight modifications, and in the end the British extracted a treaty from Siam which turned that country into more or less of a British protectorate.

But these were reflex actions, born of long imperial practice. Beyond them the British had to face the necessity for substantial changes in their own manner of holding and defending their own positions. The fact was that the underlying relation of force between governors and governed had changed. The British Empire would not serve its interests by restoring, without substantial modifications, the old forms of imperial power. They could no longer rely as much on the old tactic of granting minimum reforms in the face of maximum pressure. Shaken, challenged, and weak, the British faced nothing less than the problem of building a new imperial framework in which their economic and political power could in greatest possible measure be preserved. Now, more perhaps than ever before, when the British promised their subjects some kind of new dispensation, they had to be serious about it.

In the days of their undisputed world leadership, the British had always been best served by internal divisions within their colonies and spheres of influence. No external threat, compelling unity, had ever been as strong as the constant internal threat of popular resistance to continued subjection. If internal divisions were not sufficiently inherent or aggravated, it was always possible, by luck, invention, or carefully plotted happenstance, to set subjects tearing at each other's throats when otherwise they might have been unitedly attacking the British. That was how, in the Middle East, rival Arab tribes, dynasties, and nations were kept satisfactorily divided, and Jew was pitted against Arab, so that Britain might be forever required to keep the balance and preserve the peace. That was how, for so many decades, the cleavage between Moslem and Hindu in India had served so admirably as an argument for the continuation of British rule.

But Britain's undisputed world leadership is gone, gone forever. Britain for a long time has not been winning wars but surviving them. It has survived two German threats to its hegemony in a single generation, and the Japanese threat in Asia. In each case American assistance and intervention or co-involvement were decisive in keeping the Empire alive. Out of the recent conflict, Britain emerged impoverished and weakened, and in this condition it must now face a new threat, more serious, more powerful, more dynamic than any ever offered by the Germans or the Japanese. Across the Dardanelles, across Turkey, across the border regions of Iran and Iraq, falls the shadow of the new, supernationalist Russia, renewing the old Czarist threat to British primacy along its vital imperial "lifelines" to the east.

Along this lifeline the British now need not convenient contention but friendly and satisfied stability. They can no longer stand so surely on their own feet, secure in their rulership over feeble inferiors. They need not hostile, divided subjects and vassals, but strong, united, and friendly allies whose basic interests shall be so closely tied to Britain's that they will stand with her against the Russian menace. So in the Arab world, the new British theme is the theme of Arab unity. With tentative caution they support, even inspire the Arab League. They try to satisfy the Arab against the Jew. They agree, to the consternation of the old-line Conservatives, to withdraw their forces from Egypt, while in return they seek a closer knitting of Egypt into the British defensive system in the Middle East. The British seek the Arab's willing hand in association rather than his unwilling submission to simple superior force. Similarly in India, the British can no longer sit complacently on top of a writhing heap. The defeats suffered at Japanese hands, the close call in India itself, the indifference or the hostility of Indians to British strategic interests, were all bitter lessons. Now the British must seek a stable—and friendly—India if they can still get it. India has to be transformed into a stronger, more heavily contributing partner in the business of empire.

The attempt must finally be made—and it is an ironic paradox—to knit India closer to the Empire by consenting to a loosening of its bonds within the Empire. This British need is so strong—after all India is now one of Britain's largest creditors!—that British professions of good will acquire a faint tone of urgency that they never had before.

The British Empire is weak, but it is still a potent player on the world's imperial checkerboard. The Empire is beleaguered, but it is still resourceful. It still represents an enormous stake in the preservation of the old world, with its old ideas, its old premises, its self-renewing chaos. It is still a powerful brake on the impulse of peoples everywhere to find a way out of their impasse. It is a drag even on the impulses of the British people themselves, who voted Labor into power because they wanted to break with their past. The British Empire is on the defensive, but it is by no means ready to surrender the diadem of imperial world power. In Asia, as elsewhere, the British Empire was badly shaken by the war and by the war's aftermath, but like everything else outworn in our worldwide way of life, it survived.

10 THE UNITED STATES

Victory over Japan made the United States the greatest of the Pacific powers. The moment of the signing of Japan's surrender on the deck of the battleship *Missouri* in Tokyo Bay marked the apex, the high point of American might, American power, American decision in the Far East. It marked the end of one historical epoch and the beginning of another. For an interval that could not, by its very nature, last long, the United States held in its hands the power of decision affecting directly the fate of a billion Asiatics and beyond them the fate of the rest of the world. It was a time for a great turning in human affairs. In their suffering, their fatigue, their vast inarticulate aspiration, the peoples of Asia were ready for it. They were ready to see America wave a magic wand that would turn darkness into light, permanent war into the beginnings of permanent peace. If the American dream had any reality, now was the time for it to manifest itself. If American professions and good intentions were valid, now was the time to make them good. If the American system of capitalist democracy had within it the promise of fruitful growth for the world, here, perhaps, was the final opportunity to prove it.

But the United States was not only the victor. It was also the victim of its own past, its social and political patterns and limitations, its governing conceptions of the way to organize the world. The history of power relations in Asia over a hundred years had culminated in the struggle between Japan and the United States for mastery. This war, however, had again placed on the world agenda far more than the question of who should conquer and be master in the house. It placed before us once more the whole issue of conquest and power and profit as the basis for existence on the planet. The American victory in the Pacific war was nothing less than the American opportunity to face up to that issue. Nothing in the American record of past or present, however, suggested that it was ready or able to assume the immense responsibility thus imposed upon it.

The conventional picture of the American in Asia is the picture of a well-meaning blunderer. The myth has somehow grown and persisted that the American role in Asia, and in China in particular, has been the role of disinterested benevolence. American missionaries have been concerned with Chinese souls, American sinologues with Chinese culture. American governments and politicians through the years have, by this account, been concerned almost exclusively with the welfare and integrity of China. Even American businessmen, bemused for so long by the dream of 400 million customers, have sought only the betterment of the Chinese nation. Inspired always by these high moral purposes, the United States has through the decades stood by China in firm friendship, helping it ward off the attacks of the predatory wolfpack of nations preying upon it.

While a broad streak of deliberate hypocrisy runs through this conventional picture of American-Chinese relations, it is also true that this myth has certain roots of its own. Americans are in general more successful at self-deception than, say, the British. This is particularly true in the field of foreign affairs, in which Americans more often believe their own pious fictions. Thus, by their own accounts, they have often been almost the only representatives of the good, the true, and the just amid the many contending forces of evil. Or, in the more critical version, the American in China has been the well-meaning sinner whose deeds have never somehow measured up to his good intentions. This has been due in no small measure to a genuine confusion over definitions of American self-interest in China. It has also been due in part to the fact that American policy grew up largely out of circumstances created by the policies and actions of others.

American interest in China is as old as the United States itself. The China trade began with the pioneer voyage of the *Empress of China* in 1784, the year after the Republic was born. During the next century and more, the United States was still a debtor nation, overwhelmingly agricultural, and still expanding to its own frontiers. Only during the last thirty years, in fact, has the United States actually held the position of a Great Power in world affairs. It has grown almost by default. It is still, in so many ways, incapable of filling its own boots. Unlike the British Empire, it has not had a consciously consistent view of its place in the world. Unlike Japan, it has never been fiercely driven by any sense of weakness, need, or confinement. To Americans in general, up to the most recent times, the tangled tribulations of the rest of the world were an unwelcome and unwanted intrusion upon the tenor and themes of American national life. They were, in the mass, content with their remoteness, satisfied with their conviction of superiority, and unwilling to grasp the idea of the growing interdependence of all countries and peoples. Even now, after involvement in two world wars, the onset of the permanent absence of peace and the opening of the atomic age, there is still great resistance among us to the idea of the world's indivisibility. A great many Americans still believe or want to believe that American intervention in world affairs, especially in Asia, is largely philanthropic.

THE RECORD

There is not much philanthropy in the record of American affairs in Asia, or in China, which has been the principal sphere of American interest. Even the missionary colleges and hospitals have been investments; and the American missionaries themselves, like those of earlier comers, have been unavoidably bracketed with the interests of trade and national position. Small wars in the early years starting over incidents involving the freedom of missionaries to propagate their various faiths somehow always ended up in territorial or trading gains for the various powers they represented. In its early phase, the United States simply tagged at the tail of its more aggressive mercantile competitors. During the middle decades of the nineteenth century, when the privileged position of the foreigners in China was being established by wars and treaties, the United States always held self-righteously aloof from the repeated armed attacks on China but hastened always to appropriate to itself a share of the spoils.

The first American treaty with China, negotiated by Caleb Cushing in 1844, secured for the United States the special privileges exacted by Britain as a result of her victory in the Opium War of 1839–42. In 1858 the American minister, William Reed, actually waited alongside while British and French warships battered down the Chinese forts at Taku Bar, and sailed up the river behind the victors to sign an American receipt for the new advantages the others had won with their arms. Application of the "most-favored-nation" principle in these treaty negotiations simply meant, as far as the United States was concerned, the right to enjoy the spoils of aggression without participating in the aggression itself. Mumbling misgivings over the rape of China, the Americans took their turn in line whenever the process was repeated. "The English barbarians," wrote an imperial commissioner to the Chinese Emperor after one of these wars, "are . . . full of insidious schemes, uncontrollably fierce and imperious. The American nation does no more than follow in their direction." *

The United States, which had barely reached its own Pacific frontier, was not interested in territorial acquisitions. It was interested in trade and "protection" for its nationals. It took no concessions of its own but by treaty insisted upon sharing all the "rights" of the concession takers. It joined in the treaty-making which established extraterritoriality, forcibly restricted Chinese tariffs to 5 per cent ad valorem, placed Chinese custom revenues under foreign control, and legalized the opium trade.

In the middle of the century, while these treaties were being exacted, the rotting Manchu Dynasty was threatened with overthrow by the vast, surging movement known as the Taiping Rebellion. Having battered the dynasty into docility, the powers joined hands to bolster it up and keep it alive. The Americans joined the British and French in actively suppressing the rebellion. They kept the dynasty safe to emasculate China for another half-century to come. In the 'seventies and 'eighties a bleak chapter in the history of Chinese-American relations was written not in China but home in America where Chinese labor imported originally to build the Western railroads became objects of competitive fears. They were attacked in bloody pogroms and amid the flaring of race violence, they were

* Quoted by Foster Rhea Dulles, *China and America* (Princeton, 1946), p. 62. Chaps. II and IV in this new summary give details of the early treaty relations. "We not only held ourselves aloof while England and France struck a disastrous blow at Chinese sovereignty . . ." observes Professor Dulles, "but after the deed was done, we claimed our share of the plunder."

hounded and barred from the country. The "sympathetic affection" with which Americans are traditionally supposed to have regarded the Chinese was valid only at a distance of six thousand miles.

In 1898 the United States swept into war against Spain on the crest of a jingo-imperialist mood, fanned by the increasingly powerful groups of traders and bankers who were beginning to see the glitter of farther horizons. As a result of this war, the United States became a territorial power in Asia, acquiring the Philippine Islands. The circumstances in which these islands were annexed were directly related to the complicated rivalries of the major European powers, projected onto the Asiatic stage.

In the spring of 1898, the European powers were tearing at China like a pack of ravenous beasts. After Japan's first attack on China, Russia had seized Port Arthur and Talienwan (Dairen) on the southern tip of Manchuria. Germany seized Kiaochow (Tsingtao) on the Shantung coast. Britain took the port of Weihaiwei farther north, and France took Kwangchow Bay in the far south. The British, the most strongly entrenched of the powers in China, had the most to lose from these new divisions. They suddenly developed an intense interest in maintaining Chinese territorial integrity and sought in the United States a foil against the rising ambitions of France, Germany, and Russia. Britain was therefore delighted to have the United States take on territorial obligations in the Far East, and played an important role in overcoming the transient misgivings that delayed the Philippine annexation. That accomplished, the British tried to persuade America to help check the forward strides of Britain's rivals in China. This British design in no small measure inspired the famous Open Door notes issued by John Hay in 1899. It is an interesting and seldom remembered fact that these notes were not only in the main inspired by British diplomacy but were virtually drafted by a British official in Washington named Alfred Hippisley.[*]

The Open Door policy, usually regarded as the foundation of benevolent American participation in Chinese affairs, was in the

---

[*] An adequately documented record of all these circumstances appears in A. W. Griswold, *The Far Eastern Policy of the United States* (New York, 1938), Chaps. 1 and 2.

beginning a good deal more limited than most ceremonial orators of today choose to recall. It did not attack the foreign spheres of influence as such. It did not challenge the assaults on Chinese sovereignty. It merely insisted, as America had insisted before, on equal trading rights in the new foreign leaseholds and acquisitions. The notes were tentative, and committed nobody to anything. In fact less than a year after John Hay's note-writing, the powers were again united, and the United States with them, in the bloody suppression of a Chinese revolt. After the Boxer Rebellion had been put down amid much bloodshed and looting by an allied military expedition, China was forced to yield up more crippling indemnities and to give to the powers the right to maintain permanent garrisons in Peking and Tientsin and along the railway that joined them. (The United States, with a characteristic onset of post-factum conscience, remitted its share of the indemnity for educational purposes in China.) Russia, whose growing pressure in the north made her Britain's principal foe and who was, in fact, the main object of the Open Door notes, used the occasion to occupy all of Manchuria and extracted further concessions as the price of her slow withdrawal. The breakdown of the Anglo-American attempt to maintain an open door policy was so complete that even John Hay, with the ink on his notes scarcely dry, tried to enter the United States in the territorial sweepstakes, seeking an American naval base on the Fukien coast. This happened to fall within the sphere already pre-empted by Japan, and Japan balked the American move by reading back to an embarrassed Hay some of his own lofty injunctions about foregoing gains at Chinese expense. England, meanwhile, had made other arrangements for the defense of its interests. It made temporary bilateral terms with Germany in Europe and, in 1902, entered into an alliance with Japan in Asia. This primed Japan for its attack on Russia two years later.

Japan's attack on Russia had not only British but also American blessings and assistance. The Treaty of Portsmouth, under which Japan took over from Russia what Russia had taken from China, was negotiated and signed on American soil under American auspices. The United States silently acquiesced when Japan then compelled China to sign new pacts validating the new Japanese gains. Then it went further and entered into a secret compact with Japan on its own.

Strictly in the style of the European freebooters, this was a memorandum signed in July, 1905, by William Howard Taft and the Japanese foreign minister. In it the United States recognized and accepted Japanese control over Korea in return for a Japanese pledge not to assail the American position in the Philippines. This was followed in 1908 by the more formal Root-Takahira agreement, under which the United States recognized the "status quo" in China, thereby formally accepting Japan's "special position" in Manchuria.

During the next few years, however, American attempts to establish capital footholds in Manchurian railways and in joint loans for capital development in China all came to nothing. The Japanese, replacing the Russians of 1900, had now recognizably become the principal obstacle to a more prosperous American position in China. And it also had become plain that this obstacle could be overcome only by force of arms. "I do not believe," said Theodore Roosevelt in 1910, "in our taking any position anywhere unless we can make good; and as regards Manchuria, if the Japanese choose to follow a course of conduct to which we are adverse, we cannot stop it unless we are prepared to go to war, and a successful war about Manchuria would require a fleet as good as that of England plus an army as good as that of Germany. The Open Door policy in China was an excellent thing, and I hope it will be a good thing in the future . . . but as has been proved by the whole history of Manchuria, alike under Russia and Japan, the Open Door policy, as a matter of fact, completely disappears as soon as a powerful nation determines to disregard it and is willing to run the risk of war rather than forego its intention." *

With the outbreak of the European war in 1914, Japan seized the advantage it offered. As already noted, Japan attacked and captured Germany's holdings in China and in the South Pacific and tried, with its Twenty-one Demands, to reduce all of China to the position of a Japanese vassal. The United States countered weakly, first acknowledging Japan's "special relation" to China and then resorting to the doctrine of non-recognition, first enunciated in May, 1915, by Secretary of State William Jennings Bryan. Japan, however, had already in a series of secret agreements with Britain, France, and Russia,

* Quoted by Dulles, pp. 128-9.

secured prior acceptance of its new gains in return for its assistance
in driving German interests out of Asia. In 1917 it sought similar
assurances from the United States. The result was again an American
equivocation. In the Lansing-Ishii notes of that year, Japan genuflected
toward the Open Door and the United States announced its recognition of Japan's "special position" in China, especially in "the part to
which her possessions are contiguous."

At Versailles the Japanese insisted upon writing their gains into
the peace treaty, and after much hesitation President Wilson finally
yielded. Ironically, it was this stunning betrayal of China by the
Great White Friend in the White House that unloosed the swift
currents of Chinese nationalism immediately following the war. The
American sell-out of China at Versailles was the signal for the great
student uprising of May 4, 1919, which precipitated the greatest
national struggle in China's history.

Toward the immense movement that now rose, bringing with it
the greatest promise of freedom China had ever glimpsed, the United
States, in common with all other powers, maintained an attitude of
wary hostility. It feared the new Bolshevik Russian influence. It feared
the radicalism of the aroused Chinese masses. It feared the assault
they soon began to make on all the entrenched positions of foreign
privilege in the country. The shelling of Nanking in March, 1927,
when the nationalists took that city, was a joint British-American
operation. When Chiang Kai-shek proved to be the instrument for
checking the mass movement in full stride, American interests in
China threw their support wholeheartedly behind him. In the years
that followed, Chiang Kai-shek enjoyed the financial, moral, political,
and indirectly the military support of the United States. His campaigns against the insurgent peasantry in central China were financed
in some part by American funds, spearheaded in some degree by
American warplanes and weapons, and were occasionally even directly
assisted by American gunboats of the Yangtze patrol.

Meanwhile, the United States had embarked upon a diplomatic
counteroffensive directed against Japan and had forced a wide Japanese retreat. At the Washington Conference of 1921–22 Japan was
forced to accept the short end of a 5–5–3 naval ratio with Britain and
the United States. It was forced to pull out of the Siberian adventure

on which it had embarked in 1918 and which failed because Bolshevik resistance was too strong. It was forced to give up most of its Shantung gains and to sign the nine power pact formally guaranteeing China's political and administrative integrity. The United States in fact in 1922 and 1923 imposed upon Japan a diplomatic retreat comparable to Russia's action in 1895 in forcing Japan to give up the fruits of its first war against China. In the latter case the Russian action led to war between Japan and Russia within a decade. In this new situation, the Japanese resort to arms first against China and eventually against the United States was equally inevitable.

During the ten years between the beginning of Japan's continental drive in 1931 and its attack on Pearl Harbor in 1941, American diplomacy did all it could to balk Japanese designs while American business, ironically, did everything it could to further them. This fact by no means disproved the idea that a country is animated by its economic interests in its foreign relations. It simply testified to the shortsightedness and particular cupidity of some American business men. The government was trying to defend what it considered to be their long range economic and strategic interests. Individual businessmen, however, could not forego the profits in hand. History is filled with occasions in which patriotism has yielded to profit, long-range interests to short-range gains. It is one of the characteristic contradictions in the functioning of modern capitalist nationalism.

The American diplomatic resistance to Japan was a failure. Japan had chosen its time too well, calculated the odds too shrewdly. It had Anglo-French support on two counts: the Japanese drive promised to usher in a new dismemberment of China and the restoration of well defined spheres of influence and, secondly, Japan's drive meshed into the creation of a *cordon sanitaire* around the Soviet Union which was at that time the core of Anglo-French policy in Europe and the basis, equally, of British support for reviving German military power. Thus in the councils of the League of Nations, American pressure from the sidelines for concerted resistance to Japan was ineffectual. The League confined itself to mild acts of censure. Diplomatically isolated and unwilling and unable to go to war, the United States simply made the diplomatic record. Henry L. Stimson, then Secretary of

State, adopted the non-recognition policy initiated by Bryan in 1915. But this nowise halted the Japanese drive.

This drive, on the other hand, was immensely assisted, and in the basic sense really made possible, by Japan's ability to buy key materials on the American market. In 1938 alone, the second year of Japan's all-out offensive against China proper, the United States provided Japan with 90.9 per cent of her copper imports, 90.4 per cent of her scrap iron and steel, 82.7 per cent of ferro alloys, 76.9 per cent of aircraft and aircraft parts, 65.6 per cent of her petroleum, 64.7 per cent of vehicles and vehicle parts, and 45.5 per cent of her lead.* This American assistance to Japan continued in volume through 1940 and half of 1941. It was profitable business no matter how many Chinese lives it would cost or how many American lives it was going to cost. It continued to be profitable almost until, with the Japanese attack on Pearl Harbor, it became more profitable and somewhat more practical to sell the goods of war to the American government itself. And that did not occur until the basic antagonism, simmering so long, finally reached the point of explosion.

THE STAKE

The haggard ghosts of the 400 million customers in China still sit in at all the councils where American Far Eastern policy is made. They are still the chief American stake in China and that stake is still an unrealized dream. All the years of competition and rivalry, of wars and treaties and bloodshed and suffering have been, for the United States, based not on existing realities but on elusive expectations. The classic American defense of the "Open Door" in China, for equality of trade and position, inconsistently and falteringly maintained, has amounted to a defense of "rights" which the United States has never been able to exercise in any important degree.

Ever since 1785, when the *Empress of China* sailed back into New York harbor from its pioneer voyage with its cargo of tea and silk, the dream of wealth to be had in Asia has caught and held the

* *Shall America Stop Arming Japan?* The American Committee for Non-Participation in Japanese Aggression (New York, April, 1940).

imagination and self-interest of American traders. All the vastness of the Pacific basin, so heavily peopled, so rich with needs, so flush with the promise of fabulous profit, has seemed ever to be the ultimate domain for expanding American enterprise and American power. To a great many Americans in important places, it still does. Only this dream has been balked through the years by the self-destructive rivalry among the different powers, by the resulting perpetuation of Chinese backwardness and poverty. Great wealth has been extracted from the East by the expanding Western powers during the last two centuries, but it was done by methods and means that were self-defeating. Western imperialism stunted the development of Asia. It put a premium on Asiatic backwardness. It thwarted the often-stirring Asiatic impulses toward growth. The United States entered the game of spoliation as a neophyte, and by the time it reached its maturity, the game had played itself out. The full energies of everyone engaged in trying to profit from the wealth of Asia were employed in competition for place in a crowded field.

The classic form of mercantile imperialism reached and passed the limited peak of its possibilities long before the United States could play any appreciable role in it. The new higher-powered methods of finance capitalism, American style, encountered political and military rivals. It had to get high-powered enough to beat down its rivals. For a long time, with easier fields elsewhere to conquer, it did not feel compelled to do so. The interesting fact is that through all the many years of the gradual building up of antagonism and rivalry between the United States and Japan, Japan became and remained right up to the very eve of the war America's largest Far Eastern customer and the largest Far Eastern repository of American investment. The political-strategic elements of American Far Eastern policy far outstripped the actual American economic position.

Foreign trade has played a minor role in American economy. With its abundant resources and its huge domestic market, the United States, unlike England, Germany, Japan and other smaller countries, has never until quite recently been under relentless compulsion to achieve a large volume of exports. Nor, except for a few crucially important items, has it been very dependent upon imports. American exports in 1935 were equivalent to only about 5 per cent of the national income, and in very few categories of American production does production for export exceed 5 per cent of the total. The American share in world trade as a whole before the war was about 10 per cent. Only relatively small groups in relatively narrow sectors of American economy have had any consistently serious interest in foreign trade. In its main divisions, American economy was better served for many years by heavy restrictions on such trade, by high protective tariffs which limited international exchanges and fostered the growth of competitive industries within its own borders.

Of this relatively small American foreign trade, Far Eastern trade was one of the smaller parts, running to about 19 per cent of the total. In the peak years of 1927–31 America's Far Eastern trade came to an annual average of just under one billion and a half dollars. In the years 1931–35 the average dropped to about half that sum. This trade with immense Asia was only about half as great as trade with tiny Europe. In 1935 the United States sold more to the 11 million people of Canada than it did to the hundreds of millions of the Far East.*

There are some striking facts about this trade. The bulk of it was not with China, the dreamland of 400 million friendly customers, but with tight, tiny, hostile Japan, which became America's third best foreign customer. Again, the most important American imports came not from China, its greatest potential friend, nor from Japan, its major potential enemy, but from Southeast Asia, the colonial domain of Britain and Holland, from the Indies and Malaya which provided this country with 90 per cent of its crude rubber and more than three-quarters of its tin. American trade with the 400 millions of China was about equal to its trade with the 16 million people of the Philippines, each accounting for 19 per cent of the total American Far Eastern trade.

Another notable fact is that America's imports from Asia were more important than its exports to Asia. The silk, crude rubber, tin, tung oil, hemp, coconut and palm oils, carpet wool, spices, that it secured from the East were of a strategic and industrial importance out of all proportion to their specific dollar value or their importance in the American foreign trade picture as a whole. In most of these

* Miriam S. Farley, *The American Stake in the Far East* (New York, 1938).

specific instances, American industry was almost wholly dependent
upon Far Eastern sources. Only in the recent wartime experience did
necessity mother substitutes which may in time alter the degree of
this dependence. American exports to Asia, on the other hand, consisting in the main of cotton, wheat, tobacco, relatively small quantities of machinery and machine products and petroleum products,
were, with the possible exception of cotton, of no great importance
to American agriculture or industry as a whole. Such, at any rate, was
the picture up to the eve of the war with Japan. Since then American
production and national income have more than doubled, and if these
higher levels are to be maintained foreign trade will have to play a
larger part in American calculations than ever before.

American investments in the Far East similarly have never
attained any great relative importance. Precise figures on foreign
investments are apparently not easy to determine, to judge from the
wide disparities in various studies made of the subject. But the proportions shown in the following tables * give an approximately accurate picture of the relative position of American Asiatic investments
to American foreign investments as a whole and to the investments
of other countries in China in particular. The third table shows the
distribution, by percentage, of American investments in the different
countries.

U. S. INVESTMENTS IN ASIA IN RELATION TO TOTAL
U. S. FOREIGN INVESTMENTS, 1930

	Per cent
Europe	31.44
Latin America	25.57
Canada and Newfoundland	25.15
West Indies	7.87
Asia	6.53
Australia and New Zealand	2.68
Africa	.76
	100.00

* Adapted from tables in *Economic Handbook of the Pacific Area* (New York,
1934), pp. 336, 340, 355.

U. S. Investments in China in Relation to Other Foreign Investments, 1931

	Per cent
Great Britain	36.7
Japan	35.1
Russia	8.4
United States	6.1
France	5.9
All others	7.8
	100.00

U. S. Investments in Asiatic Countries, 1930

	Per cent
Japan	43.4
Netherlands East Indies	19.7
Philippines	16.3
China	12.7
Others	7.9
	100.00

These figures are sufficiently eloquent of the minor place occupied by American investments in all Asia and especially in China. Again, Japan is seen to have been a more fruitful and attractive source of investment than China. In China the total American investment of about $200 million was a negligible fraction of the prewar holdings there of other powers. As a sum it comes to only two-thirds of what Americans were spending annually for ice cream in 1939. The entire American investment in Asia, amounting to something between $800 million and $1 billion, is smaller than the total spent by Americans for cigarettes in a single year. China, the great reservoir of untapped hopes and unrealized profits, drew this small amount of capital because it offered small certainty of return. The interpower rivalries and the chronic internal dislocation largely due to these rivalries have made China a bad risk. Thus, about two-thirds of the whole American interest is concentrated in the single city of Shanghai, and most of the balance in the city of Tientsin. Right up to the time of the war with

Japan the great Chinese hinterland was still largely innocent of contact with the American investment dollar.

Measured against these figures alone, or for that matter against the total figure of American foreign investment, the cost of the recent war assumes particularly grotesque proportions. The United States spent more in a single day of war than the total of its whole investment in China. It took only three days to spend as much as its total investment in all Asia. This comparison suggests something of the insanity of the system under which we live. Still even this fact has to be looked at consistently: the United States was not defending what it had in Asia. It was defending what it wanted in Asia. The immense disproportion suggests merely that while war is not exactly a profitable way of securing investments, it has been apparently the only way of preventing a rival from securing them. In any case, it is the people as a whole that pays for wars. The major investors who profit from foreign investment profit immensely from war as well.

The American economic stake in China, however, is not at all the piddling trade that has been built up there or the negligible investments that American interests have made there. The stake is in the future of Asia as these interests see it. It lies in the relation between the ultimate industrialization of that vast continent and the role therein that American capital and capital goods can play. If, they persist, American enterprise and capital could operate unchallenged and in a stable field, the possibilities would be limitless, the promised profits beyond calculation. Such has been, and such still is, for what it is worth, the real economic stake of American capital in Asia.

The only territorial stake of the United States in Asia has been the Philippine archipelago, a tight swarm of warm islands lying in the South China Sea and inhabited by some 16 million people of Malay origin. The 48-year American colonial enterprise came to a formal close on July 4, 1946, with the grant of the islands' long-promised political independence. The orators of the day and the editorial writers viewed the occasion in a fine glow of vindicated morality as a triumph for American-style democracy and proof of the non-imperialist character of American power. The high virtue of the

American role in the Philippines has long been a cardinal source of American self-satisfaction, both at the classroom history level and in the interplay of Asiatic politics. This role has, of course, not been above reproach, but the American-Philippine relationship has unquestionably been different in many ways from the classic colonial relationship; and these differences are worth examining.

The islands were taken from Spain in a simple act of imperialist grab carried out in the classic tradition. American missionaries at the time hailed the event with thanksgiving, looking upon it as an assumption of greater American responsibility in the Far East, assuring greater protection and greater support for American mission enterprise. American traders thought the islands would be an outpost through which they could funnel an ever increasing flow of American goods into Asiatic commerce. The leading jingo patriots of the time, led by Theodore Roosevelt and Henry Cabot Lodge, regarded it as the logical extension, across the Pacific, of America's manifest destiny. Whether it was for some or all of these ends, the United States did take over the islands, ruthlessly put down the Filipino independence movement led by Aguinaldo in a bitter war that lasted for several years, and then endeavored, by trial and error, to fit the new colony into the American Pacific scheme of things.

This did not prove simple, nor could it be made to fit the conventional colonial formula. The relationship of the huge United States, with its population of more than a hundred million, its industrial and agricultural abundance, to a tiny archipelago with scarcely a dozen million people, could not be compared, say, to the relation of tiny Britain to huge India or tiny Holland to the populous Indies. In the latter cases, the economic tie between mother country and colony was of vital importance to the mother country. The colonies formed an integral and even indispensable part of the imperial economy. This never was and never could become true of the tie between the Philippines and the United States. On the contrary, the development of the principal Filipino cash crop for export, sugar, collided with powerful competition in the United States, the Hawaiian sugar interests, the beet sugar growers of the West, and American-dominated Cuban sugar interests. Throughout the decades of American rule in the Philippines, these interests lobbied powerfully for severing the link to the islands and placing them outside the American tariff walls. It is to the American sugar lobby above all that the Filipinos owe the independence which they have now been granted.

American financial interest in the islands remained small. On the eve of the recent war, American investments in the Philippines totalled about $200 million. American trade with the Philippines amounted, in 1932, to 4.3 per cent of America's total foreign trade and 19 per cent of the American Far Eastern trade. Imports from the Philippines (sugar, hemp, coconut oil and other coconut derivatives, etc.) accounted for about 5 per cent of all American imports. American exports to the Philippines (cotton goods, mineral oils, iron and steel products, meat and dairy products, etc.) accounted for two per cent of all American exports.

But while this American economic interest remained small, and from the over-all standpoint of American economy was of negligible importance, for the Philippines it became the be-all and end-all of economic existence. Philippines trade with the United States forming only 4.3 per cent of American foreign trade amounted to 74 per cent of the Philippines foreign trade. The entire economy of the islands was shaped by the production of its export crops, primarily sugar, which alone accounted for half of all Filipino exports, provided some 40 per cent of all the island railway revenues and paid in about 15 per cent of the total island tax revenues. The lack of balance in the economy became so acute that despite the islands' large rice production it became necessary to import in varying degrees and quantities virtually every item of food in the Filipino diet.*

Politically, the American performance as a colonial power was in some ways an improvement on that of other powers, but it was still not quite the show of disinterested benevolence described in the Fourth of July oratory. For nearly twenty years after the conquest, the Americans ruled by force, sitting on top of a persistent independence movement by sheer weight. The gradual grant of freer political institutions after 1916 fostered the growth of an unsavory political cliquism dominated by the island ruling class, an amalgam of mestizos, or mixtures of various bloods, offshoots of the old Spanish bureaucracy, and, in the role of landlord, banker, and money-lender, the

* *Economic Handbook of the Pacific*, pp. 84, 121.

Catholic Church. The Filipino peasantry and plantation workers remained in a condition of serfdom, largely illiterate and with no economic or political rights. The political régime that took shape under the beneficent hand of American democracy was the one-party dictatorship of the Nacionalistas, dominated by Manuel Quezon. Under this régime all political oppositions and popular or radical movements were held down, by legal or illegal means.

Strategically, the islands were in theory at least a bastion against Japanese expansion. The military value of the islands was, of course, never exploited. This was due in part to the inherent checks within the United States on military preparedness, in part to the constant internal American pressure against retaining the Philippines, and in part to the general underestimation of Japanese military strength that pervaded American military circles right up to the time of Pearl Harbor. So when the Japanese did finally attack the islands, they proved indefensible. Some Filipino forces fought to the end alongside the weak American garrison. After the Japanese victory some of these elements, joined by much larger insurgent peasant bands in the interior, carried on guerrilla war against the conquerors.

While these people fought in the hills, however, the ruling caste produced for the Japanese a large body of willing collaborators. Almost the entire Filipino government bureaucracy entered into the new Japanese dispensation. The only real continuing resistance to the Japanese came from the peasants who had been forcibly suppressed under the old régime, were bitterly hunted down by the Japanese, and were attacked again after the American reconquest. Organized into the Hukbalahap, these peasants often seized power in their villages, took over the land, set up local communes. Suppression of these inconvenient radicals was almost the first item on the agenda of the new independent régime that came into being July 4, 1946.

After the American reconquest, the same men who had worked with the Japanese continued, in the main, in power. Manuel Roxas, a leading representative of the type of Filipino politico who played both sides of the street during the war, won the presidency of the commonwealth in the machine-dominated elections early in 1946. Under his rule, the same old gang of Filipino politicos prepared to make what they could out of the new condition of independence.

The conditions of the grant provided a period of twenty years during which Filipino products would gradually pass outside of American tariff barriers. This posed for the islands the problem of recasting their entire economy. Their course would be shaped in part by the continuing internal struggle of the peasants for the land and the people generally for a higher standard of living. It would be shaped more decisively, perhaps, by events outside that would determine what kind of world the Philippines could take their place in as a new independent state.

For the time being their position is defined by the fact that the American military-strategic hold in the islands has been carefully retained. Whatever their internal development, they are still expected to form part of the chain of island bases with which the United States apparently now intends to gird itself for future struggle in the Pacific.

THE MYTH GLORIOUS

Such has been the record and such the stake of the American interest and the American position in the Far East. Out of this history came the collision with Japan and it came as unavoidably as the climax of a Greek tragedy. Out of this collision came the victory, the establishment of American supremacy in the Pacific basin. The consequences of this victory, the present role and policies of the United States in the Pacific, flow just as inescapably from this pattern of the past. They are shaped by the same competition for power which has marked the whole course up to now. The bumbling, the contradictions, the stupidities, the errors, and the failures, do not modify this historical conception. They are simply part of it.

Alongside this American reality there has also grown up the American myth. Part of this myth is the conception that Americans have of themselves. But even more important in it is the conception of Americans acquired by Asiatics in varying forms and degrees. This myth is in the main an unsubstantial dream filled with unrealized images. But it acquired objective reality because so many people believed in it. In the aftermath of the war with Japan for a brief time it guided the thinking and acts of millions.

The American myth in Asia was compounded of many things. It was made up of remoteness: the United States was a distant and shining temple of virtue and righteousness, where men were like gods amid unending plenty. It was made up of awe: the United States was unimaginable power, a country that could suffer crushing blows and then come back to the skies and coasts of Asia, conquer the mountains, batter down the seemingly invincible conqueror of only a few years before. It was made up of half-truths: the United States was a country that believed in freedom. Its own people were free. It was granting freedom to the Philippines. It had nothing, nothing at all in common with other Western countries, or Japan, which lived by the fruits of colonial slavery.

In a continent heavy with superstition and ancient beliefs, and scant in its knowledge of the outside world, the belief grew and existed that the United States would be both altruistic and wise: altruistic enough to side with the cause of freedom for its own sake, wise enough to see that continued imperialism in the British, Dutch, French, and Japanese style would bring no peace anywhere. A great many people who had heard about it seriously believed that the Atlantic Charter meant the end of the colonial and semicolonial system. Some believed that the United States, if only out of enlightened self-interest, would stand by the Charter and thereby guarantee their liberation from foreign rule.

There was also another belief: that Americans were a different breed of men, practicing democrats who stood for and fought for and would deliver justice for everybody. Few Americans who came among the Indians, Burmese, Chinese, Koreans, Indochinese, and Indonesians in the various honeymoon periods of initial contact could fail to be affected and even a little exhilarated by the way they were set apart from all other Westerners as the bearers of the torch of liberty. This mood, to be sure, never lasted very long on either side, but it was always there, like an elusive asset that somehow could never be turned to account.

These ideas existed in varying forms at different levels. They percolated in a kind of mist that rose obscurely and drifted among the shifting winds of the time. It would be difficult to trace them precisely. The vast majority of Asiatics had little or no direct contact with Americans before the war, and limited contact with them after the war began. Where they came, they came like men from another planet with their fabulous machines, their speed, their shattering force and energy that flew over and cut through mountains and filled the skies with roaring power. A minority, largely urban, had an earlier set of impressions, gained from missionaries, from closer contact with American business, from moving pictures, from wartime radio propaganda, from the speeches and personality of President Roosevelt, from the broadcast and rebroadcast phrases of the four freedoms and all the pledges for the future painted in shining colors. What kind of mind image filtered down to the great masses in the limitless countrysides of Asia would be difficult to say. But in varying degrees and permeating greater or lesser sections of the various populations, it is a fact that the name of the United States clearly represented a distant dream that would one day spring alive and bring with it felicity for all.

This idea had no basis in fact. All history contradicted it. All experience flouted it. Yet the belief in it was so pervasive that it became a political factor of the first magnitude. It is not an exaggeration to say that on the morrow of Japan's collapse this represented by far the greatest political asset ever enjoyed by any nation anywhere in our time. The swift dissipation of this asset right after the victory over Japan was by the same token one of the most extravagant and prodigal examples of conspicuous waste ever recorded in the annals of the nations.

A great deal of this feeling about the United States was naïve, like all simple notions of good and evil. But there was often a lot more to it than that. Many lifelong nationalists, politically experienced and sophisticated, shared much of the general hope. They did not do so because they thought the United States would act in Asia solely out of sentimental principle or humanitarian impulse. They calculated, in their own way, from considerations of American self-interest and their own self-interest as they saw it. Their reasoning went about as follows:

The United States had no stake at all in the restoration of the old imperial, colonial, or semicolonial status quo. On the contrary, after defeating Japan, the United States would have every real interest in supporting sweeping change right across the face of the continent. In the first place, the old system of divided and balanced power had led directly to the bloody, costly war. This war had not only imperiled America's position as a world power but might indeed have imperiled its national existence. In this war, moreover, the old system had exposed its fatal weaknesses. Under Japan's attack early in 1942 the colonies proved indefensible. With relatively small forces the Japanese inflicted swift and humiliating defeats on the Americans, the British, the Dutch. They had not even had to fight the French, who capitulated earlier without a struggle. The various colonial administrations had proved feeble, corrupt, corroded, incapable of commanding any assistance or solidarity among the peoples they governed. Singapore was more than a demonstration of British imperial degeneration. It was the symbol of the end of an era that could never be resurrected. The subject peoples, without a stake in the struggle, stood passively by or else helped the Japanese invaders, accepting the promise of "Asia for the Asiatics" or more cynically seeking to gain what they could from this providential falling out between the contenders for mastery. Everywhere the Japanese experienced no difficulty in enlisting willing collaborators. The Japanese failure to exploit these advantages, already examined in these pages, had equally shown in its own way that colonial or colonial-type domination in Asia could not longer work satisfactorily.

The United States, surely, the argument went on, would understand this much of the lessons of these gigantic events. Preservation of a more stable peace would now, surely, be a more compelling factor in American policy than preservation of the old empires in whatever form. This had to mean American support for full national independence for the colonial countries. Whatever the unsettling effects of such a radical change, it would still offer more real security than a restoration of the status quo ante or the acceptance of a long-drawn-out contest in which the ruling powers would seek to preserve the essence while yielding some of the form of their sovereignty. Moreover, the years of Japanese domination had left most of the countries of Asia economically prostrate. The British, French, or Dutch ability to meet the needs of reconstruction—not to say expansion—simply did not exist. This reconstruction, in southern Asia as well as in China, would be immensely profitable to American economy, ensuring full American employment and production, and it would be stable and fruitful because built on a new foundation of political equality.

Such, as far as it can be reduced from scores of conversations all the way from Delhi to Seoul to Saïgon to Batavia, was the hopeful picture of the American position seriously entertained by many conscious Asiatic nationalists. From it they concluded that American postwar aims would necessarily coincide with the aims of Asiatic nationalism. From it they concluded, at the very least, that while they could not trust the promises of the British, the French, or the Dutch, they could trust the Americans. But they were disappointed. They were confused. They began, in a short span of time, the passage from belief to doubt to open hostility. This process took place everywhere. It was the most spectacular fact of the first postwar months, the puncturing of the American myth, the rude destruction of hopes that never had any foundation in the first place. Watching it happen, in country after country following Japan's collapse, was like witnessing the crumbling of castles in the sky.

THE MYTH PUNCTURED

In the broadest and most fundamental sense, the chief American failure was the failure to stand for change. The United States had spoken for a new order of things. It acted now for the old order of things. By what it did and by what it failed to do, the American victory brought no beginning of a solution, nor the promise of a solution, to the problems of dislocation, upheaval, conflict, and nationalist aspiration. In the struggles that erupted among colonial peoples to prevent the return of their old masters, the United States stood in fact not with the rebelling subjects but with the returning rulers. In every actual political situation in which it became involved, the United States stood not with the partisans of social change but with the defenders of archaic conservatism. Peace itself remained elusive since the United States passed out of its victory over Japan headlong into a fresh competition for power with Russia.

There was no serious attempt in the councils of the victors to grapple with the question of colonies, which lies so close to the heart of the war-making rivalries of imperialism. Instead the issue was submerged, in the United Nations, in a purely abstract discussion of the idea of trusteeships. This idea, first advanced at the Yalta Conference in February, 1945, was extremely limited. It was to apply only to former League of Nations mandates, to territories seized from the enemy in the Second World War, and to such other territories as any nation might voluntarily place under trusteeship through the United Nations. This left untouched the whole issue of colonies held by Allied powers. It provided, in effect, only for a new system of control to replace the old mandate system. It left the older empires unaffected. At the San Francisco Conference a few months later, there was a long debate over the proposal to include in the United Nations charter an innocuous declaration that committed nobody to anything but included the idea that the ultimate goal for colonial territories would be their independence. In the end the issue was settled by a shoddy little compromise which equivocally bracketed the terms "self-government" and "independence" as vague goals for the indefinite future. Every suggestion that in the slightest way threatened to limit the governing power of the colonial nations was hedged and qualified to leave these nations complete latitude to deal with their colonies as they saw fit. The fate of the subjected peoples of the world was left up to the good will and good intentions of their rulers. This was not confronting the colonial problem. It was abdicating it.

The United Nations charter left it entirely up to the powers to do whatever they found it useful or necessary to do to safeguard their interests. This was being accomplished in the manner of the past, by private agreements slicing up territories, fixing spheres of influence, pressuring for offensive gains or countering with defensive alignments. It was at the same Yalta conference that the Americans secretly handed over to Russia, at its demand, not only recognition of its "preeminent position" in Manchuria but outright possession of the Kuriles, in itself a violation of the trusteeship plan first outlined at the same meeting. Sometime during the war, similarly, Roosevelt and Churchill obviously exchanged quids and quos concerning the respective American and British spheres of interest in Asia. This has not yet shown up in the documents and it may take quite some time to do so. But the course of events has plainly enough confirmed the existence of such an understanding. Roosevelt evidently assured Churchill a free British hand in the affairs of all southern Asia and secured from Churchill acknowledgment that all of the rest of Asia, including China and Japan and the Western Pacific, would be the predominant concern of the United States.

In any case, the fact is that the United States associated itself with the Pax Britannica imposed upon Southeast Asia after Japan collapsed. This included armed resistance (with American lend-lease weapons and equipment) to the attempts of the Annamites in Indochina and the Indonesians in Java to prevent the return of the French and Dutch to power. French troops returned to Indochina, carried from France in American ships, and marched into battle against Annamite insurgents armed, from .45 caliber revolvers to tanks and artillery, with American weapons, and dressed, from head to foot, in American uniforms. In Java, the British fought the Indonesians, bombing and strafing their villages, using American lend-lease fighter planes and maintaining supply and liaison with American lend-lease transport planes. Their vehicles, tanks, weapons, were in considerable measure of the same origin. Although not maintaining any troops in the area, the United States was in fact formally associated with the Southeast Asia Command throughout most of the period of these operations. The American flag flew alongside the British, French, and Dutch over the headquarters at Cathay House in Singapore and in front of the British headquarters in Batavia.

If there had ever been any thought among American policy makers of seeking any new dispensation in Southeast Asia, it disappeared long before the war ended. While the East Indies were still within the prospective military jurisdiction of MacArthur's command, he signed a civil affairs agreement with the Dutch which acknowledged that civil administration in Indonesia, when invaded and reconquered by the Allies, would pass at once into Dutch hands. With respect to Indochina, Roosevelt had once publicly intimated the possibility of a new status for that colony as a result of the French capitulation to Japan. But when it came down, in the wake of the war's end, to a strong Annamite rebellion against returning French power, the United States promptly concluded a credit arrangement with France for supply of vehicles and other "relief" equipment to French authorities in Indochina. To the stunned Annamites this agreement came as a virtual American endorsement of the French reconquest. Protests and appeals were unavailing.

When press reports from Java made it too embarrassingly plain what use American military equipment was being put to by the British, the State Department finally acted: it asked the British to remove American insignia from the offending equipment! The United States never took a step to check the cynical British use of Japanese troops to fight both the Annamites and the Indonesians. The British course was to force the nationalists by all and any means to accept the return of their old sovereignties first and to negotiate some new status afterward. By its every visible act in the eyes of the fighting nationalists, the United States associated itself wholly with this policy.

It was while blood was flowing freely both in Indochina and Java that President Truman made his declaration of foreign policy principles in a speech on October 27, 1945. Among his "twelve points"—drawing again on the language of the Atlantic Charter— the embattled Annamites and Indonesians could read the following:

We believe in the eventual return of sovereign rights and self-government to all peoples who have been deprived of them by force. . . .

We believe that all peoples who are prepared for self-government should be permitted to choose their own form of government by their own freely expressed choice without interference from any foreign source. That is true in Europe, in Asia, in Africa, as well as in the Western Hemisphere. . . .

We shall refuse to recognize any government imposed upon any nation by the force of any foreign power. . . .

On their bloody little battlegrounds, the Annamites and Javanese could only conclude that formal American policy was one thing, and actual American practice was another; that in principle America was on their side, while in fact it was on the side of the British, the

French, and the Dutch. If they resisted the full tide of their disillusionment, it was only because they still hoped against hope that they had not been so entirely wrong in their expectations. After all, they needed help, so badly.

The American policy in Japan, so persuasively expedient from the standpoint of a MacArthur, was also a little difficult for many people in other parts of Asia to understand. It looked to them very much as if the Americans were ready to allow the hated Japanese more relative self-government, freedom, and independence, than they were willing to see granted to any of Japan's recent victims. Koreans and Annamites and Javanese considered themselves at least as capable as the Japanese of running their own affairs. After all it was not they, but the Japanese, who had plunged all of Asia and the world into the bitter agony of invasion and war. It was not they, but the Americans, the British, the Japanese, the French, and the Dutch who had proved incapable of organizing any kind of secure peace in the Far East. Nevertheless after the war with Japan had been fought to its close, the Japanese Emperor was allowed to sit on his throne. Japan retained not only its national identity but the essence of its old régime, while in the colonies the efforts of subject peoples to achieve their national identities were uniformly frustrated. And as a further shocking and cynical indignity, the victorious powers did not hesitate to use Japanese troops in this process wherever they lacked sufficient force of their own to suppress nationalist movements. This was not quite the picture people had of what American victory over Japan would mean in Asia.

In India, hopeful feelings had long since dissolved. In the beginning, in 1942, many Indian nationalists had actually looked upon the American troops arriving there as an army of liberation that would free them from British rule. The mission of William Phillips, the next year, heightened the impression that the United States intended to intervene in Indian affairs on the side of the nationalists. But the American army proved to have no interest in Indian matters, and American soldiers, on the individual level, scarcely behaved like apostles of freedom. The Phillips mission, moreover, was abortive. Their naïve notions exploded, the Indian nationalists swung sharply to an attitude of hostility. After the war, while the British were probing for a settlement that would be most satisfactory to them, Pandit Nehru publicly declared that the United States was "underwriting the British Empire" and that this would lead to new wars in Asia.

In Korea, as we have seen, the Russian-American partition established after the war's end smothered the hopes of freedom that sprang so brightly into life with Japan's collapse. Koreans felt that freedom was in their grasp after forty years of subjection to the Japanese. Instead they found themselves helplessly caught between the Russian and American millstones that pressed upon them. Americans who had been greeted as liberating heroes in September were stoned in the streets in December.

In China, similarly, American policy and practice was dictated primarily by the exigencies of its competition with Russia. In their determination to keep the ultrareactionary Kuomintang in power, the Americans became embroiled in a civil war. American transport, by air and sea, played a key role in reestablishing the Kuomintang hold on most of the country. While sponsoring negotiations for a Kuomintang-Communist truce and seeking, with utmost difficulty, to achieve some kind of internal balance that would assure a Chinese régime friendly to American interests, the Americans threw their main weight behind the Kuomintang. When the Communists came close to conquering Manchuria, it was American transport that moved government forces into more favorable positions. It was American pressure, in short, that kept the internal struggle for self-determination in China from finding its own level.

To the millions of Chinese who, rightly or wrongly, for better or worse, followed the Communist leadership because the Kuomintang was so corrupt and oppressive, the United States emerged as the backer and supporter of Chinese reaction. American involvement in a shooting civil war looked to them a good deal more like old-style imperialist intervention than anything resembling a defense of democratic progress. Looked at in terms of the American-Russian competition, implicit in the whole situation, the American acts were such that Russia gained by doing nothing, or nearly nothing. The American-made mess in China would sooner or later be of utmost service in the developing design of Russian policy. Meanwhile in every Chinese city, soldiers of the United States, the stanch friend and ally of China, were being invited and urged by huge demonstrations to get out of China.

The engrossing idea of "security" dominated all these American acts. This was the basis of the bloc with England and the consequent disregard of the interests and aspirations of the colonial peoples. This lay back of the intervention in Chinese internal affairs. It governed in important measure the policy in Japan. It was also the reason for the American program for a new string of Pacific bases. Preoccupation with security is just another way of saying preparation for war. And preparation for war allows little room for preserving the rights of others or maintaining moral pretensions.

The Pacific bases plainly demonstrate this fact. They have put the American government into an embarrassing position. The official American position during the war was to disclaim any territorial gains. But with the war over and in the frenetic drive to insure maximum favorable position in the Pacific *vis-a-vis* Russia, the American army and navy insisted upon holding some of the bases it had taken by arms during the war. Since these bases are wanted under exclusive control the United States was not in a position to go too far along even with the mild and limited program for international trusteeship over seized territories, hemmed in and hedged in as it is by every possible protection for the "national" interests of the prospective trustee powers.

The official American preoccupation after the end of the war was not the rebuilding of a world out of the ruins but the fear of Russia and the need for "security" against the Russian threat. America would have kept its armies if immense pressure from the ranks and from among the people at home had not forced swift demobilization. But on the other hand it could go ahead with the manufacture of atom bombs, with provocative Arctic maneuvers, with the Bikini demonstrations of its new atomic power, and a diplomacy in West and East based entirely on the premise of a redivided world. In this there was no impulse to seek a revision of the world setup which would give the renewed threats of conflict a chance to evaporate, no tendency at all to stand on a program to meet the demands of the peoples. In the darkness of the new American-Russian antagonism, there was no glimmer for hopes of peace.

This left the Asiatic peoples in their unrelieved misery. The articulate and decisive minorities among them, at least, had believed that America would stand for change. They discovered that it stood for the status quo. They believed the United States would lead the way to a total revision of national and international relations in Asia upon a wholly new foundation. They discovered that America placed a higher premium upon its bloc with the Western powers than upon upsetting the colonial system. They thought America would stand with peoples fighting for their own freedom. They found that America in reality stood with the powers which limited that freedom. They thought that American principles would ensure American support for a daring program of progressive change. They found that America in practice always supported conservative reaction. They thought America would organize the peace. They found that America was intent upon establishing its own strategic positions by new blocs, new alignments, new land, sea, and air bases, in preparation for further war. They thought America would promote international order. They found that in all its acts it promoted international anarchy.

As these facts dawned, the belief and hope in America that had spread so far and cut so deep began to dissolve. The onset of this disillusionment dominated the postwar aftermath right across Asia. It was visible to the naked eye and audible to the open ear anywhere. The peoples of Asia were discovering America. They were discovering that it offered them no way out nor the beginning of a way out, no new organization of the world that meant anything, no break or promise of a break with the prevailing system of world anarchy. They were discovering that the United States was a Great Power, now the Greatest Power, playing the Great-Power game. There was nothing in it for them but the role of pawns or victims and the prospect of more conflict to come.

11 RUSSIA

Russia is not only the biggest new fact in the world. It is also the most controversial. Unless you are wholly remote from the world of politics, religion, and even literature and the arts—and who is?—you are in one degree or another apologist or opponent of the Soviet Union, critic or defender, friend or foe. Or else you are wondering which you are. This is by no means an academic problem. If you live in Europe you have to decide right now, or else the choice has already been made for you. If you live in the Middle East or China, you will have to decide tomorrow. If you live in the United States, you may have to decide by the day after tomorrow.

Around the question of Russia swirls a host of ideological and emotional arguments, fears and prejudices, honest convictions, and special pleadings. Russia for some represents the specter of communism, for others the betrayal of communism. It is the hope of the future, and it is the blight on the future. It is a beacon for all men or a burden on all men. It can do no right. It can do no wrong. It is totalitarian tyranny and it is the new freedom, full-blown, untarnished and untarnishable. It is socialism wholly made. It is socialism in the making. It is socialism stifled. It is socialism stillborn. It is not socialism at all. It is a firm pillar of world peace. It is the greatest menace to world peace. It is virtue and evil, truth and legend, liberal myth and reactionary fact. It is the birthplace of man's aspirations in our time. And it is their tomb.

This is not the parlor game of twenty questions. It is a matter of the fate of the peoples of the world. Its issues reach into every American home and into the life of everyone everywhere. The development of American relations with Russia will shape the future of the coming generations. The conflict already in course in Europe between the Anglo-American bloc and the Russians has occupied the foreground of international affairs ever since the collapse and surrender of Nazi Germany. But however uneasy and unsettled European affairs remain because of it, the decisive issues between Russia and the

243

United States lie not in the West, but in the East; not in Europe, but in Asia.

Russia is not merely one of the intervening factors in the affairs of Asia. Russia is itself an Asiatic power. The greater part of Russian territory, all the vastness of space between the Urals and the Pacific Ocean, is part of the Asiatic continent. Siberia is broader by a thousand miles than the United States, and in area it is three times larger than China. There are about fifty million Russian Asiatics, all the many tribes blending across the frontiers of Russian and Chinese Turkestan, all the related Mongol strains from Lake Baikal to the Chinese Great Wall. The southern frontier of Asiatic Russia extends from the edges of Afghanistan, where Russian Pamir reaches close to India's northwestern border, to the Amur River, that bounds Manchuria, and to Possiet Bay, just below Vladivostok, facing the Japan Sea. This is a distance of more than 4,000 miles, the longest continuous land frontier on earth.

In the time of the Czars most of Asiatic Russia was a vast wilderness, more primitive and backward than China. In our time this is no longer true. Siberia is already a heavily developed area capable of sustaining itself in war and peace, and its real potentialities for further industrial growth have barely been tapped. Russia is not merely an Asiatic power. It is the greatest Asiatic power, the largest, the strongest, and by pre-atomic weapons, militarily the most unassailable. This fact can never be overlooked in considering the role of Russia in Asia. America and Britain are interlopers from afar, tied to Asia only by the thin lines of global communications. But Russia is resident in Asia, occupying the largest quarter of the largest continental land mass on our planet.

The history of Russian relations with non-Russian Asia falls broadly into three phases: the Czarist imperialist penetration which acquired aggressive form in the nineteenth century and came to an abrupt end with the revolution in 1917; the experimental and short-lived Soviet internationalism which guided Soviet policy on the whole from 1919 to 1927; the Soviet imperialist expansion now taking place.

Czarist imperialism intruded upon China at a time when Russia had barely penetrated and opened its own Siberian wilderness. Early contacts and treaties had to do with fixing the boundaries between the two countries. The Russian entry into the competition of the powers in China took place in a spirit of adventurist grabbing. It was, of course, part of Russia's expansion to its own Pacific frontier, and the effort to secure an all-year Pacific port was a logical outcome of that expansion. But this effort under the Czars in the nineteenth century and in the first years of this century was hopelessly premature when considered in terms of Russia's ability to secure, to defend, and to exploit such an outlet. Internally backward and ruled by a semi-medieval autocracy, Russian power had size and weight, but little more. The Czarist adventures in China were limited, fumbling, and almost always ended in failure. Great lumbering Russia could extort advantages from weak China, but it could not hold its own even against tiny, aggressive Japan. In the closing years of Czarism, Russia actually occupied the junior place in a partnership with Japan for the mutual defense of their respective spheres of influence.

Like the United States, Czarist Russia shared in the middle of the last century in the advantages won in China by the armed forces of Britain and France. Indeed, the Russian and American ministers waited together while the Anglo-French fleets attacked the Chinese forts at Taku Bar in 1858. Together they followed the victors up the river and together they waited their turn to get China's unwilling signature on treaties surrendering large slices of Chinese power and sovereignty. Later when the Russians finally began to build the Trans-Siberian Railway, the principal object of their policy in China became to open a short cut by rail across northern Manchuria to Vladivostok and to secure an ice-free outlet in southern Manchuria. This made all of Manchuria and Korea as well their projected sphere of influence.

When Japan intruded upon this sphere as a result of its victory over China in 1895, it was Russia that organized the diplomatic counteroffensive. Japan was forced to disgorge the positions it had won by force, to give up the Liaotung Peninsula, the ports of Port Arthur and Talienwan (later called Dalny and still later Dairen). The Russians then promptly appropriated these gains for themselves. By "agreement" with China, Russia in 1898 acquired leaseholds at Port Arthur and Talienwan, and the railway rights it sought across

Manchuria. The Boxer Rebellion, in 1900, was the Russian pretext for occupying all of Manchuria and its slow evacuation, spreading over two years, was punctuated by new "agreements" adding to its positions.

In these closing years of the century, all the powers were tearing at the old Chinese Empire like a pack of wolves at the carcass of a downed victim. France had taken Annam and Cambodia. Britain had established its rule over Burma and now took the port of Weihaiwei while Germany took Kiaochow, on the coast of Shantung. But, as we have already noted, it was primarily the Russian advances in Manchuria that motivated the Open Door policy initiated by the United States, under British urging, in 1899. Japan, coveting Manchuria and Korea for its own, ardently supported the Open Door doctrine and finally, in 1904, attacked Russia. The Russians went down to ignominious defeat. A year later they were forced to disgorge what they had earlier forced Japan to disgorge. All the loot passed back to the Japanese, including Port Arthur and Talienwan and the South Manchurian railway rights. Korea became a Japanese protectorate and five years later an outright Japanese colony. China was given no choice but to submit. Russia retained the Chinese Eastern Railway crossing Manchuria in the north, and accepted as its sphere all of northern Manchuria and Mongolia while acknowledging Japanese supremacy in the south. On this basis Russian-Japanese relations were more or less stabilized.

Between 1907 and 1916 Russia and Japan entered into a series of secret agreements culminating in an alliance for the mutual defense of their spheres against the attack of any third party. This partnership ended abruptly in 1917 when Czarism fell. The advent of the Soviet State in Russia upset all the power relationships in China. For more than a decade after the revolution, the Western powers, despite their continuing conflicts among themselves, were compelled in the main to combine against the common menace of Russian Bolshevism.

INTERNATIONALIST RUSSIA

This menace was something new under the sun. The Bolsheviks in those first bitter, bright, costly years of revolution and civil war, were hard-headed internationalists, the first of their kind in the world. For Lenin and Trotsky the revolution did not merely signalize the end of Czarism in Russia. It heralded the downfall of the capitalist system throughout the world. It was the beginning of a new world order based on the social ownership of the means of production. The Bolsheviks did not in the least consider that they were engaged in building a new national power in Russia. They were seeking an end to all national power. They were building not a new Russia, but a new world. Theirs, they believed, was the first in a necessary series of international, socialist revolutions. The break in Russia, as they saw it, was only the snapping of the weakest link in the chains of world capitalism. Lenin said and repeated a thousand times in 1917 and afterward that socialist Russia could not survive alone in a hostile capitalist world. "World revolution" was neither catch phrase nor by-product. It was a necessity. It was, they believed, the only road to the reorganization of the world, the end of national antagonisms and collisions based on conflict for colonies, markets, raw materials. It was the beginning of the use of the world's physical and human resources for advancing society to a higher plane.

Lenin just after the revolution defined internationalism as "the subordination of the interests of the proletarian struggle in one nation to the interests of that struggle on an international scale, and the capability and readiness on the part of one nation which has gained a victory over the bourgeoisie of making the greatest national sacrifices for the overthrow of international capitalism." * For a brief, intense period, this was the spirit which animated Russian Bolshevism, and it brought arrayed against it all the entrenched powers of the world.

The Russian revolution was like a deposit on world socialism, valid only for a short period. That revolution had to extend or else retreat upon itself. It had to become in fact international or else reassume, in some new form, its purely national identity. The Bolsheviks were victorious in the civil war in their own country, and they fought off the military intervention of the powers which lasted until 1922. They triumphed in Russia. But elsewhere their cause failed. Central Europe erupted in revolutions, in Hungary, Austria, Germany, but one after another they fell short of their purpose.

* Statutes of the Third (Communist) International (Moscow, 1920), p. 70.

Russia was in fact isolated. It had to adapt itself to lone existence inside a bristling rim of hostility. Its people weary, its land ravaged, it needed a truce. Internationalism was a tender flower that had to grow strong swiftly or else be choked in the weeds of renewed nationalism. First subtly, then headlong, this choking process began to take place within the Russian Bolshevik régime. It began the shift, now slowly, now perceptibly, now swiftly, from the radical world view to the conservative national view. Out of the desperateness of Russia's isolated situation, it was almost inevitable that instead of "making the greatest national sacrifices for the overthrow of international capitalism," the régime began to seek from elsewhere the greatest international sacrifices for the preservation of Russian national socialism.

This transformation in the character and emphasis of Soviet policy took place over a period of several years. It was not until Lenin's death in 1924 that his uncompromising internationalism began to give way openly to the idea of "socialism in one country" advanced in that year for the first time by Joseph Stalin. During these first years the currents of socialist internationalism and Russian nationalism were in constant conflict and contradiction. It was not until after 1927 that Russian national interests were finally enthroned openly and unabashedly and without contradiction as the foundation of Soviet policy. In the course of this time, there were ample, striking glimpses of what revolutionary diplomacy could look like when applied on the world scene.

This diplomacy produced rage, consternation, and embarrassment in all the imperial chancelleries of the world. From their radio at Tsarskoe Seloe in 1917 and 1918 the Bolsheviks broadcast and rebroadcast the novel notion of a peace without annexations or indemnities. They proposed the end of all subjugation of one nation by another anywhere in the world. In behalf of Russia, the Bolsheviks acted promptly on their own proposal. They publicly repudiated all treaties ever made by the Czarist government at the expense of other nations. To the mortal discomfort of everyone concerned, they pulled out of the Czarist archives and published all the secret treaties concluded before and during the First World War by the various

Allied countries, all the deals for territory and position, for seizures, and for payments.

The Russian Czarist position in China was in particular repudiated and disavowed. Attitudes expressed by Lenin years before in the obscure underground press now became Soviet policy. In 1900, at the time of the suppression of the Boxer Rebellion, Lenin denounced the rulers of Russia for placing "their greedy paws upon China," for robbing China "as ghouls rob corpses." Warning that imperialist policy in China would lead only to further wars, Lenin wrote: "The policy of the Czarist government in China is a criminal policy which is impoverishing, corrupting, and oppressing the people more than ever." * In 1905 Lenin hailed the defeat of the Czarist government at the hands of Japan as "the catastrophe of our worst enemy." Compared to Czarism, he found Japan was "progressive and advanced," and he looked upon Japan's victory as "a blow to backward and reactionary Europe." † It was in this spirit, in 1917, that the leaders of the new Russia approached the issues of international politics. The effects went deep and wide.

The Russian revolution had an enormous indirect influence on all the politics of Asia. The impulses it radiated reached from Mongolia to the farthest Indies, fusing with the deepest roots of the newly growing nationalist movements in all those countries. Its influence was felt to one degree or another in the wave of nationalist rebellions punctuating the postwar decade after 1918 throughout the colonial East. Direct Russian participation or direct Russian influence in most of these events was negligible, existing for the most part only in the frightened newspaper dispatches and headlines of the times. The Communist International was then but newly formed. Most of its parties in the East had scarcely come into being. The catalytic force provided by Russia in the progress of Asiatic nationalism was not the often cited Moscow gold or the machinations of omnipresent agents. It was the force of an example and an idea that assaulted the foundations of imperialism everywhere.

When they turned eastward in search of the support they had failed to win in the West, the Bolsheviks gave their most active at-

* W. I. Lenin, *Works* (Eng. ed.), Vol. IV, pp. 60–63.
† W. I. Lenin, *Sämtliche Werke* (Wien-Berlin), Vol. VII, 1929, p. 57.

tention to China. In a declaration on July 25, 1919, the Soviet government specifically annulled and repudiated "all the secret treaties concluded with Japan, China, and the former Allies: treaties by which the Czar's government, together with its allies, through force and corruption, enslaved the peoples of the Orient, and especially the Chinese nation, in order to profit the Russian capitalists, the Russian landlords, and the Russian generals." Again on October 27, 1920, the Soviet Government in a note to China said:

The Government of the Russian Socialist Federated Soviet Republic declares as void all the treaties concluded by the former government of Russia with China, renounces all the annexations of Chinese territory, all the concessions in China, and returns to China free of charge and forever all that was ravenously taken from her by the Czar's government and by the Russian bourgeoisie.

Three and a half years later, in May, 1924, the Russians finally succeeded in outmaneuvering Japan and the Western powers and wrote this policy into a new treaty with China. It was a revolutionary document. At a blow, it canceled out the whole past unequal relationship and substituted for it a basis of complete equality. It surrendered all the Russian concessions and the privilege of extraterritoriality. The treaty did have certain equivocal features reflecting Russia's nationalist tendencies. The Russians did not return wholly the Chinese Eastern Railway. But they did substitute for the former exclusive Russian control a new Sino-Soviet partnership with an agreement for eventual sole Chinese ownership. Russian policing and garrisoning rights along the line were given up without reservation. In this treaty the Russians also acknowledged Chinese sovereignty over Outer Mongolia, which had actually proclaimed its independence two years earlier during the bitter struggle that took place there between Russian Red forces and the anti-Bolshevik White forces under Baron Ungern von Sternberg. Red troops subsequently withdrew from the country, and Mongolia remained in fact independent and tied to Russia rather than to China. While these provisions left certain problems unsolved, the treaty as a whole was for China unique and without precedent. It was the first equal treaty signed by China with an outside power in modern times. It was the first and only treaty in which China was treated on a basis of complete reciprocity. The effect in China was dazzling. To the other powers, which had done everything in their power to balk the signing of the pact, it was a smarting blow. For the Russians it was an immense propagandistic victory, if only because it showed that they practiced what they preached and were the only real foreign friends of Chinese nationalism.

The new currents of Chinese nationalism, however, were beginning to flow not in Peking where the pact between governments was signed, but in Canton where Sun Yat-sen was leading an open rebellion against the Peking government. The Russians entered into an agreement with Sun through their envoy, Adolf Joffe, in 1923. The next year Sun's moribund party, the Kuomintang, was completely reorganized, armed with a radical nationalist program. Soviet political and military advisers, headed by Borodin and General Bluecher (known as Galen) arrived in Canton. A military school was set up under Russian auspices at Whampoa. A new army was organized. But most important of all, the newly formed Chinese Communist Party was put to work for the Kuomintang. A mass movement of the workers and peasants was arising out of a natural confluence of historic and economic forces and was already stirring considerable areas in south China. The Communists, working within and for the purely bourgeois Kuomintang, became the principal organizers, leaders, and fighters of this movement, which paralyzed the British port of Hong Kong by a general strike that lasted for more than a year, and which cleared the south of dissident militarists.

Thus opened a gigantic revolutionary opportunity. The victory of an anti-imperialist revolution in China might have transformed the entire world picture of the time. It could have been a major defeat for the British, who were still the dominant Western power in the East. It might have forced realignments of all the contending forces in the world. Most of all, it might have embarked the giant China upon a new course in which it could begin to realize the strength it possessed. Such events would have changed the face of the earth. But they did not come off. The Russian influence, instead of increasing the chances of success, ensured failure.

The story of this failure is long and complex. We have already reviewed these events in outline in an earlier chapter, but it may be useful to summarize them again in the present context.* The essence of the matter comes down to this: the Russian influence on the Chinese revolution came into full play at a time (1926–27) when in Russia power had passed to the conservative and nationalist bureaucracy led by Stalin. They wanted a revolution in China, but they failed to grasp the dynamics of the struggle there, even as most of them had failed to understand what had really happened in Russia in 1917. Interested primarily in securing an ally in the East and setting up an Asiatic bulwark against the anti-Soviet West, the Russian leaders placed their entire reliance upon the bourgeois leaders of the Kuomintang. They acted on the premise that the Kuomintang leaders were the only possible leaders of the anti-imperialist revolution. They believed, moreover, that these leaders would have to see the revolution through to its conclusion and could not do otherwise. This conception was imposed upon the young Chinese Communist Party, which dutifully subordinated itself to the leadership of Chiang Kai-shek who had meanwhile made himself the leader and the most commanding figure in the nationalist movement.

Swept forward by the mass movement, the Kuomintang advanced northward in 1926. It aroused millions of workers and peasants. It defeated or absorbed the armies of the old militarists who opposed it. It appeared to be on the verge of conquering the entire country when, in the spring of 1927, Chiang Kai-shek reached Shanghai, conquered for him by an insurrection of the workers in that major industrial port. The movement threatened to go far beyond the simple limits of anti-imperialism. It menaced the whole semi-medieval structure of land tenure in China, and in the cities the workers made small distinction between Chinese and foreign factory owners. Chiang Kai-shek, established in Shanghai, made his deal with the Chinese bankers and foreign interests there and then turned on the movement he led. He smashed it. The Russians retreated from the field in total rout. They clung vainly for a few months to the Kuomintang "left wing" at Hankow. But there, in turn, all their specious doctrines, arguments, promises, and optimistic assertions

* The reader is again referred to the author's *The Tragedy of the Chinese Revolution* for a detailed account and treatment.

collapsed in the face of political realities. The "left wing" capitulated to Chiang Kai-shek. The Russians pulled out, leaving the Chinese Communists, the union leaders and peasant leaders, the thousands of active revolutionary militants in the cities and the countryside to pay the price of failure under the swords and muzzles of Chiang's executioners. Diplomatic relations between Russia and China were also severed. The Russians reacted convulsively and directed the Chinese Communists into a series of desperate uprisings, culminating in the Canton Commune in December, 1927, where some 5,000 Chinese workers and a number of Russians were slaughtered in the streets. The Russians had failed, by their own errors, to achieve their end in China, and the effort they made had brought tragic disaster upon the cause of the Chinese revolution.

NATIONALIST RUSSIA

The defeat in China hastened the national-conservative evolution of the Soviet bureaucracy. In that same year, 1927, the left wing opposition in the Bolshevik Party, led by Trotsky, was liquidated, its members dispersed to exile or concentration camps. The bureaucracy shaped itself into a wholly totalitarian police régime. This new bureaucratic power consolidated itself in the following years by terror, by mass political deportations, by physical liquidation of oppositions accompanied by all the bizarre claptrap of frameup trials. Total power, economic, political, social, and even literary, passed into the hands of the bureaucratic caste. This caste elevated itself far above the people, beyond serious challenge and with all the controlled means of production as its base and its weapon. It became a superclass far more powerful than its counterparts in bourgeois society because it controlled the entire economy and enjoyed undivided control of the state power. It proceeded belatedly to begin the industralization of the country, and it accomplished its purpose to an extraordinary degree by an immense wrench and at infinite pain and cost to the people.

The object of this program was to strengthen Russia, to gain time for Russia, regardless of the cost not only to the Russian people but to the revolutionary and Communist movements in other countries as well. The foreign Communist parties were converted into pliable tools, serving eagerly and blindly every changing requirement in the long and difficult course of Soviet foreign relations. The criterion was not the advancement of the cause of socialism in these non-Russian lands but the preservation and safety of the Russian Soviet State. These aims conflicted, because the prime object in foreign policy of the Soviet bureaucracy was the maintenance of the status quo. Russia wanted respite, not turmoil. It wanted alliances with existing states, not dissolution in upheavals whose outcome was not guaranteed. Russia wanted bastions of support for itself, not revolutions which would want support from Russia. Russia wanted to make herself acceptable as an ally of the strong, not suspect as an ally of the weak. The victory of Fascism in Germany in 1933 was a mortal blow to the world socialist movement, but insofar as it sharpened the antagonisms between the Western Powers, it was rationalized in Moscow as a gain, not a loss, for Russian interests. In Spain, the Russians intervened not in support of the workers' revolution but in support of respectable, though impotent, bourgeois republicanism which proved unable to withstand the Fascist assault despite the limitless heroism of the anti-Fascist workers. In France, the Russians signed a pact with Laval in 1935. Consequently the next year the French Communists deliberately dammed the flood tide of the great general strike which brought the country to the edge of revolution. Russia preferred to gamble on its pact with French capitalism rather than risk the uncertainties of a struggle for a Soviet France. Russia maneuvered, power against power, in a thoroughly cynical and self-centered program of self-preservation. It achieved its end, but at the cost of revolution in Europe.

The Russians wooed the Western powers, with proffered pacts, with People's Fronts, with the demonstrative transformation of French, British, and American Communists into ardent supports of their respective régimes. In the Far East, after intermittent skirmishing with the Japanese along the Manchurian frontier, the Russians bought off Japanese pressure by selling the Chinese Eastern Railway to Japan's Manchukuoan puppets and with Japan itself signed a non-aggression pact. While this more or less stabilized the eastern front for the time being, in the west sharp turns had to be made. Russian

wooing came to naught at Munich, where Britain and France bargained with Hitler to turn the sharp edge of his sword against
Russia. Russia promptly countered by coming to terms with Hitler
on its own account, securing for itself a new partition of Poland and
turning Hitler's pressure back on the British and French.

The war, when it finally came, was, as Russia had hoped, a collision of the great national powers in the West. Hitler, belatedly
trying to buy himself out of that war by attacking in the east in
1941, reached too far. His paranoiac genius failed him. His defeat
followed. Out of that conflict Russia emerged in the full panoply of
national power. With the war's end, Russia's role on the stage of
world affairs was not that of a proponent of a new world order but
that of a powerful claimant to the spoils. It spoke not for international communism, but for Russian national "security" and aggrandizement. Out of Moscow came no echo of "peace without
annexations or indemnities" but a deliberate program of maximum
annexation and maximum indemnities. Russia established its power
across eastern and southeastern Europe and reached out to the Elbe
and beyond. It looked again, as the old Russia had long looked, out
across the Dardanelles to the Mediterranean and the Middle East. It
reached across the Amur River into Manchuria and spilled over into
Korea. It drove out into the Pacific to the farthest of the Kuriles.
Russia faced its erstwhile allies across the ruins to match grab for
grab, deal for deal, mile for mile of strategic territory.

The new Russia picked up out of its past not the broken thread
of Bolshevik internationalism which it had dropped in the first decade
after the revolution, but the thread of classic Russian imperialism
which the Bolsheviks thought they had severed forever in 1917.

The new Russia appears on the world scene now as an infinitely
stronger and more dynamic claimant to the spoils once won or lost
or coveted by the Czars. It has embraced and absorbed not only the
political-strategic aspirations of Czarist imperialism, but its moral
attitudes, its sentimental patriotism, its glorification of its past. It
has enshrined again every idol that the Bolsheviks tore down. The
brief interlude of socialist internationalism is gone, like a forgotten
spasm. In its place stands the Soviet Russian fatherland, more power-

ful, more autocratically ruled, more ruthless, more successful than the Czarist fatherland ever was.

For the Russians today the return to Manchuria is triumphant vindication for the Russian army and fleet that went down before the Japanese four decades ago. In the winter of 1944, a long novel called *Port Arthur* was published in Moscow. A review of the novel filled three columns of the Soviet publication *Literature and Art,* and concluded as follows:

> The Russian army and the best representatives of the officer corps of that period displayed great love of their fatherland and bravely rose up to repulse Japanese aggression. . . . Port Arthur was to the officers and men defending it the same thing as Sevastopol has been for the Black Sea sailors —not a city or a port, but more than that. It was the very symbol of the fatherland of Russian soil, as precious and holy to Russia as the soil of Tambov and Ryazan.*

On September 2, 1945, the date of the formal Japanese surrender, Stalin said in a radio speech:

> The defeat of the Russian troops in 1904, in the period of the Russo-Japanese war, left grave memories in the minds of our people. It fell as a dark stain on our country. Our people trusted and awaited the day when Japan would be routed and the stain wiped out. For forty years we, the men of the older generation, have waited for this day. And now this day has come.†

This was a far cry from the attitude of Lenin, decades earlier, when he denounced the Czar's government for placing "greedy paws on China" and robbing it "as ghouls rob corpses." It had even less in common with the Bolshevik act in 1919 annulling all Czarist treaties which "through force and corruption enslaved the Chinese nation in order to benefit the Russian capitalists." All that had been greedy and corrupt and enslaving in the eyes of the Russian Bolsheviks has now in the eyes of Russia's present leaders become as "precious and holy" as it was in the eyes of the Czar. The Russian conquests scornfully repudiated by the Bolsheviks as ugly relics of

---

* Quoted by Harrison Salisbury, "Will Russia Fight Japan?" (*Collier's,* November 18, 1944).

† Radio Address of Generalissimo Stalin, Soviet Embassy Information Bulletin (Washington, D.C.), Sept. 6, 1945.

a discarded past have been reestablished as the holy rights of the new Russian state.

When Stalin sat down with Roosevelt and Churchill at Yalta in February, 1945, to discuss Russia's coming part in the war against Japan, he laid down his terms. These were explicitly the restoration of the long-lost acquisitions of the Czars in Manchuria. The three leaders signed their secret treaty, similar in tone, content, and purpose, to the many secret treaties which the Bolsheviks uncovered for the world in the archives of St. Petersburg and repudiated in 1918. In the Yalta pact signed on February 11, 1945, and not made public until one year later, Stalin demanded and Roosevelt and Churchill agreed that in return for Russian entry into the war against Japan "the former rights of Russia, violated by the treacherous attack of Japan in 1904, shall be restored."

These, as previously noted, were specified to include the return to Russia of the southern half of Sakhalin, the establishment of Sino-Soviet control over the Manchurian railway system, the internationalization of the port of Dairen, the restoration of the Russian lease on Port Arthur as a naval base, and the safeguarding of Russia's "preeminent position" in the entire region. As a bonus, the pact threw in what the Czars had never had, the Kurile Islands.

As in the past when Chinese territory and sovereignty were kicked around in foreign chancelleries, the Chinese were given no choice in the matter except to submit. In the Yalta pact Roosevelt bound himself to "obtain" the concurrence of Chiang Kai-shek but this concurrence was purely formal, for the agreement added: "The heads of the three Great Powers have agreed that these claims of the Soviet Union shall be unquestionably fulfilled after Japan has been defeated." Chiang Kai-shek's concurrence was duly "obtained," and the Yalta terms were embodied in the Sino-Soviet treaty signed in Moscow on August 14, 1945.

Thus the Soviet Union, the first modern state to sign an equal treaty with China after the First World War, imposed the first and only unequal treaty on China after the Second World War. By reacquiring its lease on Port Arthur, the Soviet Union achieved the distinction of sharing with Britain alone the possession of Chinese territory. For Hong Kong, seized again by the British immediately after Japan's collapse, and Port Arthur, are now the only foreign territorial holdings in China. Russia laid its heavy hand on the Chinese at a time when even Britain and the United States, and after them all the other powers, had already felt compelled to relinquish their concessions and settlements and extraterritorial rights. Formally and legally at least, China had at last rid herself of the more obvious and more obnoxious aspects of her semicolonial status. Only Britain's Hong Kong and Russia's Port Arthur and Russia's officially recognized "pre-eminent position" in Manchuria were excepted.

The gulf between the revolutionary conceptions of international freedom and equality represented by the Bolsheviks in 1919 and the system of "rights" and "pre-eminent position" in 1945 measures the extent of the transformation of the Soviet State in the intervening years. And the new Soviet imperialism has only begun to make its impact felt. In Europe and the Middle East it confronts and challenges Great Britain. In Asia it confronts and challenges the United States. It measures its "pre-eminent position" in Manchuria against the American position in East China. It measures its ability to manipulate and use the Chinese Communists against the American ability to dominate the Kuomintang. It opposes its ability to dominate the Asiatic continent against the American ability to dominate the Pacific Ocean. The new cycle has only just begun. It has a long and tortured path yet to follow.

Supporters and apologists of the new Russia frequently argue now on the basis of Russia's "rights" which stem from her position as one of the Great Powers of the world. Russia has as much "right," it is argued, to seek control of Europe as Britain has. Russia has as much "right" to positions in the Mediterranean as Britain has, or to a share in Persian oil. Russia is just as "entitled" to its special position in Manchuria as the United States is "entitled" to its special position in the rest of China. Russia has the same "right" to hold and fortify the Kuriles as the United States has to extend and fortify its Pacific bases. Russia, in sum, has as much "right" to expand in its own strategic-political-economic interests as the Anglo-American bloc has to expand in its interests.

Actual or potential Russian expansion in Europe, the Middle East, and Asia is not, it is argued, old-fashioned imperialism but the legitimate establishment of Russia's minimum security. Security is the thing. Russian security requires control of the Dardanelles, just as British security requires control of Gibraltar and Suez. Russian security requires a naval base at Port Arthur just as American security requires bases at Saipan, Okinawa, and in the Aleutians.

But what is unique about this Russian "security"? When did any expanding power act for any reason other than its "security"? Japan attacked China in the first place, it told the world, to defend its "security." Hitler attacked Poland for the same reason. Britain's wars and intrigues for a century from London to Suez to Singapore have invariably been in behalf of British "security." The American program for Pacific bases and for position in China is no less a program for American "security."

In the interests of its security, it is argued, Russia has the "right" to ensure "friendly" régimes in neighboring countries. But this is by no means a Russian monopoly, nor is it a new development in world politics. The history of the British Empire is speckled with the creation of "frendly" régimes in Egypt, Transjordan, the Indian states. France long made use of kings and beys in Africa and Asia. There were puppets and puppets and puppets long before the day of Vidkun Quisling. Germany in Europe and Japan in Asia did of course develop the idea of "friendly" neighbors to a notable degree in recent years. The United States, for its part, has been known to take a hand in creating "friendly" governments in Latin America and is engaged right now in trying to assure itself a "friendly" government in China.

But what kind of "rights" are these, and what kind of "security" do they provide? If you accept the logic of this argument, you have to accept its premises. You have also to accept its consequences. The premises are national power, national aggrandizement, national position in the world. If Britain and the United States are granted these "rights," then Russia must be granted the same "rights"—but this means that all issues between them depend upon the relationship of force that lies between them. For as long as the world is not dominated by any single great power, it means division of the world between rival blocs of power. And while rival blocs may precariously balance each other for longer or shorter periods, they cannot coexist indefinitely. The consequences are wars. The kind of "security" provided by this system is precisely the kind of security which has led to war after war in the last hundred years. Its purpose is power, economic power, strategic power, military power. Its mechanism is power politics. Its weapon is war, land war, sea war, air war, atomic war, bacteriological war. If the basis is competition, the outcome is hostility; and against the inevitable collision, the rivals must arm and arm, expand and expand. The logic of this kind of "security" is more "security." The logic of expansion is more expansion. The logic of force is more force. This is no theoretical conclusion any more, nor a speculative analysis. We have seen it happen repeatedly, twice on the grand scale in our own generation. Millions of the buried dead and the living, and all the ruins from Chapei to Guernica to Coventry to Bremen to Hiroshima are the evidence.

If Anglo-American imperialism and Russian imperialism have the "right" to expand, to control, to dominate, to establish their zones of influence or, if you will, their zones of "security," then they also have the inalienable and inescapable "right" to collide with one another. Given our advance into the age of atomic weapons, the results of such a collision are now clearly imaginable. The peoples of the world, that is those that are left when the issue is finally decided, will be left with the "right" to be dominated by the one camp or the other. For most of us and for most of our children, that will be a very academic choice.

IS SOCIALISM THE ISSUE?

There is a further argument and it is, perhaps, the most serious one of all. This is the argument, still advanced by some Russians and by some of their supporters abroad, that Russia represents socialism and is therefore not only more dynamic but more progressive than Anglo-American democratic capitalism. It is because Russia is socialist that the capitalist nations mortally hate and fear it. The Russian cause, it is argued, is the cause of world socialism. Every Russian victory is a victory for socialism, every mile of Russian expansion is a gain for socialism. In the ultimate collision of the two great blocs, therefore, the victory of Russia would be for the greater ultimate benefit of mankind.

To anyone who is willing to consider that socialism is a way out of the present confusion and frustration, this is a serious proposition. The idea of a socialist transformation of our society is a powerful, persuasive idea which has captured the imagination and loyalty of struggling people everywhere. It proposes to eliminate capitalist competition and the inequities of capitalist profit based on wage slavery. It proposes to release the creative and productive energies of people to make things for use and not for profit, and promises thereby an immense increase in productivity and the elevation, on a worldwide scale, of the human standard of living. It proposes to strike mortally at the causes of war that lie in the race for markets and materials by marshaling the whole world in a common effort for the common good. It promises to free man from the struggle for survival by progressively ensuring his survival. It would free him to advance to farther scientific and intellectual horizons.

This promise has had in it the magic of hope in the limitless capacity of man. It has proposed liberation from the greed and cruelty which in all history have been regarded as attributes of human nature instead of attributes imposed on men by the societies in which they have lived. It has seemed to have in it the way to a way out of recurring wars and crises and chronic insecurity and inadequacy in the lives of all people. It has offered, above all, the only program for the progressive leveling of the national barriers that now strangle the world, proposing to reorganize on the basis of the rational exploitation of wealth through a world commonwealth of peoples. Socialism has represented, in short, a bold and vaulting program of the highest moral purpose and libertarian ideals.

Russia seemed, for a short while, to concretize these hopes, to make them real, to stand for something sharply and radically new in the world. These were the ideas of the men who made the Russian Revolution and who appealed to the rest of the world to join them. But that appeal failed. The revolution remained isolated, and isolated, moreover, in one of the most backward countries of the modern world. Out of that isolation and out of that backwardness grew the totalitarian régime, the bureaucratic and police state which is the Russia of today. The broadest kind of internationalist aspiration was transformed into the narrowest kind of nationalist concentration of power. Revolutionary Russia failed to become the herald of world socialism. It became instead a new supernationalist police state. Instead of creating a new kind of political freedom, it became a new form of political tyranny. It ended the rule of one class and substituted the rule of a superclass.

This superclass, an all-powerful and self-reproducing bureaucracy, achieved great successes of its own kind. It shattered the medievalism of the old Russia and took great forced strides in the industrialization of the country. It established elementary literacy in a largely illiterate land. And with considerable foreign help, it successfully defended the country against invasion.

But it also obliterated the development of any real social democracy. This ruling class has maintained itself and its power by terror and by an enforced unanimity. We have watched it grow into a materially favored class at the expense of a mass of workers held to an abysmally low standard of living. In 1932–33 we saw it carry out forced collectivization and subject millions of people in one of the richest farm areas in the world to decimation by famine. We have watched it drop, one after another, the ideas and practices of internationalism and replace them with all the worst features of blind and even fanatical and religious nationalism. We have watched it blot out the bold beginnings that were made in creation of new and higher norms in social relations, in marriage and divorce and education. We have watched it stifle the spirit of independent inquiry and craftsmanship in science and the arts. We have seen this "monolithic" state smother all political opposition. We have seen its purges, its liquidations, its mass deportations, its bizarre trials, its substitution of power for justice in its control of the lives of individuals. We have watched Russia develop under this régime into a land where men do not speak their minds or act for fear of the secret police.

It is possible to describe this evolution in many ways. It is possible to surround it with many myths and tortured rationalizations. But to call it socialism is like calling the Inquisition Christianity.

There is still, of course, endless debate over the simplest facts of the internal reality of Russia, a debate nourished by the enforced insulation of the country from the rest of the world. But there is scarcely as much room for argument over Russian acts outside Russia's own borders. In the years before the war we saw Russia eviscerate surging popular movements in China, Germany, Spain, France, in the interest of the transient requirements of Soviet foreign policy. We have watched Communists and a pathetic host of liberal intellectuals transform themselves into grotesque puppets, capable of turning 180 degrees in their thinking at a nod from Moscow. We have seen Russia carve up Poland by agreement with Nazi Germany, and eventually we saw the Soviet army swallow up all of eastern Europe like a conquering horde. If all this was still "socialism," then what was the stripping of conquered countries of their industries? Or looting "friendly" territory, like Manchuria, of its machinery? What kind of socialism is involved in the burden of reparations that Russia is trying to lay on the backs of the workers of Italy, Rumania, Hungary, and Germany? Precisely what ideal of international proletarian brotherhood is being served by Russia's part, together with the United States, in the strangulation of tiny Korea?

Is this, conceivably, the challenge of socialism to the world capitalist order represented by the United States and Great Britain? The supporters of Russia insist that it is. They declare that whatever the iniquities of Russia, they ultimately serve the good cause. They point to the fact that in some of the countries where Russian control has been established since the end of the war against Germany, land relations have been revised, as in Poland, and that in some degree capitalists have been expropriated and production nationalized. This, they argue, is the essential process, this is the long-term gain. These are the foundations of the truly socialist order that will eventually emerge from the totalitarian welter. It may be true, they sometimes admit, that people are not more free and perhaps are less free under the new dispensation. A few may even be killed off or shipped to Siberian exile. But in return for yielding themselves wholly up to the guidance and total control of an all-powerful ruling caste, they are on the road to acquiring some new eventual measure of relative economic security. If they must suffer now under the iron heel of a police state in which no man may speak his mind, it is only to assure to their more or less distant progeny the ultimate flowering of a new existence under socialism.

This is perhaps as good a way as any to rationalize the anti-human quality of so much of our current history. Perhaps there is comfort in it, especially if one does not have to wait for the day of glory while living under Russian rule. But it is another version of the old Wobbly song about the promise of pie in the sky when you die. For people who are looking for a way out of the jungle now or in the graspable future, pie in the sky is not enough. After the experience of the last twenty years, we have to insist more than ever before that the road to greater freedom does not lie through lesser freedom. The tread of the secret police cannot be made to sound like the march toward the brave new world. Mere nationalization is not socialism. German fascism also nationalized a large part of German economy and also offered its people pie in the sky. Mussolini nationalized and incorporated. Even in Chiang Kai-shek's China, state-owned industry far outweighs the private ownership of the means of industrial production. Nationalization without greater democracy is tyranny. The earmark of socialism is not the nationalized means of production but the kind of social régime that people can establish on the basis of nationalized means of production, economically, culturally, and physically. The Russian totalitarian oligarchy is no yardstick by which to measure the promise of a socialist order in society. It is only the yardstick by which to measure a totalitarian oligarchy. The Russian example does not prove the good or evil of socialism. It does not prove anything about socialism at all except that it cannot be built in a single country, especially a huge, backward country. All that Russia teaches us is what happens when a socialist revolution is isolated and consequently falls back on a national police power instead of going ahead to create a broader democracy.

If this totalitarian monstrosity has indeed taken title to the terms "socialism" or "communism," if it is no longer possible to rescue those names and restore to them their original content of high moral and social purpose, then it would be far better for socialists to surrender their terminology and find new language in which to describe their program and voice their aspirations.

The crucial thing in any case is not the label but the fact. And the fact is that we are confronted now by Russian nationalism, by a new and greater Russian state. Whatever its hypnotized non-Russian supporters delude themselves into believing, its premises are Russian national interests. It wields its power with brutal scorn for its own and for the lesser peoples of the earth. In the postwar huggermugger it demands its indemnities, its control of territory, its "strategic" rights. It loots, strips, oppresses, and it plays the classic imperialist game with its own brand of cruel cynicism and with embellishments of its own creation. Not the least of these is its ability to manipulate popular movements in other countries and to prostitute honest social struggle abroad to its own national ends.

This is a new national power in the world arising in a time when national power is the brake of all brakes on human progress. It confronts and challenges the national power of the United States, and the peoples of the world are caught helplessly in the vacuum thus created. To the extent that this is a clash between two "systems" it is a fraud upon humanity, because neither one is pregnant with any decent promise for mankind. Democratic capitalism, Anglo-American style, has shown conclusively enough in these past three decades that amid great abundance it cannot adequately clothe or house or feed enough of its people. It cannot any longer keep society viable and functioning. It cannot make its immense productive machinery work with any reasonable efficiency except for purposes of war. Russian totalitarianism, on the other hand, is a new form of national power which offers a limited solution of the economic impasse, but at the price of driving people into political and social thraldom on a level lower even than that which prevails in the so-called democratic West.

It is on the basis of this poor choice that we find the world dividing between these two immense hostile blocs. What is taking place is an enormous concentration of rival national powers which not only are incapable of creating any basis for ultimate stability in human life for a decently prolonged period, but cannot even arrive at a temporary modus vivendi. What they are doing instead is bringing to its penultimate conclusion the epoch of the powerful national state in human history: a world divided in two. The ultimate is the collision between them. Such is the road we are traveling. The problem is to find a turning.

12 PERMANENT WAR OR PERMANENT PEACE

To try to think reasonably about the present state of the world is to assume that reason has something to do with the case. But every "reasonable" approach soon halts before a stone wall of unreasonable fact. We are caught in a tangle of cause and circumstance that is sweeping us toward everything that nobody wants. For ours is the time of the triumph of the irrational. It is difficult to wander anywhere on the face of the earth without being assailed by a sense of being in a madhouse where delusions govern amid hopeless and needless suffering, where myopia and fear have obscured the most elementary demands of true self-interest. It is as though we had an object in life—say, freedom, peace, security—and actually devoted our most intense energies to the business of placing obstacles in our own path.

Still, there is a great deal of reasonableness in the world. There is the reasonable and overwhelming desire of ordinary people everywhere for the chance to live and grow in peace. There is the reasonable weariness of a generation that is tired of destruction and muck, fears, tensions, and uncertainties. There is the profoundly reasonable desire for change, for something that will work a little better than what we have had or what we have now. There is, in short, the deepest and most creative and most reasonable force in the world, the urge of men to better their estate.

Yet everything that is done or that happens, including our own acts, conspires against us. Such is the gross contradiction, the dementia of our time, a mighty unhinging of our social faculties. It results from our inability to use our knowledge and resources to create a society that will work. This is the dislocation that has produced two world wars in a single generation and confronts us with not much more than the threat of a third, or offers us at best a prolonged and paralyzing absence of peace. In the shortening interims, meanwhile, nothing works. The simplest needs of the greatest majority of all people cannot begin to be reasonably satisfied.

This is most acutely the case in Asia, but the problems of war and peace in Asia obviously cannot be considered apart from the problems of war and peace in the world as a whole. The present pattern of events in the East has been shaped in large degree by the evolution of the West during the last few centuries. Asia's future now depends, in even greater degree, on what the Western "barbarians" do with the world they dominate.

The society that has given us the kind of history we have been surviving for the past forty years is a mortally sick society. It is a society in convulsion, rent by conflict between its ability to produce things and its ability to use what it produces. Our productive capacities and our socio-political institutions are at war. Instead of generating growth by their mutual interaction, they are capable now of generating only friction. This friction generates heat that is consuming people and things with steadily increasing ferocity.

What we are witnessing is the extinction of the national state as an instrument of national economy. The process is proving to be prolonged, bloody, and exhausting. It is more destructive than any comparable period of great change of the past, because there is so much more to destroy and because our powers of destruction are so much greater. Science has brought whole nations and perhaps the globe itself within the sights of its new weapons, carrying to the ultimate extreme the common perversion of human reason and ingenuity. At the service of the national state in our time, it could not do otherwise.

The epoch of the modern nation-state as an instrument of national economy came into being after a period of wars and dislocations that lasted for centuries. For nearly three hundred years it served as a more or less reasonably sufficient instrument for fostering the growth of industrially productive forces. It created a power-economy that transformed the face of the earth and yoked all of more backward Asia and Africa to the West. During its development many wars took place, but they occurred within broad areas of possible expansion. They were part of the process of growth. However, by 1914—to choose a conveniently arbitrary turning point—productive power had far outstripped the national-economic structure of society. All the weaker peoples of the world were brought into subjection, all the backward areas occupied and colonized. Capitalist competition, developing by its own inner logic, broke through and across national boundaries. Concentrated economic power within the nations developed into cartels, into international and world-wide monopolies. These bred greater inter-nation conflicts. These conflicts were, in their own twisted way, an expression of the new need to enlarge the economic units of the world. They proved that national political economy had become a shackle on growth. The war of 1914–18 established that the world itself was the minimum unit of necessary change.

We have already remarked in these pages that the Russian revolution of 1917 was an attempt to open the door to the beginning of this needed change in the direction of a new kind of international society. But when the Russian revolution proved unable to preserve its initial impulse and intent and reverted to an intense nationalism under a new kind of oligarchic dictatorship, the door was slammed shut. The years of the Long Armistice that followed tend now to be telescoped into a simple punctuation between the wars. But the events of those years still have much to teach us. Those were the years in which Western capitalism displayed its total inability to create any workable balance in the world, driving itself instead into the suffocating depths of an unprecedented world economic crisis that led inexorably to Fascism and war. Those were also the years in which the peoples stirred and moved, in many ways and by many paths, seeking other solutions for the global impasse.

That was the time of the profound and almost universal turn to simple pacifism. It was translated and perverted at the higher levels of politics into the disarmament conferences, the gestures of the Kellogg-Briand Pact, and the solemn farce of the League of Nations. It was the time of a great literature of disillusionment and clarity about the motive forces of society, in novels, the social sciences, history, and biography. It was also a period marked by great political upheavals in which people in the mass tried by one means or another to break new historic ground. In Europe between 1918 and 1936 there were revolutions in Germany, Austria, and Hungary, the general strike in England, the overthrow of the monarchy and the civil war in Spain, and the general strikes in France. In Asia likewise, the end of the First World War touched off waiting impulses of gigantic force. Huge masses of poverty-ridden colonial slaves entered the political arena in search of independence in India, Java, Korea, Indochina, and most spectacularly, in China in 1925–27. These movements brought to the threshold of revolutionary mass action more millions of people than probably ever stirred before in any comparable period of human history.

But in varying ways all these impulses and actions aborted. The Eastern European revolutions following 1918 were crushed by the direct and indirect action of the victorious Western allies. In Germany, between 1918 and 1933, the Socialists and Communists managed between them to dissipate the chance they had to assume the leadership of the movement toward a unified Europe. It was only when they had utterly failed that disoriented millions in Germany surrendered themselves to the psychotic desperation of Hitlerism. Hitler's challenging attempt to become master of Europe was, in its own grotesque way, an alternate attempt at an answer to the need for European unification. Only he offered Europe unity in German chains. Against this the peoples of Europe, most notably in France and Spain, spent their energies in desperate and futile challenges. Russian nationalism refracted through the Communist parties, the liberal and Socialist leaders of the People's Fronts who feared social change, and the guardians of national power in London, Paris, Rome, Berlin, Moscow, and Washington choked off these revolutionary impulses. Having blocked dynamic and progressive change, and instead having nourished the totalitarian fanaticism of Hitler, the Western Powers found themselves faced with another German challenge to Anglo-French domination of Europe. Thus ended the Long Armistice.

In Asia similarly, Western imperialism proved hopelessly incapable of fostering growth, but it was still strong enough to drive progressive Asiatic nationalism back into the suffocating soil of social and economic backwardness. It was able to prostitute various colonial and semi-colonial ruling classes to its own purposes. The result was to open Asia to the heavy tread of a Japan advancing to challenge its

Western rivals. Japan moved into the vacuum of chaos in Asia and tried, in its own way, to weld that continent into a political and productive unit under Japanese domination.

The issues were thus yielded up to the decision of another holocaust. Germany and Japan tried to elevate themselves to the final two peaks of rivalry for domination of the world. But they failed to make their challenge good. Amid immense slaughter and suffering, their Western rivals prevailed and the issue of world power was suspended instead between the greater Powers of Russia and the United States. What survived the war was national and economic power in its most highly concentrated form. Two decades ago there were half a dozen contenders for world power. Today there are only two. All the other empires and nations live on in the shadow, pawns and satellites or helpless victims, each one trying feebly to nurse its own incurable ills.

The needs of society are again relegated to the background, for while national power survives it chokes off the growth of the world political economy that must somehow replace it. The decisive foreground is occupied by all the mutual and well grounded fears, military preparations and maneuvers, threats and counter-threats, weapons and counter-weapons, struggle for spheres of influence and power over strategic materials and territory. Every diplomatic argument is a skirmish, every conference a battle. This kind of hostile jockeying can go on for a long time. Between Britain and Germany and between the United States and Japan it lasted for decades. But the ultimate conclusion of it is war. Meanwhile it produces an absence of peace that is almost as paralyzing as war. There is nothing "reasonable" about this historic chain of circumstance. Yet it is the unreasonable fact.

Even among the men of position and power in the world who carry the prime responsibility for it, the prospect inspires terror. Only the most demented and demoralized among them actually want war, for it has become evident, even to many of them, that war has grown too costly to yield adequate returns on the investment they must make in blood and treasure. The character of the new weapons, the atomic bombs and others more terrible to come, has aroused some fear in the most debased and most cynical of the politicians. Still, so long as their basic premise remains the preservation and strengthening of the national economic unit—whether it be Anglo-American capitalist or Russian statist—their antagonism remains basically insoluble. It arises out of the miasma of the past decades, the enormously developed fear that one huge national power inspires in another, the long and tangled history of clashing political and ideological interests, the angry reach for strategic boundaries, bases, power on the ground, in the air and in the sub-microscopic heart of the nucleus of the atom. It is no longer, as it was in 1914, a relatively simple collision between contenders for markets and commercially profitable territory. It has gone beyond that to the all-embracing issue of power capable of organizing the world. While this issue remains unresolved, all other problems wait and, waiting, grow more acute. In the interim, half-measures make no impression on the enormous bulk of the unsolved problems of mankind. The world is driven deeper into an epoch of permanent war. This epoch will have to last until somehow, in some form, and on some terms, a new society emerges that can be made to work.

This is not a condition that can be met with half-solutions and expedients. What we are up against is the fact that all the old ideas, all the old practices, all the old premises, and all the old leaderships are bankrupt. This applies to those who have ruled and governed and shown themselves capable only of waging war and perpetuating chaos. It applies equally to those who have led the oppositions and sought other paths, the many-hued liberals, the pusillanimous Social-ists, and the degenerated Communists, who have proved capable only of leading people down blind alleys, leaving them there in the dark-ness of compounded confusion.

The best, by act and by pressure, that they could produce out of the cataclysm of the war was the United Nations Organization. Yet the United Nations, like the League of Nations before it, is barely even an acknowledgment that the world must function on a unified basis or not at all. It is a crude expedient, resting essentially on the old ideas, the old practices, the old premises, the old leaderships. Even more barefacedly than the League and with many fewer reserva-tions, the United Nations leaves the fate of the mass of the weak in the hands of the few strong. It is at best a mild check on rapacity, at worst a thin cloak for it. It is a mirror of our world, not an instrument for changing it.

And change—drastic, radical change of the whole structure of society—is the need. The problem is not one of "controlling" atom bombs or other weapons of war, but of rooting out the causes of war. It is not a matter of smoothing out the jagged edges of self-expanding spheres of influence but of abolishing such spheres altogether. It is not a matter of adjusting boundaries or economic barriers but of leveling them. It is not a matter of creating a euphemistic system of "trusteeship" to cloak colonial and strategic expansion but of ending once and for all the whole colonial system and any form of subjection of one people by another. It is not a matter of treaties, goodwill, or moral purpose. It is a matter of the whole context of society. It is a matter of transforming the world and the way we all live in it.

To such a program of change even the war made its own peculiar contribution. To summon the strength needed to beat down the threat of German and Japanese power, the United States in effect transformed its own economic system. American industry and agriculture were harnessed to a common need and a controlled program of production. Under this program, with all its gross inefficiency, swollen overhead, and super-profits for the dominant corporations, actual production rose to astronomic proportions. Methods of operating international economy were similarly transformed. The United States, Britain, and their allies and satellites joined in a group of combined boards. In varying degrees these boards pooled and controlled shipping, food, raw materials, and to some extent production itself. Driven to it by the most imperative common need, the Western allies in practice junked all the most precious tenets of their so-called free capitalist system. They were compelled to abolish much of the anarchy in production and exchange. They had to substitute for it some semblance of an orderly and systematic program for the production and movement of needed goods. This operation was subject to a constant undertow of mutual rivalries and antagonisms, of fear and intrigue and defense of special economic interests and positions, particularly as between the United States and Britain. There was monumental waste and super-monumental bungling. But by and large it worked.

The output of this stupendous productive surge was for the most part exploded into nothingness. The immense communal effort it represented spent itself in the greatest frenzy of destruction so far known in human history. Yet within this convulsion a smothered miracle took place. The paretic economy of the Western world was transformed into a vital, functioning force. There was nearly unlimited demand and in the end the system produced enough to meet it with broad margins to spare. Bridges of ships spanned the oceans. The globe was laced into a network of air transport created out of nothing in less than two years. The thin, sluggish, inadequate arteries of world communications were expanded, almost overnight, into a gigantic system that destroyed forever the illusion of remoteness in any corner of the earth. Scientific knowledge took gargantuan strides forward, dissolving the mysteries of sea and sky, exploring vast realms of the unexplored, and yielding staggering results, everything from better insect repellents to cures for pneumonia and syphilis, from electronic gadgets and radar to the split atom. Even more spectacular was the war's discovery of the untapped resources of human energy and intelligence. Men were snatched from routines of simple manual labor and were converted, by millions, into highly skilled technicians. Use was found for all the latent richness of the sense of responsibility in men, their capacity to act and to think and to lead. Before it destroyed them amid total meaninglessness, the war exposed glimpses of all there is in men that could be so meaningful. It drew upon and dissipated their profound capacity for devotion and comradeship and sacrifice. It is perhaps the most irrational paradox of all that the years of the most destructive war in history were also the years of the most concentrated creative and productive effort ever known. Our society could produce effectively only to destroy. Only the insanity of a global war could force men to the sanity of worldwide common effort.

All this passed, like a movement during a spastic convulsion. With the war's end the weak and designedly temporary framework of common effort fell to pieces. The war had not been fought to liquidate national economic power. On the contrary, every effective action taken was in the direction of restoring the previous condition of national and international anarchy. The Byrneses, Bevins, and

Molotovs may be seeking in all earnestness to find some workable arrangement for the world in the next period. But they take as their point of departure the re-creation and reinforcement of the national political and economic unit. This is like trying to avoid the recurrence of a volcanic eruption by rolling back the lava and pouring it down the still-smoking crater.

Almost everyone, to be sure, talks now about "one world." Almost everyone in the political firmament, president, premier, dictator, street-corner politician, or editorial writer, genuflects daily in the direction of some one world or other, like a devout Moslem facing Mecca to pray. Not so long ago it was the lonely dream world of the unheeded radicals. Today it is a crowded realm indeed. Bank presidents and preachers and princes of industry jostle each other outside its pearly gates. Even Winston Churchill calls for a United States of Europe. A lot of this is plain hypocrisy. Much of it is self-delusion. Some of it is honest aspiration. But all of it is an acknowledgment that the old catchwords are obsolete, that the national mythos has to be replaced by the world mythos if the people are to be satisfied that a real effort is being made to build the peace.

But if such an effort were in fact in progress, the current agenda of international relations would have quite a different character. Issues like the Balkan boundaries, Trieste, reparations would not be fought like battles aiming at the creation of a new strategic balance of power. They would assume their more proper proportions as small details that would settle themselves once a new structure was built into which they could fit. The frame of reference would not be the aggrandizement of national power but the foundations of a new world political economy. The immediate concern would be the problem of making world-wide economic cooperation effective in peace rather than in war. The peacemakers would be considering practical ways of meeting the world's constructive needs. It is not a question of wholesale panaceas or full-blown solutions. It is a matter of taking the first steps in the desired direction. It is the business of recognizing that peaceful and productive growth is no longer a matter of the individual acts, policies, or interests of this or that country, but a matter of the entire reorganization of society.

It is sometimes argued that the settlement of problems like Trieste is a necessary prelude to coming to grips with the broader problems. The only trouble is that settling on the status of Trieste has nothing to do with unifying Europe. It has to do with locating the south European pivot of the Eastern and Western spheres of influence. It has nothing to do with establishing peaceful relations between Italy and Yugoslavia. It has to do with determining who shall control the Adriatic against future economic and military contingencies. It is not a first step toward peace but another step toward war.

First steps toward peace or toward a new world order—they come to the same thing—would involve such matters as setting up world-wide pools in food, raw materials, shipping, air transport, communications, and some sectors of production. They would have to do with abolishing all armed forces, shedding military budgets, and refitting industrial machines to the needs of a shattered world. They would have to do with the creation of new world agencies for the rational allocation of goods and services on the basis of these needs. They would be concerned with liquidating the colonial system and devising new methods and new machinery for meshing the needs and resources of the backward areas of the world with the needs and resources of its more advanced sections. This would call for regional bodies to plan in common, to function in common, to meet common local, regional, and world needs. New political machinery, based upon this expanding economic order, would have to be created to conform to and serve this new kind of world economy.

In the current reality, a certain amount of lip service is duly paid to all these objectives, but they remain remote from the sphere of action. The problems of the social context are in fact relegated to the most obscure and impotent of the committees of the United Nations and to other equally impotent international bodies, while the centers of real power contend with one another on the basis of national interest. Thus the American and Russian negotiators could not agree on the further evolution of German economy, much less of world economy. They could not erase an arbitrary boundary they themselves created across the body of tiny Korea, much less level national barriers across the world. They could not agree on who should have Trieste, much less open the way to a freer, more unified Europe. They could not, without greatest difficulty, reopen trade along the Danube, much less open the sluices of fuller international exchange for all countries. They could not agree on terms and conditions of their "trusteeships," much less cauterize the infection of colonialism.

The Powers have not failed, moreover, to act on the implications of this impasse. Amid talk of disarmament and "control" of sources of atomic energy, the United States has gone on making atom bombs. It is spending billions to develop even newer and more terrible weapons. It is seeking networks of strategic bases in both oceans and is openly exploring the requirements and conditions of future war across the polar icecap. Russia, on its part, has swallowed up huge territories and yoked millions of people to its totalitarian machine. It has stripped conquered lands of goods and machinery. It has expanded its military power, cynically established its total political control over neighboring countries. It seeks feverishly to overcome the American atomic advantage and in expectation of being able to do so, it leans threateningly across the borders of Turkey, Iran, and Manchuria. While all this goes on, all talk of peace, security, stability— to say nothing of human freedom—is ephemeral nonsense. Europe continues to suffocate under its crazy-quilt patchwork of outworn national and economic barriers and Asia is condemned to more sterile and inconclusive strife.

There is no such thing as a "local" solution any longer, and in our times "local" problems easily assume continental proportions. There are staggering domestic issues in every country in Asia. Scarcely any of them can be domestically resolved. The whole vast problem of China's internal economy and political balance germinates in the deep and remote and molecular life of the Chinese village. Yet the fate of the Chinese peasant in great degree depends on what happens in New York, Washington, and Moscow. India, Indochina, Indonesia, Burma can by tortured struggle achieve measures of greater national independence. But such gains will be empty and fruitless unless these peoples can take their places as components in a new world order capable of nourishing their growth.

It is difficult to avoid the feeling that events in Asia seem already to be sweeping beyond any chance of reasonable retrieval. Asia has not yet begun to figure as a major item on the postwar agenda of the

Great Powers. The chief protagonists are still wrestling for the soul of Europe. Asia waits, the scene of a far greater struggle to come. But conflicts do not stand still. All the tight knots are meanwhile pulled tighter. In China, civil war has already cut deeply into any chance that existed for relative peace. In this civil war the United States stands as the committed supporter of one side, the decadent, brutal, incompetent, tyrannical side whose only visible virtue from the official American point of view is its opposition to the Communists. For many Americans, in and out of official position, the Communists' only serious vice is their affinity to Russia. The broader implications of the civil war in China are plain enough. It is already, in essence, a masked border war between Russia and the United States.

In southern Asia, the rebelling colonial peoples have been left to wrest, unaided, whatever concessions they could from their returning masters. They have proved so relatively strong and their masters so relatively weak, that the British, French, and Dutch have been compelled to make substantial concessions. But the adjustments have taken place within the hated and stifling imperial structures which survived the war. For this survival, the colonial peoples hold the United States responsible. America is already the whited sepulcher in which their overbright hopes lie buried.

Official American thinking about Asia is already oppressed by the seemingly hopeless and hostile disorder of the continent. Americans cannot even as yet "do business" on any serious scale anywhere in the Far East, and least of all in China. It seems to many of them a poor kind of victory that does not afford opportunities to turn over a quickly multiplying dollar. American military thinking is already heavily colored by the "realistic" theme which finds in the relative order of Japan a far more attractive strategic investment. These quarters view Japan as capable eventually of becoming an armored shield, the forward line of offense and defense against the dark and dangerous and impenetrable land mass of Eurasia.

Russia, since the war, has been largely intent upon achieving and extending her immense gains in Europe. In Asia, the Russians have so far contented themselves with the franchise they bought so easily at Yalta, gains that would have been worth a war to win. Having eviscerated industrial Manchuria, they are guarding their new "rights" with troops at Port Arthur. Presumably they are planning to, or have already begun to, transform Sakhalin and the Kuriles into their own Pacific buttresses facing the threatening arc of American bases. Out of choice or necessity, or both, the Russians have meanwhile played a passive game and they have been amply rewarded for doing so. Every American policy, every American act has so far served the Russian rather than the American interest in Asia. Thus Russia has held itself largely aloof from the developing civil war in China, although not so aloof that its influence is wholly unfelt. The Communists may have expected more immediate Russian support than they received. Russia's act in stripping Manchurian industry must have come to them, too, as a rude blow, since they must have hoped to make that industrial area the base for their own expanding strength. Nevertheless, the Russians gave them access to Japanese arms in great quantities. The Russians balked and delayed Nationalist troop movements into Manchurian ports. This was not negligible help and it suggested the promise of more when, as, and if it should suit the Russian interest to grant it. Meanwhile the more untenable the American position becomes, the greater is the potential advantage to Russia. The deeper the American commitment to the Kuomintang, the surer the guarantee of unresolved turmoil in China and the better for Russia's ultimate interest. Time is the principal element in immediate Russian policy in Asia. The principal object of that policy remains maximum positional advantage in relation to the United States. When events favor or allow more active Russian intervention to serve this object, it will be forthcoming.

For the Russian-American cycle in Asia has only just begun. If right now one side is being canny and the other stupid, if either one is blind or inept, shrewd or successful, the direction in which both are moving is quite plain. Whatever the mumbo-jumbo about territorial integrity, defense, offense, or security, it adds up to eventual conflict for mastery in Asia.

Such are the unreasonable facts. It still seems necessary to ask the reasonable question: Can this conflict be avoided and if so, how? Here again, it is a question of how much reason has to do with the case. By every reasonable criterion, another world war is the most unthinkable, undesirable, and most unwanted of all prospects. Yet the unreasonable facts are paramount and they make the prospect of such a war in the foreseeable future, given present acts, policies, and premises, a very real prospect indeed. So much so that any assurance that war can be avoided already sounds either pious or fanciful. Yet it is obviously *possible* to avoid it. It is obviously possible to retrace steps already taken, to find a new starting point, and to head off anew in some more hopeful direction. It is possible to do it. Most of us undoubtedly want to do it. The question is whether we can do it.

Anybody who tries to talk reasonably about getting us off the rails that lead toward another world war has to talk about taking a turn of one hundred and eighty degrees. We have to reject the futile and petulant business of playing "you first." The American people are not without a certain hard appreciation of the current realities. Opinion polls taken early in 1946 showed that 68 per cent of those polled expected another world war within twenty-five years. Another poll, reported in November, 1946, asked Americans whether they thought Russia or the United States or both were responsible for the danger-ous friction between them. Of those polled 74 per cent replied: "Both." If this is a fair and accurate cross-section of American opin-ion, then it proves again that the people are wiser and infinitely more honest than the experts, the dopesters, the newspapers, and the poli-ticians. For it is precisely on this score that we can afford no provincial illusions. The mote and the beam have to be removed at the same time. If we are to talk reasonably about a reasonable peace, then we have to talk about rectifying the acts and policies of the castes and classes which rule in both the United States and Russia. We have to assume that they can be compelled to make the one-hundred-eighty-degree turn that is needed or else be replaced by regimes that will be willing to make it.

If we can accept this assumption, then we can talk about first steps toward peace. These steps would involve for both Russia and the United States a general retreat from the advanced positions they already occupy along the road to war. In Europe, obviously, Russia would have to yield much more than the United States. It would have to remove its heavy hand from the countries it has occupied and absorbed. It would have to relieve the pressure that is preventing Europe from unifying itself on a new, free, and workable basis. In Asia, on the other hand, it is the United States that would have to give infinitely more ground.

The Asiatic provisions of such a joint move toward the beginning of peace would have to include at least the following:

Russia and the United States would have to agree mutually to the cancellation of the secret Yalta agreement under which the United States bargained away Chinese territory in return for Russian assistance in the war against Japan. Russia would have to abrogate the unequal treaty it signed with China as a result of the Yalta deal. It would have to yield up its "pre-eminent" position in Manchuria. It would have to surrender its renewed hold on the Liaotung Peninsula. It would have to withdraw its troops from Port Arthur and forego its "right" to joint control, with China, of the Manchurian port of Dairen. It would have to abandon any plans it has for militarizing Sakhalin and the Kurile Islands. Russia would have to carry out total disarmament.

The United States would have to withdraw its troops, marines, and naval contingents. It would have to withdraw its political and economic support from the Kuomintang government and allow the internal balance in China to find its own level. The United States would have to drop its entire program for establishing strategic bases in the great Pacific arc stretching from Guam to the Aleutians. It would have to stop making atom bombs. It would have to destroy the stock of atom bombs it has already produced. It would have to disarm totally and abandon all experimental development of new weapons.

Both Russia and the United States, in other words, would have to give up their attempts to win and hold special strategic positions aimed at each other. They would have to stop talking peace and preparing for war and substitute a common policy of talking peace and preparing for peace.

Taken by themselves these measures would pump out a good deal of the foul air that hangs over Asia now. But they would be only the beginning. Into this newly created vacuum, it would be necessary to breathe new life. Russia and the United States would have to join with other countries in a common political and economic program that would place Asia in a wholly new relation to the Western world.

Such a program could begin by assistance in establishing and guaranteeing the independent national identities of the Asiatic peoples. That would mean ending all colonial power. That would mean recognition of the freedom and independence of India, Indochina, Burma, Malaya, Indonesia, and Korea. Indeed, the very first and immediate and very least of the tokens of such a common policy would certainly have to be the removal of the artificial line cut across Korea and the withdrawal of Russian and American forces from that country. Similarly, all British forces would have to quit India, the French would leave Indochina and the Dutch would evacuate the Indies.

It would of course be absurd to take this to mean that a new set of bristling and hostile nationalisms should be created to replace the bristling and hostile imperialisms of the past. On the contrary, the peoples of Asia have to make the leap from colonial slavery into a world order. That is not going to be accomplished easily or swiftly. It is, in fact, one of the most difficult transitions history has ever imposed on people. But it is, nevertheless, the only way they can emerge from their backwardness and start forward. If it is true that great Powers like the United States and Russia cannot stand alone in the world, let no one expect backward India or tiny Indochina to do so. They have to fit into a world that will help them grow instead of exploiting them. If no such world opens up to them, they are doomed to strangle by themselves or else become submerged within the orbits of the greater contending nationalisms. Freedom is an expanding element. If it cannot expand, it turns into its opposite. That is as true for Venezuela as for Russia, for the United States as for Siam. There is no escaping it. Nor, in a reasonable world, would we want to escape it. We would be intent, rather, upon absorbing all the freedom that men can create.

There is no intention to suggest here that all we need is moral goodwill to march forward to a glistening future. Higher moral values among men will be an indispensable part of the common effort that is needed. But morality is a product of social circumstance. We know that men are capable of acting from the loftiest impulses.

We know also that men can act like cruel, unthinking animals. Our society has enthroned many moralities but it lives in fact by the amorality of the jungle. If the world we have reduces men to the level of beasts, then we have to seek moral standards in terms of the world we want. The struggle to achieve a higher estate for man is, indeed, a struggle to achieve a morality by which men can honestly live. On the way, meanwhile, we must somehow absorb human weaknesses as well as human strength. We have to start from what we have and what we are.

The blueprints we need for that future we want will call upon the skills of many draftsmen. They would involve immense, wrenching change, perhaps greater change than we can hope to realize in the time that remains. In both Russia and the United States it would require acquisition of power by the people, in the one case by the liquidation of the totalitarian police state and in the other case by the abandonment of anarchic capitalism. The process would be complex and difficult. Its forms, content, methods, problems would be varied and would assume shapes that we can now see only in broadest outline. But even now it does not seem wholly impossible. For is it really impossible to apply to purposes of peaceful growth the gigantic energy that was poured into waging war? Is it really impossible to apply the conquests of science to the improvement of man instead of his destruction? In the face of all the realities and the likelihoods, one is still reminded of those famous characters who said the world was flat, who said man could not fly, who said there was no such animal as a giraffe. Big corporations have formed cartels and controlled the international production and distribution of chemicals, oil, rubber, tin, and steel. Why should it be impossible for equally big but socially controlled combines to organize the international production and distribution of chemicals, oil, rubber, tin, steel? If our existing governments could set up combined boards to run a war, why is it impossible for the peoples of the earth to set up combined boards to run the peace? By these same premises, it is certainly possible to organize the world into great regional federations and to frame them eventually into a United States of Asia, a United States of Europe, a United States of the Americas, combined for all necessary purposes into a United States of the World. This is not a picture of a dim utopia. It is a picture of a world using the resources already at its disposal to feed the people of the world, to clothe them, house them, to educate their young. It is a world that opens the way to a limitless future.

There would, surely, be obstacles on a scale commensurate with the goals. There would, for example, undoubtedly be a huge bureaucracy, almost as bad, possibly, as the bureaucracy created in Washington in recent years to carry on what was called the "war effort." It lumbered and blundered and it groaned with the corruption of special interests. It also managed to produce a not inconsiderable "war effort." There would be waste, which over a long period of years might barely equal the waste that occurred in the world in the brief time between 1939 and 1945. There would always be the danger of abuses of power and freedom, but these could hardly be comparable to those which keep so much of humanity today in a condition of moral or physical slavery. There would be friction, but less friction, possibly, than was generated in the course of one short war in which fifty million people were killed and hundreds of billions in treasure blown to bits.

A program for the future along these lines is filled with a variety of dangers. There is danger in it for the profit system of capitalism because such a world order would have to be keyed to mass needs rather than individual profits. There is danger in it for the rulers of totalitarian states because such a world order would be built on foundations of expanding democratic freedoms. There is danger that the competitive spirit of man will be transferred from the realm of the simple, brutal struggle for survival to the higher realms of physical, cultural, and moral advancement. There is the danger that some of the still untried ideas of socialism might be introduced into the way the world is run. These are all mortal risks. The question is whether they are more mortal than the risk of another world war.

It is by now past time to listen to the scornful snorts of the "realists," to say nothing of all the experts on human nature. This program, this whole idea, is fantastic, visionary, dangerous; and anyway, if it is not all of these things, it is certainly impossible. Capitalist America will never give up its profit system or abdicate its military position in the Pacific. Statist-totalitarian Russia will never give up its police machine, will never yield up its conquered territories, or cease trying to impose its power on other lands.

These "realistic" critics are possibly right. They are even probably right. But let us understand clearly what this kind of realism means. If it is not realistic for Russia and the United States to take the first moves toward reducing the danger of conflict between them, then it is simply not realistic to talk about peace in Asia or peace in the world. If such is the case, then the new epoch of permanent war must run its course. The rival national-economic powers will have to continue the costly process of canceling each other out. Russian national-economic power or American national-economic power must in the end prevail and create a new world order in the image of the final victor. That, too, will be a solution of a kind. But it is reachable only through another and greater inter-continental war that will decimate the race and leave a good part of the world in ruins.

On the credit side, such as it is, there are only two items. One is time. How much time we do not know. We are at the mercy of circumstances and the shifting relationships of force. The question of time is defined now by such factors as the time it might take Russia to master the secrets of the atom bomb, the rate and pace of Russian economic reinforcement, the possible course of the American internal economic cycle. The experts figure and calculate and speculate and from their various slide rules come up with estimates of how long we have to live. Five years? Ten years? Twenty? We do not know, except that it adds up to time, an x quantity of time that seems measurable at least in years if not in decades.

The second credit item is the universal will of people for a better future than they are now offered. The popular will is the largest and most powerful element in the whole compound. Events have pulverized it again and again. It is dispersed, undefined, and amorphous. Nevertheless it still exerts enormous pressure. It still embraces whatever hope there is for men in our time. The question is whether it can be translated, in the x period of time that remains, into action that will alter the prospect, prolong the respite, or avert the catastrophe.

It does not lack motion and in some cases neither does it lack direction. In Asia masses hammered into docile submission by centuries of adversity show again and again their readiness to rise from their knees. In Europe people victimized and pauperized by successive wars display a truly awesome resilience.

The people of England, to take the most notable example, gave an overwhelming mandate of change to the Labor Party. The Labor leadership has so far given no sign that it will do more in the sphere of world affairs than try to hold on to the British imperial franchise. The British people, consciously and by free democratic action, gave power to a government committed to a socialist program. But limited domestic reforms at home coupled with imperialism abroad will by no means give the British people the changes they so clearly demand. If by the same democratic methods the British people can force their government to move beyond its present limited policies, or create a government that will, then perhaps they will give the world an example of a kind of progressive political action that can even now be successful. If they allow the Labor politicians to continue their present drift, then the British people are simply heading for the same kind of futile compromise and frustration and failure that accompanied the Social Democratic experiments on the European continent after the last war.

In the United States, the people have as yet provided themselves with no choices more significant than the biennial or quadrennial selections of Republicans or Democrats to run the country's government. Probably in no country is the angle of refraction between depth and surface of popular feeling more acute than it is in the United States. It is difficult to see in the American swing to the Republicans an expression of the profound mood of protest, weariness and rejection deep among the people. Yet it is there. The American people are peculiarly endowed, materially and historically, to assume a leading position among the peoples of the world. But their impulse and intent to transform the broad notions of American democracy into a dynamic force, at home and abroad, are still far from realization. The United States is still the citadel of capitalist conservatism. The American people have yet to fashion for themselves even the beginning of a new leadership capable of facing the responsibilities of this epoch instead of leading the country down the road to more crisis, more war.

Of the Russian people, we know little. The occasional journalistic contact produces every evidence that the Russian people desire no less than any other to be free to grow. But the extent of their submission to the Russian police state and to their own nationalist myths is difficult to measure. The chances of the transformation of the Russian police state, by popular action of the Russian people, are simply unknown.

Elsewhere the leftward surge of the people is enveloped in the bitterest paradox of our time. The movement toward the political left absorbs the best energies and hopes of those who want change. But in many countries of Europe, as in China, it ends up in the cold embrace of Communist totalitarianism. In local or domestic terms, the Communists become radicals, patriots, agrarian reformers, or defenders of the status quo, or whatever expediency demands. But in one thing they are uniformly consistent: they are all instruments of the Russian national state. Because of this, the enormously progressive instincts of the people are diverted and perverted wherever Communists exert effective influence.

Everywhere honest liberalism, a weak and quavering political quantity at best, is shattered by the moral and political contradictions of Russian totalitarian tyranny parading as socialism. There is not much liberalism left in the liberal democrat who adapts himself, politically and philosophically, to the reality of the Russian dictatorship, the police regime, the smothering of independent and spontaneous political and cultural development among the people. In practical politics, the Communist parties, functioning as tools of Russian national policy, become the most divisive and demoralizing obstacles in the path of the progressive political left. They block the common effort to find a way out by means of a serious internationalism. They reduce left-wing politics to a matter of choosing sides between the contending nationalisms. This is the worst and most fateful consequence of the development of the Russian national super-state. Coming on top of conservative inertia and resistance, this is the heaviest of the adverse pressures on the conscious will of great masses of people in many countries who with prodigious stoicism still seek a way out.

The practical problems of organizing the necessary political struggle seem so great and the time seems so short. Still, we can draw certain very definite lessons from the experience of the last three decades. We learned from the example of the European social democracy (and in a lesser way from the Rooseveltian New Deal in the United States) that progressive programs tied to compromise with the status quo are doomed to failure. On the other hand, we learned from the example of the Soviet Union that progressive programs tied to rule by dictatorship are doomed to lapse into tyranny. What we have yet to discover is a course of action that will steer us safely past the Charybdis of compromise and the Scylla of totalitarianism.

We also learned that leaders who represent classes of society that stand to lose most by change will keep on leading us, if we allow them, from one impasse to another, from one catastrophe to another. We have to transfer power to representatives of the great masses of labor and the people at large, for they have the most to gain from progressive change. We have to make this transfer by democratic means and resort to force only if we have to, and then only in defense of the clearly established majority interest. We have to try to create new political mechanisms, new parties, new political standards. We must employ means consonant with our ends. We have to find out how to serve the general interest of progressive change and at the same time erect maximum possible safeguards against the twin corruptions of power and violence. We have to go forward without yielding any of the freedoms we already have, least of all the freedom of dissent. We need new norms for political struggle if we are ever going to achieve any new norms in social relations among men.

The challenge is overwhelming. It cannot be denied that it seems now almost beyond our power to meet. But the issue is man's future and we cannot settle for less, because less will not do. The shape of that future depends on whether we can still organize the world more rationally, pool its resources and its needs, federate its races, nations, and cultures, and remove from the sphere of inhuman competition the food, the resources, the products of labor, the things by which men live. If this be a dream, then we had best make the most of it, for it is the only stuff that survival is made of.

INDEX

Abe, Noboyuki, 93, 95
Aguinaldo, 229
Aleutians, 259, 280
Ambonese, 130
American soldiers, 7–34, 81–82, 240, 241
Anglo-American bloc, see Russian-American Relations, United States
Anglo-Japanese Alliance (1902), 189, 199, 218
Anglo-Indians, 14, 111
Annam, 143, 149, 165, 170, 246
Annamites, 104, 130, 134–176, 238, 239; see Indochina
Arab League, 211
Arabs, 210–211
Arnold, Maj. Gen. Arch, 95, 96
"Asia for the Asiatics," 127, 155, 194, 234; see Japan
Atlantic Charter, 119, 132, 174, 206, 232, 238
atomic war, 182–185, 260, 270, 276, 284
Attlee, Clement, 120, 132, 209
Aung San, 208

Bandung, 123, 131
Bao Dai, 149
Batavia, 13, 122–123, 128, 129, 130, 235, 237; see Indonesia
Bekassi, 132
Bengal famine (1943), 119
Bevin, Ernest, 182, 209, 273
Bhamo, 19, 21
Bikini, 182, 183, 241
Bluecher, Gen., 251
Blueshirts, Chinese, 50
Bolsheviks, 190, 220, 221, 246–251, 255, 256, 258; see Russia
Bombay, 107, 108, 119, 121
Borodin, Michael, 55, 56, 59, 251
Bose, Subhas Chandra, 105, 207–208
Boxer Rebellion, 218, 246, 249
Bryan, William Jennings, 219, 222
Buck, Pearl, 46

BURMA, 31, 69, 103, 108, 145, 155, 207–208, 276, 281; British in, 103, 129, 202–204, 208, 209, 246; race attitudes in, 15–21
Burma National Army, 208
Burma Road, 27, 67, 68, 70
Byrnes, James, 182, 273

Cairo Conference (1943), 85, 86, 205
Calcutta, 11, 12, 13, 14, 121
Cambodia, 140 n., 143, 162, 170, 246
Canton, 29, 57, 66; Chiang Kai-shek coup (1926), 59; Commune (1927), 59, 253; May 30 Massacre (1925), 56
Caobang, 149, 164
Caodaoists, 155
capitalism, 247, 254, 260–261, 263, 265, 268, 271, 272, 283, 285
Catholic Church (Philippines), 230
Cedile, Col., 153, 175
Chang Chin-chiang, 55
Changchun, 41
Chengtu, 25
Chennault, Maj. Gen. Claire, 68
Chiang Kai-shek, 26, 29, 41, 43–80 (biographical sketch, 45–67), 166, 168 n., 220, 252–3, 257, 264; see China, Communists
Chiang Kai-shek, Mme., 26
CHINA, 37–42, 43–80, 104, 257–259, 276–277, 286; American soldiers in, 14, 17–34, 241; army, 17–21, 24, 27–32, 69; Britain, 56, 201–202, 203, 210, 216, 217–220, 251, 257–258; early imperialist invasions, 52, 215–220, 245–246; Indochina, 142, 143, 151, 162, 166–169, 172, 176; Japan, 44, 62, 64–67, 70–71, 189–193, 194, 218–222, 245–246; Kuomintang-Communist conflict, see Communists; Kuomintang regime, 23–30, 48, 60–63, 166, 191, 278; Kuomintang, United States support of, 43–44, 67–80, 181, 240, 258, 277, 278; Manchuria, 37–42, 43, 44, 62, 78, 190–192, 240, 257,

Date Due

8337	Oct 7	NOV 12 '53	
8337	Oct 19		
8474	Nov 11	DEC 15 '53	
"	Nov 29	FEB 4 '54	
8474	Dec 15	JAN 4 '55	
8043	Jan 17	JAN 21 '55	
	Jan 31		
NOV 3 '50			
DEC 5 '50			
JAN 4 '51			
JAN 22 '51			
DEC 10 '51			
DEC 14 '51			
JAN 18 '52			
JAN 19 '52			
NOV 1 '52			
NOV 15 '52			